Pattern Recognition and Image Processing

"Talking of education, people have now a-days" (said he) "got a strange opinion that every thing should be taught by lectures. Now, I cannot see that lectures can do so much good as reading the books from which the lectures are taken. I know nothing that can be best taught by lectures, except where experiments are to be shewn. You may teach chymestry by lectures — You might teach making of shoes by lectures!"

James Boswell: *Life of Samuel Johnson, 1766* (1709-1784)

"Mathematics possesses not only truth, but supreme beauty – a beauty cold and austere like that of sculpture, and capable of stern perfection, such as only great art can show.

Bertrand Russell in *The Principles of Mathematics* (1872-1970)

DAISHENG LUO

Dr. Daisheng Luo was born in 1947 in Sichuan in the Republic of China. He read for a degree in Electrical Engineering at the University of Sichuan in the Department of Electronic and Electrical Engineering and gained his BSc in 1970. His ability and quality were immediately recognised with the award of a Research Fellowship in that same department, being promoted to Assistant Lecturer in 1978 where he gained an interest in the area of imaging systems, and was awarded a Diploma for Imaging Processing and Pattern Recognition (IPPR) by the University of Shanghai Jiaotong in 1980. In 1983 he was promoted to the post of Lecturer at the University of Sichuan.

In 1989 he came to Scotland with the appointment of Honorary Research Fellow in the Department of Electronic and Electrical Engineering at the University of Glasgow, being made Research Assistant in the Department of Civil Engineering in the same University from 1992-1995. In 1996 he moved to his present appointment of Researcher at the Clinical Research Initiative, Institute of Biomedical and Life Science, University of Glasgow where he is now Research Fellow.

Daisheng Luo has a wide range of research interests, especially in image processing, pattern recognition and software development. He is well-known and highly respected for his reputation in these areas and has published 21 research papers in several recognised journals, and was awarded six prizes from the Chinese Provincial Government for his excellent research achievements.

Pattern Recognition and Image Processing

DAISHENG LUO
Department of Electronic and Electrical Engineering
and
Institute of Biomedical and Life Sciences
University of Glasgow

WP

WOODHEAD
PUBLISHING

Oxford   Cambridge   Philadelphia   New Delhi

Published by Woodhead Publishing Limited,
80 High Street, Sawston, Cambridge CB22 3HJ, UK
www.woodheadpublishing.com

Woodhead Publishing, 1518 Walnut Street, Suite 1100, Philadelphia,
PA 19102-3406, USA

Woodhead Publishing India Private Limited, G-2, Vardaan House, 7/28 Ansari Road,
Daryaganj, New Delhi – 110002, India
www.woodheadpublishingindia.com

First published by Horwood Publishing Limited , 1998
Reprinted by Woodhead Publishing Limited, 2011

British Library Cataloguing in Publication Data
A catalogue record for this book is available from the British Library

ISBN 978-1-898563-52-5

Contents

Preface   ix

Acknowledgements   x

Chapter 1   Introduction   1
1.1   Image Processing   1
1.2   Pattern Recognition   2
   1.2.1   Pattern Recognition Methods   2
   1.2.2   Pattern Recognition System Design   3
1.3   Relationship Between Image Processing
     and Pattern Recognition   4
1.4   Image Processing and Pattern Recognition
     in Object Analysis   6
1.5   About This Book   7
References   9

Chapter 2   Object Detection   11
2.1   Introduction   11
2.2   Image Restoration   11
   2.2.1   Inverse Filter   12
   2.2.2   Wiener Filter   12
   2.2.3   Constrained Least-Square Filter   12
2.3   Image Enhancement   13
   2.3.1   Smoothening   13
   2.3.2   Sharpening   14
   2.3.3   Image Equalisation   16
2.4   Image Segmentation   18
   2.4.1   Region Segmentation   18
   2.4.2   Boundary Segmentation   20
   2.4.3   Other Extensively Developed Methods   23
2. 5   Object Detection and Labelling   23
References   24

Chapter 3   Shape Analysis   27
3.1   Introduction   27
   3.1.1   Shape Representation   27
   3.1.2   Irregular Shape Representation   27
   3.1.3   Shape Representation in Image Processing   33
   3.1.4   Shape Representation by Convex Hull   33
3.2   Convex Hull   34
   3.2.1   Introduction   34

3.2.2   SPCH Algorithm for Convex Hull Finding   35
   3.2.2.1   Stair-Climbing Method for Simple Polygon Finding   37
   3.2.2.2   Properties of the Simple Polygon   40
   3.2.2.3   Sklansky's Algorithm for Convex Hull Finding   43
3.2.3   The Validity of Convex Hull Finding   44
3.2.4   Conclusions   47
3.3   Convex Hull Based Shape Representation   47
3.3.1   Boundary and Convex Hull   48
3.3.2   Description Function   49
3.3.3   Feature Extraction and Shape Classification   52
   3.3.3.1   Measurements   54
   3.3.3.2   Feature Extraction   56
   3.3.3.3   Shape Classification   59
3.3.4   Examples of Shape Analysis   59
3.4   Fractals   71
3.4.1   Introduction   71
3.4.2   Definition   71
3.4.3   Self-similarity   73
3.4.4   Fractal Dimension   74
3.4.5   Multi-fractals   74
3.5   Fractals Based Shape Representation   74
3.5.1   Boundary and Fractal Dimension   74
3.5.2   Region and Fractal Dimension   75
3.5.3   Example of Shape Analysis   75
3.6   Summary   78
References   79
Appendix 3A   Find the Simple Polygon by Stair-Climbing Method   83

Chapter 4   Roundness/Sharpness Analysis   85
4.1   Introduction   85
4.1.1   The Problem of Roundness Analysis   89
4.1.2   The Problem of Circle and Arc Detection   89
4.2   Hough Transform   90
4.2.1   Introduction   90
4.2.2   Definition of Hough Transform   91
4.2.3   Algorithm of Hough Transform   91
4.2.4   Circular Hough Transform   92
4.3   Algorithms for Circular Hough Transform   92
4.3.1   Curve Detection   92
4.3.2   Basic Method   93
4.3.3   Directional Gradient Method   94
4.3.4   Centre Method   96
4.3.5   Gradient Centre Method   100
4.3.6   Radius Method   101

4.4   Threshold Function *T(r)*   104
4.5   Sharp Corners   106
4.6   Examples of Roundness/Sharpness Analysis   106
4.7   Conclusions   116
References   117

Chapter 5   Orientation Analysis   121
5.1   Introduction   121
   5.1.1   Problem of Orientation Analysis   121
   5.1.2   Development of Orientation Analysis   122
5.2   Directed Vein Method   123
   5.2.1   Directed Vein Image   123
   5.2.2   Orientation of a Vein   125
   5.2.3   Algorithm   126
5.3   Convex Hull Method   130
5.4   Principal Component Transformation   131
   5.4.1   Theory of Principal Component Transformation   132
   5.4.2   Orientation by Principal Component Transformation   135
5.5   Moments   136
   5.5.1   Theory of Moments   137
   5.5.2   Central Moments   137
   5.5.3   Orientation by Moments   138
5.6   Examples of Orientation Analysis   140
5.7   Discussion and Summary   151
References   153
Appendix 5A.1   The Double-boundary Method   156
Appendix 5A.2   Lemmas and Propositions   157

Chapter 6   Arrangement Analysis   159
6.1   Introduction   159
   6.1.1   Aggregates   160
   6.1.2   Examples of Arrangements   160
6.2   Extended Hough Transform   165
   6.2.1   Hough Transform   165
   6.2.2   Extension of Hough Transform   168
6.3   Simplified Extended Hough Transform   169
6.4   Arrangement Features   169
   6.4.1   Orientation and Position   170
   6.4.2   Description in Hough Space   170
   6.4.3   Feature Extraction   186
6.5   More Arrangements And Features   188
   6.5.1   More Arrangements   188
   6.5.2   Measurements   190
   6.5.3   More Features   203

Contents

6.6   Description and Classification of Arrangements   205
    6.6.1   Description   205
    6.6.2   Classification   207
    6.6.3   Further Development   210
6.7   Summary   210
References   211
Appendix 6A   The Consistency Ratio R_θ of θ 213

Chapter 7   Conclusions   215

Computer Programs   217

Index   241

Preface

Although they have been developed for a few decades, image processing and pattern recognition are still hot subjects in science. In many fields people have been trying to employ image processing and pattern recognition to solve their own problems. Thus, books and papers were published to encourage their applications. However, some of the theories, techniques, and approaches seem to be the date-of-art, but they can deal with only theoretic or ideal problems. Some of them seem to be good, but they can solve real problems at low levels or in simple cases. Some can treat only special problems encountered by professionals. Therefore, the available theories and techniques are still far from meeting the needs of dealing with real problems. People have always been glaring at markets to look for new theories and techniques.

Object analysis by image processing and pattern recognition is also a hot subject. This is because, in many fields, in many cases, especially in daily life, people have to deal with problems of object analysis (description, recognition, classification). With the dramatic development of computers, they dream that everything, without exception of object analysis, is processed automatically by electronic brains. Therefore, they yearn for finding the date-of-art theories and techniques concerning object analysis by computers. However, bits of theories and techniques were published here and there in literature, there is no single book presenting especially object analysis in markets.

This book is the only one presenting particularly object analysis. It is an entrance leading to the object analysis world. It will be a toolkit for the readers working in the fields, where object analysis is needed, such as computer vision, robotics, artificial intelligence, remote sensing, civil engineering, geology, geophysics, biology, physiology, medical, environment, marine, agriculture, industry, etc.

This book represents initially some theories and techniques of image processing and pattern recognition for object analysis. More specifically, the aim was to present some methods for analysis of the shapes, orientations, and arrangements of objects: these three are very important properties, which are used for description, recognition, and classification of objects. The book presented here was based principally on analysing the individual objects in two-dimensional images.

In this book, first a brief review of image processing and pattern recognition and their previous applications in object analysis is given.

Then, for object analysis, image restoration, image enhancement, image segmentation, and object detection and labelling are introduced.

Next shape analysis of objects is presented. A convex hull based shape description and classification is presented. A new algorithm, SPCH, is presented for finding the convex hull of either a binary object or a cluster of points in a plane. This algorithm is efficient and reliable. Features of pattern vectors for shape description and classification are obtained from the convex hull and the object.

These features are invariant with respect to coordinate rotation, translation, and scaling. The objects can then be classified by feature-space method, for example here, by minimum-distance classification.

Forth, the roundness/sharpness analysis of objects is presented. Three new algorithms, referred to as the Centre, Gradient Centre, and Radius methods, all based on the Circular Hough Transform, are presented. Two traditional Circular Hough Transform algorithms are presented as contrasts. Examples of the three new methods successfully applied to the measurement of the roundness (sharpness of corners) of two-dimensional objects are also given. The five methods are compared from the points of view of memory requirement, speed, and accuracy; and the Radius method appears to be the best for the special topic of sharpness/roundness analysis.

Fifth, the orientation analysis of objects is described. A new method, Directed Vein, is proposed for the analysis. Another three methods: Convex Hull, Principal Components, and Moments, are also presented. Comparison of the four methods shows that the Directed Vein method appears the fastest; but it also has the special property of estimating an 'internal preferred orientation' whereas the other methods estimate an 'elongation direction'.

Finally arrangement analysis of objects is introduced. A new method, Extended Linear Hough Transform, is proposed. In this method, the orientations and locations of the objects are mapped into extended Hough space. The arrangements of the objects within an aggregate are then determined by analysing the data distributions in this space. The aggregates can then be classified using a tree classifier.

Taken together, the methods presented in this book provide a useful toolkit for analysing the shapes, orientation, and arrangements of objects such as those seen in two-dimensional images.

Acknowledgements

I would like to express my thanks to Professor J. Barker and Dr. James. E. S. MacLeod, in the Department of Electronics and Electrical Engineering, and Dr. Peter Smart, in the Department of Civil Engineering, University of Glasgow. They gave me good suggestions and comments for the earlier version of this book. Dr. Smart supported also with a very good laboratory, powerful equipment, and some carefully selected soil micrographs.

I would like to thank Professor J. C. MacGrath and Craig Daly, APU, IBLS, University of Glasgow, for their provision of research facilities in the late work of this book.

I would like to thank my son, Mr. Ji Luo, in University of Cambridge. He did much and very good work on wording, editing and prof reading of this book.

Finally, I would like to express my heartfelt thanks to my wife, Zhang Li Wu, who supported me with all her strength in this work. Without her support, this work would not have been successful.

Daisheng Luo
APU, IBLS
University of Glasgow
August, 1998

1

Introduction

1.1 IMAGE PROCESSING

Sight is a human being's principal sense. A visual image is rich in information from the outer world, and receiving and analysing such images is part of the routine activity of human beings throughout their waking lives. At a more sophisticated level, human beings may generate, record or transmit images. These activities together comprise image processing.

Theories and techniques of image processing originated in the study of optics and optical instruments. However, the advent of digital computers opened vast new possibilities for artificial image processing. By the mid-1960's, third-generation computers offered the speed and storage necessary for practical implementation of image-processing algorithms; and in 1964 the capabilities of digital image processing were spectacularly demonstrated when pictures of the moon transmitted by the Ranger 7 space probe were processed to correct various types of image distortion inherent in the on-board television camera (Gonzalez and Wintz, 1987).

Since that date, the field of image processing has experienced vigorous growth. Digital image processing techniques are used today in a wide range of applications that, although otherwise unrelated, share a common need for methods capable of enhancing pictorial information for human interpretation and analysis. These applications include: remote sensing; security monitoring; medical diagnosis; automatic inspection; radar; sonar; detection of military targets; robotics; business communication; television enhancement (after Jain, 1989); civil engineering; etc. In civil engineering, it has been used for structural monitoring, hydrology, and soil microstructure. In this book, it will be introduced based on a specific request to provide improved methods to analysing and classifying micrographs of soil.

In image processing, after acquiring a digitised image, the main tasks are: enhancement or rectification; segmentation; measurement; and data analysis, as indicated in Figure 1.1. Image enhancement and image rectification are often used to emphasise certain features and to remove artefacts respectively. Two types of measurements are made: feature measurements are taken off individual objects which have been defined by a segmentation process, and field measurements are obtained globally from complete images. Finally, these feature and field measurements must be analysed. In this book, some methods of rectification and segmentation were presented, but the emphasis being on measurement and data analysis.

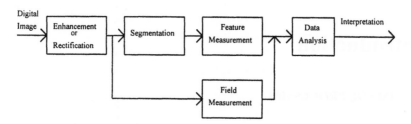

Figure 1.1   Diagram of image processing for object recognition.

1.2   PATTERN RECOGNITION

1.2.1   Pattern Recognition Methods

In communication with the outer world, one of the most important goals for human beings is to recognise objects. For example, from an image, image set, or image sequence of objects, we need to recognise which directions the objects are oriented toward, where they are located, how they are arranged, what size and shape they have, and what sorts of things they are.

During the past 30 years, pattern recognition has had a considerable growth. The need for theoretical methods and experimental software and hardware is increasing. Applications of pattern recognition now include: character recognition; target detection; medical diagnosis; biomedical signal and image analysis; remote sensing; identification of human faces and of fingerprints; reliability analyses; socioeconomics; archaeology; speech recognition and understanding; machine part recognition; automatic inspection; and many others (Young and Fu, 1986).

Pattern recognition by computer is, in general, a complex procedure requiring a variety of techniques that successively transform the iconic data to information directly usable for recognition (Haralick and Shapiro, 1992). Many methods of artificial pattern recognition have been proposed, applicable in general not only to objects in a visual image but also to other types of real world entity. Traditionally, these methods are grouped into two categories: *structural* methods and *feature-space* methods. Structural methods are useful in situations where the different classes of entity can be distinguished from each other by *structural* information, e.g. in character recognition different letters of the alphabet are structurally different from each other. The earliest-developed structural methods were the *syntactic* methods, based on using formal grammars to describe the structure of an entity. Some other methods which may be described as structural are machine vision methods such as those based on point distribution models, active contours, etc.

In feature-space methods, a set of *measurements* (typically numerical) is made on each real-world entity (or *pattern*), and from the measurement set there is extracted a set of features which together characterise the class of patterns to which the given pattern belongs. The features are regarded as the elements of a vector drawn from the origin in a multi-dimensional *feature* space. Ideally, the measurements and features are so chosen that (a) the extremities of the vectors representing patterns belonging to the same class tend to cluster together in a region of feature space, and (b) the extremities of the vectors representing patterns belonging to different classes tend to occur in distinct such clusters in distinct regions of feature space. A *classifier* can then assign an unseen real-world pattern to a particular class according to the region of feature space in which the vector representing this pattern falls.

The traditional approach to feature-space pattern recognition is the *statistical* approach, where the boundaries between the regions representing pattern classes in feature space are found by statistical inference based on a *design set* of sample patterns of known class membership. An unseen pattern can then be classified simply by determining the region of feature space in which it lies. An alternative approach is to use a mathematical or physical model of the *pattern generating mechanism* to predict the regions: this approach is useful in situations where it is costly or impossible to obtain sufficient numbers of design samples to allow statistical conclusions to be drawn from them with any degree of confidence. A third possibility, which appears to be due to the Author, is to choose features so that the total hypervolume of feature space within which feature points can occur is known *a priori*. The whole of feature space can then be partitioned according to some suitable scheme for the problem in hand. This approach might be useful where there exists a continuum of pattern classes, rather than a set of discrete classes. This approach is considered towards the end of Chapter 3 with respect to the problem of classifying objects

Feature-space methods are useful in situations where the distinctions between different pattern classes are readily expressible in terms of numerical measurements of this kind. Such a situation often exists, for example, in the study of soil microstructure, where, for example, important distinctions between soil particles, required by soil engineers, are based on such considerations as roundness versus angularity. These and other aspects both of the nature of a soil particle and of soil structure lend themselves to numerical measurement, and there was an urgent need for numerically based classification for immediate comparison with numerical properties of the soil. The feature space approach is the one that has therefore been used in this research.

1.2.2 Pattern Recognition System Design

Figure 1.2 (a) gives a simplified and generalised view of a pattern recognition system. Unclassified specimens are the specimens which are to be classified. Pattern analysis is the process of extracting the characteristics of the specimens; these characteristics might be measurements or structured observations. Training samples are specimens whose class membership is taken as known *a priori*; in almost all cases, it is the set of characteristics obtained from these specimens which is used. *A priori* definitions are definitions of the classes which have been set up in advance, either on the basis of some theoretical analysis or in an entirely arbitrary fashion depending on the nature of the problem. The criteria are definitions of the closeness with which an unclassified specimen must match the definition of a particular class in order to be placed in that class; if no class is sufficiently closely matched, the specimen may be rejected i.e. not placed in any class. These criteria may be set to broad or narrow limits depending on the use to which the results of the classification will be put. Decision making is the process of comparing the actual characteristics with those on which the classification is to be based. In some cases, it is appropriate to monitor the lack of fit, i.e. the error, and to use this to modify the set of characteristics which is actually being used for classification.

Figure 1.2 (b) is a simplified and generalised view of the process of designing a pattern recognition system. Here, a pattern is the set of characteristics which is inherent in a sample. These patterns may be taken from real samples; but some synthetic patterns designed to test the system may be included. Here, pattern analysis is the process of extracting the actual set of characteristics to be used in the classification. The *a priori* definitions, training samples, and criteria, are the current versions of these parts of the system; but during the design process, these may not yet have been finalised. The general procedure is to use the current version of the system to classify the patterns supplied to it. The results are then inspected to see whether they are judged to be satisfactory. If not, the error is fed back to modify the current versions of the parts of the system.

1.3   RELATIONSHIP BETWEEN IMAGE PROCESSING AND
PATTERN RECOGNITION

Image processing is concerned with the qualities and measurements of images of objects. Pattern recognition is concerned with the description and classification of entities. In object or picture recognition, the entities are objects in an image and image processing and pattern recognition are complementary.

Image processing is often a necessary pre-processing stage preceding pattern recognition. In order to provide patterns which are effective and efficient descriptions of objects, image processing is required to improve the qualities and measurements of an image. For example, filtering is used to remove noise and measurement redundancy; segmentation is used to obtain individual objects; representation is conducted to produce measurements; and so on. Then a set of characteristic measurements and relations among these measurements are extracted for the representation of patterns. On the basis of this representation, the classification of the patterns with respect to a specific goal is performed.

Conversely, pattern recognition can be a main-stream processing procedure in image processing. In order to determine a good set of characteristic measurements and their relationships for the representation of objects, pattern recognition is sometimes needed to classify or cluster primitives or measurements of the images. For example, classification by the statistical method is used for texture segmentation; clustering analysis is used for region segmentation; an hierarchic method is used for scene segmentation; etc.

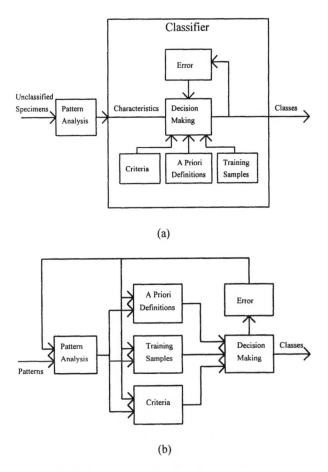

Figure 1.2   (a) Operation of a pattern recognition system; (b) Designing a pattern recognition system.

The output data of image processing for object recognition is a set of measurements. The input data of pattern recognition for object recognition is a set of unclassified patterns, each of which is defined by a set of features. The patterns are selected and/or extracted from the measurements by data analysis. The data analysis can be a separate procedure linking image processing and pattern recognition; it can also be a part of image processing or a part of pattern recognition.

Therefore, in object or picture recognition, the general procedures are image processing (which may apply pattern recognition methods), data analysis, and pattern recognition. The diagram of this procedure is as shown in Figure 1.3.

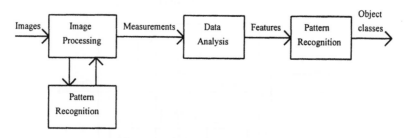

Figure 1.3   Diagram of object recognition.

1.4   IMAGE PROCESSING AND PATTERN RECOGNITION IN OBJECT ANALYSIS

In many case, individual objects will be described and classified for some purpose. For example, in soil micromorphology, the amount, size, and shape of soil particles, pores, and voids were analysed by manual methods such as point counting started in 1940s. Since 1960s, computers have been used in the analysis. Now, because many powerful computers with very large memory and very high speed have been developed, it is much faster and more efficient for object analysis by computer than by hand.

In object description and classification by image processing and pattern recognition, objects for certain purpose are first prepared. Then their images are acquired by digital imaging systems, such as CCD camera, optical microscope, electronic microscope, magnetic resonance scanner, CT, etc. The acquired images are then processed to reconstruct the object models. For each object model, its features (or pattern) are extracted and classified by image processing and pattern recognition theories and techniques. The flow chart of object description and classification is shown in Figure 1.4.

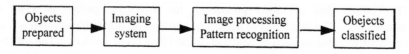

Figure 1.4   Flow chart of object description and classification.

1.5   ABOUT THIS BOOK

This book is specifically aimed at object shape, orientation, and arrangement analysis and classification: these three are very important factors for object classification.   For example, they are used both for description, recognition and classification of soil particles and voids, and for studying the relationships between the soil structures and physical, chemical, geological, geographical, and environmental changes, based on the electron micrographs of soils selected and published by Smart and Tovey (1981) and focused on the individual particles and voids.

Chapter 2 is concerned with object detection.   First, the most popular methods: inverse filter, Wiener filter, and constrained least-square filter are introduced to image restoration.   Then image smoothening, sharpening, and intensity equalisation are introduced to image enhancement.   Finally, region segmentation and boundary segmentation are introduced to image segmentation.   Object detection and labelling are introduced at the end of this chapter.

Chapter 3 is concerned with shape description and classification of objects. The shape description is first focused on the convex hull method.   A new convex hull algorithm is introduced for finding the convex hull of either a binary image or a cluster of points in a plane.   The measurements of an object in an image are obtained from the convex hull of the object and the object itself.   The pattern of the object is selected and extracted from the measurements.   The classification of the objects in an image is conducted by minimum distance classification method. Shape description is also discussed briefly based on fractal/multi-fractal method.   The principle concept of fractals is first introduced.   Then how to measure the fractal dimensions of an object is presented.

Chapter 4 is concerned with sharpness/roundness analysis of objects.   Three new algorithms, Centre, Gradient Centre, and Radius methods, of the Circular Hough Transform are introduced for the analysis.   Two traditional Circular Hough Transform methods are presented as well.   Comparison of the five algorithms, the Radius method appears to be the best for the special topic of sharpness/roundness analysis.

Chapter 5 is concerned with orientation analysis of objects.   A new method, Directed Vein, is introduced for the analysis.   Another three methods: Convex Hull, Principal Components, and Moments, are also presented.   The latter two are the most popular methods.   Comparison of the four methods shows that the Directed Vein method appears the fastest; but it also has the special property of estimating an 'internal preferred orientation' whereas the other methods estimate an 'elongation direction'.   It is suggested that in some cases, estimates of both properties of an object should be used simultaneously for classification.

Chapter 6 is concerned with the classification of aggregates of objects.   A new method, Extended Linear Hough Transform, is introduced; and a method of analysing the arrangement of objects within an aggregate is developed from this method.   The orientations and locations of the objects are mapped into extended Hough space.   The arrangements of the objects are then determined by analysing the data distributions in this space.   The classification of the aggregates is performed by a tree classifier according to the characteristic arrangements of the objects in the aggregates.

Chapter 7 gives the conclusions from the methods presented in this book.

Some examples of experiments are given in the relevant chapters.   Some computer programs written in C/C++ are listed in Computer Programs at the end of this book.

The literature on individual topics is reviewed in the relevant chapters, beginning with object detection.

References

Gonzalez, R. and Wintz, P. (1987) *Digital image processing*. Addison-Wesley, Reading.
Haralick, R. M. and Shapiro, L. G. (1992) *Computer and robot vision*.   Addison-Wesley.
Jain, A. K. (1989) *Fundamentals of digital image processing*. Prentice-Hall International Inc.
Smart, P. and Tovey, N. K. (1981) *Electron Microscopy of soils and sediments: examples*.   Oxford University Press.
Young, T. Y. and Fu, K. S. (1986) *Handbook of pattern recognition and image processing*.   Academic Press.

2

Object Detection

2.1 INTRODUCTION

In object analysis by image processing and pattern recognition, individual objects must be detected beforehand from their images. For object detection, many methods have been developed to segment objects from their back ground and from some other objects. Most of the detection methods can be divided into 2 classes: region detection and boundary or edge detection. In region detection, thresholding, region growing, region splitting, template matching, pattern classification, etc. can be used. In edge detection, intensity gradient, filtering, linear or non-linear transform, etc. can be used. Which methods to be used depends on the aim and the accuracy of object analysis, the complexity of the object structure, and the quality of the images. Usually, during image acquisition, the illumination is not uniform. This will cause that both the objects and the background are not intensity homogeneous. On the other hand, the noise of the imaging system will be added to the images. Both the intensity heterogeneity and the noise result in difficulties in object detection. Therefore, image restoration, image enhancement, etc. are necessary before object detection.

In this chapter, image restoration and enhancement will be first introduced. Then, image region segmentation and edge segmentation will be presented.

2.2 IMAGE RESTORATION

When an object is being imaged, the acquired image (or observed image) is usually not the same as the image of the object itself. The purpose of image restoration is to restore (or reconstruct) the object image from the acquired image. Let $f(x, y)$ denote the intensity of an object, $h(x, y)$ the point spread function of an imaging system, and $g(x, y)$ the acquired image. Then, the acquired image $g(x, y)$ is the convolution of the point spread function $h(x, y)$ and the object image $f(x, y)$:

$$g(x, y) = h(x, y) \otimes f(x, y) + n(x, y) \qquad (2.2.1)$$

where $n(x, y)$ is the additive noise coming form the surroundings, $\otimes$ the convolution operator. Image restoration is to find the object image $f(x, y)$ by solving the equation (2.2.1). However, it is difficult to solve the convolution equation (2.2.1) mathematically. Even more, the point spread function $h(x, y)$ and the noise $n(x, y)$ are unknown actually. The common way for solving this problem is first to estimate the point spread function $h'(x, y)$ of the imaging system and the noise $n'(x, y)$. Then from equation (2.2.1), estimate the object image $f'(x, y)$ which minimises the error $(f(x, y)-f'(x, y))$.

Many methods have been proposed for estimation of image $f(x, y)$. The most two popular methods are inverse filter and Wiener filter.

2.2.1   Inverse Filter

Inverse filter is the simplest filter for image restoration. It assumes that the noise $n(x, y)$ is small enough to ignore its affection on the image quality. Thus the equation (2.2.1) will become into:

$$g(x, y) = h(x, y) \otimes f(x, y). \tag{2.2.2}$$

Direct solution of equation (2.2.2) is not easy. Fourier transform provide a access to solve the problem:

$$G(u, v) = H(u, v) F(u, v) \tag{2.2.3}$$

where, $G(u, v)$, $H(u, v)$, $F(u, v)$ are the Fourier transforms of $g(x, y)$, $h(x, y)$, and $f(x, y)$, correspondingly. From equation (2.2.3), $F(u, v)$ can be obtained:

$$F(u, v) = \frac{G(u, v)}{H(u, v)} = \frac{H*(u, v)G(u, v)}{|H(u, v)|^2} \tag{2.2.4}$$

where $|x|$ indicates the module of x, and * indicates the conjugate of a complex. The object image $f(x, y)$ can be obtain from $F(u, v)$ by inverse Fourier transform.

2.2.2   Wiener Filter

The disadvantage of the inverse filter is that the denominator $| H(u, v) |^2$ in equation (2.2.4) may be zero at some points (u, v). On the other hand, when the noise $n(x, y)$ in equation (2.2.1) can not be ignored, the restoration by inverse filter may not good. The most popular method to improve the restoration is Wiener filter:

$$F(u, v) = \frac{H*(u, v)G(u, v)}{|H(u, v)|^2 + N(u, v)/S(u, v)} \tag{2.2.5}$$

where $N(u, v)/S(u, v)$ is the ratio of noise to signal. Similar to the inverse filter, the object image $f(x, y)$ can be obtained by inverse Fourier transform. An example of the image restoration by Wiener filter is shown in Figure 2.1. Figure 2.1 (a) shows an original image. Figure 2.1 (b) shows the restored image of the original image in Figure 2.1 (b) by Wiener filter.

2.2.3   Constrained Least-Square Filter

Another popular filter is the constrained least-square filter (Hunt 1973):

$$F(u,v) = \frac{H*(u,v)G(u,v)}{|H(u,v)|^2 + \gamma |P(u,v)|^2} \qquad (2.2.6)$$

where $P(u, v)$ is the Fourier transform of the Laplacian operator, and γ is a parameter computed iteratively.

2.3 IMAGE ENHANCEMENT

Usually, in image restoration by inverse filter or Wiener filter, the spread function $h(x, y)$ is mainly concerned with the imaging system. To improve further the image quality, image enhancement is also necessary. Image enhancement is to enhance some information important or interested; or compress some information not important or less interesting. Image enhancement can be classified mainly into three groups: smoothening, sharpening, and equalisation. Smoothening is to reduce high frequency noise. Sharpening is to enhance the edges or boundaries of objects. Equalisation is to uniform the intensity of objects or back ground.

2.3.1 Smoothening
For image smoothening, many methods have been developed. The main three methods are: low pass filter, mean filter, and median filter. The most popular low pass filters are Gaussian filter and Butterworth filter. The magnitudes of the filters are:

$$H(u,v) = \exp(-\frac{(r-r_0)^2}{c^2}) \qquad (2.3.1)$$

$$H(u,v) = \frac{1}{1 + c(r/r_0)^{2n}} \qquad (2.3.2)$$

where r is the distance to the point(u, v), r_0 and c are the mean and covariance in Gaussian filter and the nominal filter cut-off frequency and constant in Butterworth filter. The mean filter is given by:

$$f(x,y) = \frac{1}{A}\sum(g(x-i,y-j)w(i,j)) \qquad (2.3.3)$$

where $w(i, j)$ is a window function with size $n{\times}n$ elements, and A the module of the widow. The median filter is defined as:

$$f(x,y) = g_{m/2}(x-i,y-j) \qquad (-n/2 < I, j < n/2) \qquad (2.3.4)$$

where n is the dimension of an $n{\times}n$ window, $m=n^2$, and $g_k(x{-}i, y{-}j)$ ($k{=}0$, 1, ..., $m{-}1$, m) are in an increasing (or decreasing) order. Figure 2.2 shows an example of smoothening by Gaussian filter.

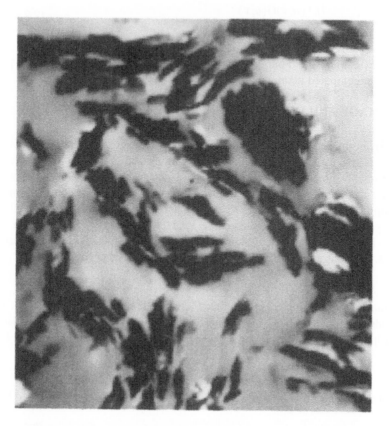

Figure 2.1 (a)   An original image of soil particles (From P. Smart and K. Tovey (1981) Electron Microscopy Soil and Sediment: examples, fig. 5.7, pp. 46).

2.3.2 Sharpening

In many cases of image acquisition, the reflection and refraction of illumination, the out-focus of camera, the limit-band frequency of imaging system, etc., may cause the acquired image blur.   Image sharpening is one of the ways to enhance the edges or boundaries.   It can be expressed by a formula:

$$f(x, y) = g(x, y)w(x, y) \qquad\qquad (2.3.5)$$

where $w(x, y)$ is a weight function.   The most popular filter is Butterworth high-pass filter:

Figure 2.1 (b)   Restored image of Figure 2.1 (a) by Wiener filter.

$$w(u, v) = \frac{1}{1 + c(r_0 / r)^{2n}} \cdot$$

(2.3.6)

Other popular weight functions are gradient operator ∇ and Laplace operator ∇^2:

$$w(x, y) = 1 + \nabla / g(x, y) \quad (\nabla = \partial g(x, y)/\partial x + \partial g(x, y)/\partial y)$$

(2.3.7)

$$w(x, y) = 1 + \nabla^2 / g(x, y) \quad (\nabla^2 = \partial^2 g(x, y)/\partial x^2 + \partial^2 g(x, y)/\partial y^2).$$

(2.3.8)

An example of image sharpening by gradient operator weighting is shown in Figure 2.3.

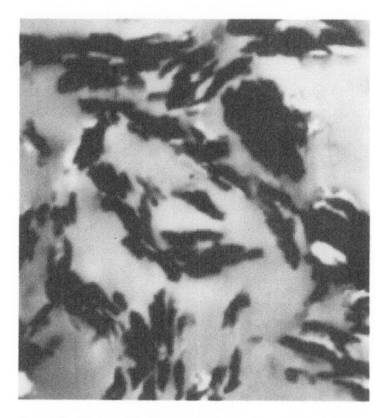

Figure 2.2   The smoothened image of the Figure 2.1 (a) by Gaussian filter.

2.3.3   Image Equalisation

Image equalisation includes contrast adjusting, intensity linear stretching, histogram equalisation, histogram specification, intensity equalisation.   The purpose of these processing is to increase homogeneity both in objects and background so that more details of objects can be obtained and more accuracy of object detection can be achieved.   For the purpose of object detection, one of the important processes is histogram equalisation (Woods and Gonzalez 1981):

$$f_i = \Sigma p(g_j) = \Sigma(n_j/n) \quad (j = 1, 2, ..., i) \quad (i = 1, 2, ..., m). \quad\quad (2.3.9)$$

Here $p(g_j)$ is the histogram of image $g(x, y)$; n_j and n are the numbers of intensity value j and total intensity, respectively, in the image $g(x, y)$; m is the number of intensity levels; and f_i is the intensity value i in image $f(x, y)$.   Another process is histogram specification (Gonzalez and Wintz 1977):

Figure 2.3   The sharpened image of the Figure 2.1 (a) by gradient operator.

$$f_k = h(\Sigma p(g_j)) \qquad (k = k_1, k_1+1, ..., k_1+l) \qquad (2.3.10)$$

where f_k is the intensity value k and l is the number of intensity levels in image $f(x, y)$ corresponding to m in image $g(x, y)$. Other process is intensity equalisation or shadow correction (Narendra and Fitch 1981):

$$f(x, y) = \alpha \, [g(x, y) - g_l(x, y)] / \sigma(x, y) + g_m(x, y). \qquad (2.3.11)$$

Here $g_l(x, y)$ is the low-pass filtered image of $g(x, y)$; $\sigma(x, y)$ is the standard deviation of $g(x, y)$; $g_m(x, y)$ is the local average image of $g(x, y)$; and α is an adjustable constant. An example of intensity equalisation is shown in Figure 2.4, where $\alpha = \sigma(x, y) = 1$, and $g_m(x, y) = 128$.

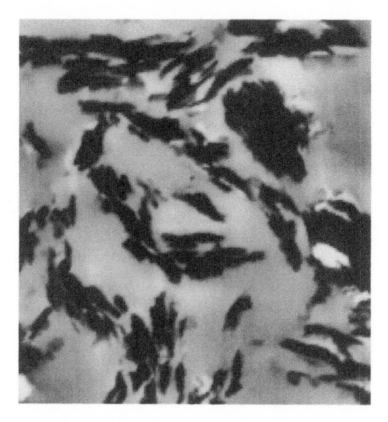

Figure 2.4   Intensity equalised image of the Figure 2.1 (a).

2.4   IMAGE SEGMENTATION

Image segmentation is one of the most important processing in image processing and pattern recognition. It is also essential processing for object detection, analysis, and classification. Image segmentation is to segment objects from background and from some other objects. For object detection, segmentation include two classes: region segmentation and boundary segmentation. In region segmentation, objects are presented by regions, while in boundary segmentation, regions are reconstructed from boundaries or objects are described by boundaries.

2.4.1   Region Segmentation

(1)   Thresholding
The simplest region segmentation is thresholding:

$$f(x, y) = g(x, y)w(x, y) \qquad\qquad (2.4.1)$$

where $w(x, y)$ is a window function defined as:

$$w(x, y) = \begin{cases} 1 & g(x,y) \ge T \\ 0 & g(x,y) < T \end{cases}.$$
(2.4.2)

Here T is a threshold value. It can be estimated form the image or the image's histogram. The segment clips the objects into grey of one and the back ground into zero. Thresholding is the simplest and it is efficient where both objects and background are or can be processed to be homogeneous. Therefore, it is a basic and a highly frequently used method in image segmentation. However, if the back ground and/or objects are not homogeneous, thresholding will not segment objects properly.

(2) Multi-level Thresholding

Multi-level thresholding segments regions into intensity bands. Similar to thresholding, the window function (2.3.8) can be modified as:

$$w(x, y) = I \quad \text{if } T_{i-1} < g(x, y) \le T_i \quad (i=1,2, ..., k).$$
(2.4.3)

In many cases, the threshold value T_i is very difficult to estimated from both the image and the histogram. In other world, it can not achieve a good segmentation by thresholding or multi-thresholding. Some part of an object may be segmented into back ground or other objects, or some parts of back ground may be segmented into objects.

(3) Recursive Thresholding

Thresholding can be implemented recursively in an image to achieve a good segmentation. In each iteration, if a region needs re-segment, find a threshold value and threshold it once again. The iteration ends if no region needs re-segment.

(4) Region Growing and Region Splitting.

Region growing (Young and Fu 1986) starts with a small region. The small region grows into a bigger region by merging its neighbouring regions if the neighbouring regions have the same properties as the small region. The growing procedure is iterated until now region needs merge. In some cases, the merging method would produce a highly fragmented segmentation. Region splitting method is a reverse process of region splitting. To improve the region growing and splitting, Horowitz and Pavlidis (1974) proposed a method of a directed split-and-merge procedure. Ohlander et al. (1978) proposed a recursive region splitting. Milgram and Kahl (1979) presented a recursive region extraction.

An example of region segmented images by thresholding is shown in Figure 2.5.

2.4.2 Boundary Segmentation

In some cases, the edges or boundaries of objects are sharp and homogeneous themselves.   Boundary segmentation can be used to detect edges or boundaries. The regions of objects can be reconstructed from the boundaries.   The edges or boundaries can also be used to present objects.

(1)   Gradient Operator

The simplest boundary segmentation is edge detection by gradient operator:

$$f(x, y) = \nabla = \partial g(x, y)/\partial x + \partial g(x, y)/\partial y. \qquad\qquad (2.4.4)$$

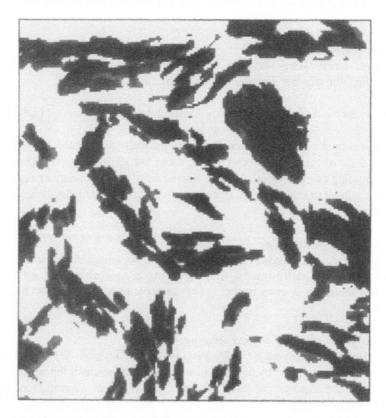

Figure 2.5   Region segmented image of the image in Figure 2.1 (a).

The values of $f(x, y)$ would be high on the edges or boundaries, and low in both objects and back ground.   If the image is blur or the edges are not sharp, the boundaries detected may be wide and disconnected.

(2) Laplacian Operator

Laplacian operator is another popular and efficient edge detection. It is defined as:

$$f(x, y) = \nabla^2 = \partial^2 g(x, y)/\partial x^2 + \partial^2 g(x, y)/\partial y^2. \tag{2.4.5}$$

The edges detected by Laplace operator would give narrower edges, because it is a secondary derivative operation. The edges may also be disconnected like the gradient operator.

(3) Laplacian-Gaussian Filter

Marr and Hildreth (1980) suggested to use a Laplacian-Gaussian filter which is defined as:

$$\nabla^2 g(x, y) = -\frac{1}{2\pi\sigma^4}(2 - \frac{x^2 + y^2}{\sigma^2})\exp(-\frac{x^2 + y^2}{2\sigma^2}). \tag{2.4.6}$$

They also suggested a *DOG* filter:

$$DOG(\sigma_e, \sigma_i) = \frac{1}{\sqrt{2\pi}\sigma_e}\exp(-\frac{x^2}{2\sigma_e^2}) - \frac{1}{\sqrt{2\pi}\sigma_i}\exp(-\frac{x^2}{2\sigma_i^2}). \tag{2.4.7}$$

(4) Template Operators

Templates or widows can be used to implement gradient or Laplace operator in edge detection (Russ 1995). The most frequently used template operators are Prewitt, Sobel, and Robert operators.

    The Prewitt operator is defined as:

$$\begin{aligned} P_x &= (F_2 + F_3 + F_4) - (F_0 + F_7 + F_6) \\ P_y &= (F_0 + F_1 + F_2) - (F_6 + F_5 + F_4) \\ P(m,n) &= |P_x| + |P_y| \end{aligned} \tag{2.4.8}$$

where P_x and P_y are the intensity gradients at point (m, n) in the x and y directions; $P(m, n)$ is the Prewitt value of point (m, n); F_k $(k=0, 1, ..., 7)$ are the intensity values at points adjacent to point (m, n) as shown in Figure 2.6.

    The Sobel operator is defined as:

$$\begin{aligned} P_x &= (F_2 + 2F_3 + F_4) - (F_0 + 2F_7 + F_6) \\ P_y &= (F_0 + 2F_1 + F_2) - (F_6 + 2F_5 + F_4) \\ P(m,n) &= \sqrt{P_x^2 + P_y^2}. \end{aligned} \tag{2.4.9}$$

The Robert operator is defined as:

$$p_{xv} = F_2 - F_6$$
$$p_{vx} = F_4 - F_6$$
$$p(m, n) = \sqrt{(p_{xy}{}^2 + p_{yx}{}^2)}.$$

(2.4.10)

An example of the edge detected image by Prewitt operator from the intensity equalised image (Figure 2.4) is shown in Figure 2.7.

$$
\begin{array}{ccc}
F_0 & F_1 & F_2 \\
F_7 & m, n & F_3 \\
F_6 & F_5 & F_4
\end{array}
$$

Figure 2.6   Prewitt operator.

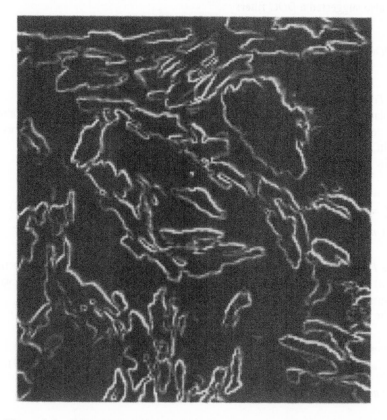

Figure 2.7   Edge detected image by Prewitt operator from the image 2.4.

2.4.3   Other Extensively Developed Methods

Many image segmentation methods have been proposed.   Javis and Patrick (1973) presented a clustering method using a similarity measure based on shared near neighbours for image segmentation.   Kettig and Landgrebe (1976) proposed a classification method for multispectral image data segmentation.   Beck et al. (1980) reviewed a theory of textural segmentation.   Besl and Jain (1988) proposed a segmentation method through variable-order surface fitting.   Beaulieu and Goldberg (1989) proposed a stepwise optimisation approach for hierarchy image segmentation.   Fairfield presented a contrast segmentation by Toboggan contrast enhancement.   Alvarez et al.   (1992) developed a method for image selective smoothing and edge detection by non-linear diffusion.   Some other methods can be found from: Davis 1975, Weszka 1978, Fu and Mui 1980, Haralick 1983, Haralick and Shapiro 1985, Young and Fu, 1986, Wilson and Spann 1988, Jain 1989, Haralick and Shapiro 1992, Morel and Solimini 1995.

2.5   OBJECT DETECTION AND LABELLING

The purpose of object detection is to get the individual region or boundary which presents the object.   The above methods of region detection or edge detection could be used, for example, if objects need to be presented by boundaries, edge detection methods will be used.   If the objects need to be described by regions, region segmentation will be used.   Combination of region and edge detection would be better than one of them is used.

   After the objects have been segmented from the image, they need being labelled.   Luo and Ma (1989) proposed a double boundary method for object labelling.   Another is called integrating method:

$$f_i(x,y) = \begin{cases} f(x,y)+i & if \quad \int B(x,y(x))dx \geq 0 \\ f(x,y)-i & Otherwise \end{cases} \qquad (2.5.1)$$

$(0 \leq y \leq B(x, y(x)))$.

In this method, The boundary $B(x, y(x))$ of an object $g(x, y)$ is collected by edge following.   The integration of the equation (2.5.1) is implemented along the boundary $B(x, y(x))$.   At a boundary point $(x, y(x))$, if the integration is greater or equal to zero, the values $f(x, y)$ at all points (x, y) in image $f(x, y)$ is added with I. Otherwise, $f(x, y)$ is subtract by i.   Here i is the i'th object.

References

Alvarez, L., Lions, P. L., and Morel, J. M. (1992) Image selective smoothing and edge detection by non-linear diffusion (II). *SIAM Journal on numerical analysis,* Vol. 29, pp. 845-866.

Beaulieu, J. M. and Goldberg, M. (1989) Hierarchy in picture segmentation: a stepwise optimisation approach. *IEEE PAMI,* Vol. 11, No. 2.

Beck, J., Hope, B., and Rosenfeld, A. (1980) *Human and Machine Vision.* New York Academic Press, pp. 1-38.

Besl, P. J. and Jain, R. (1988) Segmentation through variable-order surface fitting. *IEEE PAMI,* Vol. 10, No. 2, pp. 167-192.

Davis, L. (1975) A survey of edge detection techniques. *Computer Graphics and Image Processing,* Vol. 4, pp. 248-270.

Fairfield, J. (1990) Toboggan contrast enhancement for contrast segmentation. *IEEE 10th conference on Pattern Recognition,* pp. 712-716.

Fu K. S. and, Mui, J. K. (1980) A survey on image segmentation. *Pattern Recognition,* Vol. 13, pp. 3-16.

Gonzalez, R. C. and Wintz, P. (1987) *Digital image processing.* Addison-Wesley.

Haralick, R. (1983) Image segmentation survey. *Fundamentals in Computer Vision,* pp. 209-224.

Haralick, R. M. and Shapiro, L. G. (1985) Image segmentation techniques. *Computer Vision Garaphics and Image Processing* Vol. 29, pp. 100-132.

Haralick, R. M. and Shapiro, L. G. (1992) *Computer and robot vision.* Addison-Wesley.

Horowitz, S. L. and Pavlidis, T. (1974) Picture segmentation by a directed split-and-merge procedure. *Proc. Second Int. Joint Conf. Pattern Recognition,* pp. 424-433.

Hunt, B. R. (1973) The application of constrained least square estimation to image restoration by digital computer. *IEEE Trans. Comput.* Vol. 22, No. 9, pp. 805-812.

Jain, A. K. (1989) *Fundamentals of digital image processing.* Prentice-Hall International Inc.

Javis, R. A. and Patrick, E. A. (1973) Clustering using a similarity measure based on shared near neighbours. *IEEE Trans. Comput.* C-22, pp. 1025-1034.

Kettig, R. L. and Landgrebe, D. A. (1976) Classification of multispectral image data by extraction and classification of homogeneous objects. *IEEE Trans. Geosci. Tectron.,* Vol. 14, No. 1, pp. 19-26.

Marr, e. and Hildreth, E. (1980) Theory of edge detection. *Proc. Royal Society. London,* B207, pp. 187-217.

Milgram, D. L. and Kahl, D. J. (1979) Recursive region extraction. *Computer Graphics and Image Processing,* Vol. 9, pp. 82-88.

Morel, J. M. and Solimini, S. (1995) *Variational Methods in Image Segmentation.* Birkhauser.

Narendra, P. M. and Fitch, R. C. (1981) Real-time adaptive contrast enhancement. *IEEE Trans. Pattern Anal. Mach. Intell.,* Vol. 3, No. 6, pp. 655-661.

Ohlander, R., Price, K., and Reddy, P. R. (1978) Picture segmentation using a recursive region splitting method. *Comput. Graphics Image Process.* Vol. 8, pp. 313-333.

Russ, J. C. (1995) *The Image Processing Hand Book.* Second Edition, CRC Press.

Smart, P. and Tovey, N. K. (1981) *Electron Microscopy of Soils and Sediments: examples.* Oxford University Press.

Young, T. Y. and Fu, K. S. (1986) *Handbook of pattern recognition and image processing.* Academic Press.

Weszka, J. S. (1978) A survey of threshold selection techniques. *Computing Vision Graphics Image Process*, Vol. 7, pp. 259-265.

Wilson R. and Spann, M. (1988) *Image segmentation and uncertainty.* Research studies Press Ltd, John Wiley & Sons Inc.

Woods, R. E. and Gonzalez, R. C. (1981) Real-time digital image enhancement. *Proc. IEEE* Vol. 69, No. 5, pp. 643-654.

3

Shape Analysis

3.1 INTRODUCTION

3.1.1 Shape Representation

In image processing and pattern recognition, identification and classification of objects is often necessary.   Examples include recognising objects in satellite images; discriminating between fishing boats, merchant ships, warships, etc. in the sea; in industry, recognition of machine spare parts such as screws, nuts, etc.; in medicine, detection of cancers, ulcers, tumours, and so on.   In the study of soil microstructure, recognition and classification of soil particles, voids, bacteria, etc. is a very important task.   Smart and Tovey (1981) give further examples of these sorts of soil microstructures.   Figure 3.1 shows soil particles and soil voids typical of those studied.   To recognise and classify objects with different shapes, the objects have to be represented by their shape characteristics, so that the information extracted from the objects can be compressed.   Therefore, one of the essential procedures is so called shape representation.

3.1.2 Irregular Shape Representation

Objects generally can be classified into three categories: regular, special, and irregular shaped.   For the regular shaped objects, such as triangle, rectangle, square, circle, oval, etc., the shape representation can be easily defined.   For the special shaped objects, such as industrial spare parts, the shape representation can be designed to match their special shapes.   However, for the irregular objects, such as soil particles, it is very difficult to design their shape representation.   In this case, usually the length, width, thickness, roundness, and roughness are chosen as the basic shape representation.   Some other features, such as holes, corners, etc. can be added to give more information for the representation.   Here the discuss is emphasised on the irregular object representation, for example, soil particle representation.

In the study of irregular object, most shape representations comprise size, length, breadth, thickness, sphericity, roundness, roughness, etc.   Wadell (1932) (see Krumbein and Sloss, 1951) proposed a fundamental equation for measuring sphericity:

$$S_w = \sqrt[3]{v / v_s} \tag{3.1.1}$$

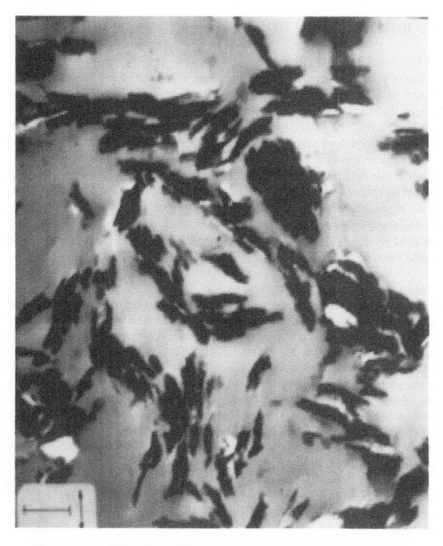

Figure 3.1 (a)   Soil particles (LH mark = 1μm) (From Smart and Tovey (1981) Electron Microscopy of Soil and Sediments: examples. fig. 5.7 pp. 46).

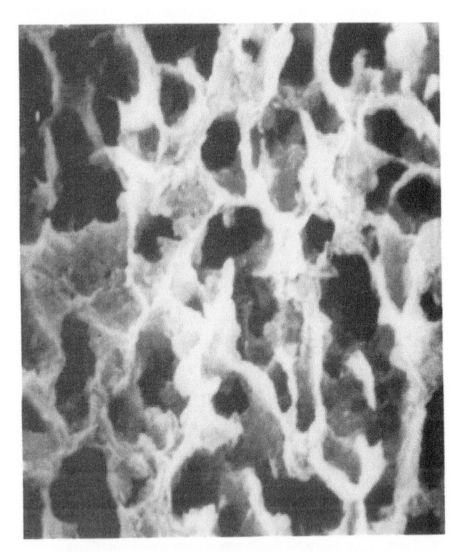

Figure 3.1 (b)   Soil voids (From Smart and Tovey (1981) Electron
Microscopy of Soil and Sediments: examples. fig. 3.6 pp. 27).

where v is the volume of a particle, and v_s is the volume of the circumscribing sphere. Smithson (1939) (see Pettijohn, 1949) adopted shape ratio:

$$S_s = l / b \qquad\qquad\qquad (3.1.2)$$

where l is length and b is breadth, to represent crystal shape. Krumbein (1941) (see Krumbein and Sloss, 1951 and Brewer, 1964) introduced the concept and measurement of pebble diameters as shown in Figure 3.2, where a, b, and c are calliper diameters, a being the greatest, b being the greatest orthogonal to a, and c being the greatest orthogonal to a and b. He then defined sphericity:

$$S_k = \sqrt[3]{bc / a^2} \qquad\qquad\qquad (3.1.3)$$

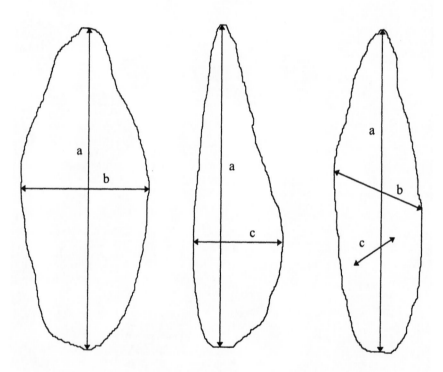

Figure 3.2 The concept and measurement of pebble diameters (see Krumbein (1941) Journal of Sedimentary Petrology, Vol. 11, fig. 2, pp. 66).

which is based on a triaxial ellipsoid as the reference shape. Pettijohn (1949) suggested that the property of sphericity might be measured by the ratio:

$$S_{pa} = s/S \tag{3.1.4}$$

where s is the surface area of a sphere of the same volume as the fragment in question, and S is the actual surface area of the object, (this ratio will be affected by surface texture). He also suggested that the sphericity might be expressed by:

$$S_{pl} = d_n / D_s \tag{3.1.5}$$

where d_n is the nominal diameter (diameter of a sphere of the same volume as the object) and D_s is the diameter of the circumscribing sphere (generally the longest diameter of the object), which is the same as equation (3.1.1). Krumbein and Sloss (1951) proposed, as a similar measure of sphericity to Pettijohn's S_{pl}, the ratio of the nominal diameter d_n to the maximum intercept a through the particle:

$$S_{ks} = d_n / a \ . \tag{3.1.6}$$

Sneed and Folks (1958) (see Brewer, 1964) measured the maximum projection sphericity:

$$S_{sf} = \sqrt[3]{c^2 / ab} \tag{3.1.7}$$

where a, b, c, are the longest, intermediate, and shortest axis, respectively. Brewer (1964) gave a close approximation to true sphericity:

$$S_b = d_c / D_c \tag{3.1.8}$$

where d_c is the diameter of a circle equal in area to the area of the projection of the grain when it lies on its largest face and D_c is the diameter of the smallest circle circumscribing the projection.

In addition to the analytical methods mentioned above, human eyes may be trained to estimate the shape of objects. Krumbein and Sloss (1951), Brewer (1964), Hodgson (1974), FitzPatrick (1984), Bullock (1985), designed standard visual charts of particles which are widely used for classification of sand grains. Figure 3.3 shows Bullock's (1985) standard view chart. This chart is a combination of roundness, sphericity and roughness of particles. Classification by eye is essential in field work, where there is no possibility of measurement; and the success of this depends on the quality of training and hence on the quality of the charts used.

Shape Analysis

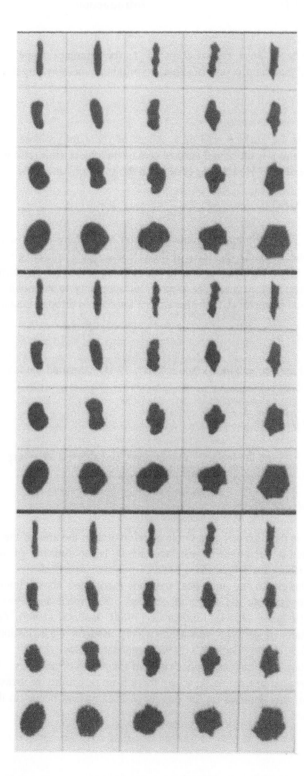

Figure 3.3   Sphericity and roundness charts combined with roughness/smoothness grades (From Bullock (1985) Handbook for Soil Thin Section Descriptions, fig. 31 pp. 31).

3.1.3 Shape Representation in Image Processing

In image processing and pattern recognition, many approaches to the problem of representing the shapes of two-dimensional objects by real-valued features have been proposed. Methods based on representing the boundary of an object include Fourier boundary encoding (Granlund 1972), curvature description using the normalised dot products of the vectors joining successive pairs of boundary points (Rosenfeld and Johnston 1973), direction chain codes (Freeman 1974), piecewise approximation e.g. using straight line segments (Pavlidis 1977), and hierarchical representation (Ballard 1981). Several authors have studied methods based on the medial axis transform (Arcelli et al. 1981, Rosenfeld and Kak 1982). Methods in which an object is decomposed into sub-regions of various shapes were investigated by Shapiro and Haralick(1979), Avis and Toussaint (1981), Ferrari et al. (1980). Papers on morphological and related methods include those by Tradhanias (1992), Shih and Wu (1992), Dai et al. (1992) and McMillan et al. (1992).

3.1.4 Shape Representation by Convex Hull

The shape representations mentioned in Section 3.1.3 are very useful for description of objects with special shapes such as machine spare parts, printing characters, geometric graphs, and so on. However, in some cases, for example in soil micro-structure study as shown in Figure 3.1, the objects to be recognised or classified have almost random shapes, and there are rarely two geometrically similar objects, let alone two exactly the same. For this reason, more appropriate shape representation methods are needed: and moreover the shape representation has to be normalised and invariant with respect to co-ordinate rotation, translation, and scaling.

Here, much use was made of the convex hull as a basis for shape representation. In this chapter, first, a new algorithm, SPCH, is introduced for finding the convex hull of the binary image of an object in two dimensional space, such as one of the soil particles shown in Figure 3.1 (Smart and Tovey 1981). In this method, a simple polygon is first constructed from the binary image of an object by a method I may refer to as *stair climbing*, the convex hull of the object is then found by Sklansky's original algorithm (Sklansky 1972). This approach is guaranteed to find the convex hull correctly even in circumstances where Sklansky's algorithm fails if applied directly to the object, which has the advantage of executing in linear time (provided the object is represented as a set of binary values) in a two-dimensional array as is usual in image processing.

A convex hull based shape representation suitable for classification of irregular objects is then described; and the basic measurements, which were taken from convex hulls of objects in combination with the original object as the shape representation, are explained.

Convex hull based shape representation is invariant with respect to co-ordinate rotation, translation, and scaling. It is useful especially for the representation, recognition, and classification of such objects of random shape, such as soil particles, sand grains, sugar crystals, etc., in two dimensional images such as those which the author has been analysing.

The convex hull can be used to obtain characteristic shape measurements to enable objects to be classified by automatic pattern recognition: the basic set of these measurements is explained towards the end of this chapter. The convex hull is also used in Chapter 5 to provide orientation measurements for pattern recognition, and it is useful when studying clustering in pattern space.

3.2   CONVEX HULL

3.2.1   Introduction

(1)   Definition of Convex Hull
In general, the convex hull of a set of points in high dimensional space is the smallest convex set which contains all of the points in the space.   In two dimensional space, the convex hull of a set of planar points is the smallest convex polygon which contains all the set of planar points and whose vertices are a subset of the planar set.

(2)   Review of Methods of Finding Convex Hull
The convex hull is a very powerful tool in computational geometry.   It is widely used, for example, in image processing (Rosenfeld 1969) and pattern recognition (Duda and Hart 1973, Toussaint 1982).   The computation of the convex hull of a finite set of points, especially in the plane, has been studied extensively over the past decade.   Two aspects of the problem were identified: (a) Finding the convex hull of a set of planar points and (b) Finding the convex hull of a planar polygon. Many algorithms for its solution exist.   The earlier work was reviewed by Toussaint (1981), Preparata and Shamos (1985), and Avis et al. (1985).   Bass and Schubert (1967) was thought to be the first proposing an algorithm for finding the convex hull.   Five years later, Graham (1972) was the first to propose an optimal $O(NlogN)$ algorithm for the convex hull of planar points and $O(N)$ for a star-shaped polygon.   The first $O(N)$ algorithm for some simple polygon was proposed by Sklansky (1972).   Subsequently, Jarvis (1973) and Eddy (1977) developed algorithms with complexity of $O(NH)$, where H is the number of vertices in the convex hull to be found.   Shamos (1978) (see Preparata and Shamos 1985) was the first to propose an $\Omega(NlogN)$ algorithm.   Further optimal algorithms were presented by such as Akl and Toussaint (1978), McCallum and Avis (1979), Preparata (1979), Boas (1980), Devroye and Toussaint (1981), Toussaint and Avis (1982).   The least complexity algorithm might be the $O(NlogH)$ presented by Kirkpatrick and Seidel (1982).   The later methods of finding convex hull can be found in the methods developed by Toussaint and ElGindy (1983), Toussaint (1985), McQueen and Toussaint (1985), Melkman (1987), Day (1988).   Apart from the sequential algorithms, many parallel algorithms have been studied thoroughly such as Jeong and Lee (1988), Miller and Stout (1988).

Most existing algorithms of finding the convex hull allow the input data points to be stored in arbitrary order (although the fast Graham's (1972) algorithm requires that the input data has to be a star-shaped polygon). The simple Sklansky's (1972) algorithm does not work on all polygons correctly (Bykat 1978). It requires that the input data must be a weakly externally visible simple polygon (See definition in Section 3.2.3 Lemma 3.4; see also Toussaint and Avis 1982, Toussaint 1985). In object analysis, the input data is always a binary image of an object. The point set can be either the boundary or the region of the object in the binary image. The distribution of the planar points may not be a star-shaped polygon, nor a weakly externally visible simple polygon. In this case, direct use of the fast Graham's or the simple Sklansky's algorithm may not find the convex hull correctly. The use of the other existing algorithms may be time consuming. Therefore, here is introduced a new algorithm, the SPCH algorithm, which is particularly suitable for use when the point set is stored as an array of binary pixels, and therefore particularly suitable for use in image processing, where this storage method is the one most widely used for binary images. Provided the point set is stored in this way, the SPCH algorithm runs in linear time. The flow chart of the convex hull finding by the SPCH algorithm is shown in Figure 3.4.

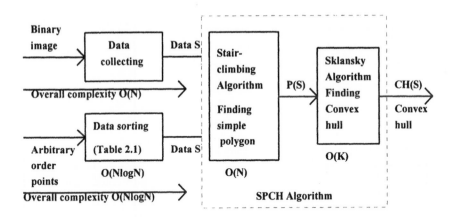

Figure 3.4   Flow chart of convex hull finding.

3.2.2 SPCH Algorithm for Convex Hull Finding

The SPCH algorithm, which finds a convex hull from a binary image, consists of two parts shown in Figure 3.4: (1) finding first a simple polygon $P(S)$ of S by a new algorithm referred to as *stair-climbing* algorithm and (2) finding then the convex hull $CH(P(S))$ of $P(S)$ by Sklansky's algorithm (1972). Here the polygon $P(S)$ is found in such a way that it is guaranteed to lack features which would cause the Sklansky method to fail.

It will be shown in Section 3.2.3 Proposition 3.3 that the complexity of the stair-climbing algorithm (stage 1) is $O(N)$. The complexity of Sklansky's algorithm (stage 2), starting from a polygon with H vertices, is $O(H)$. Thus in the cases of a binary image we are considering, the procedure for finding the convex hull of S runs in linear time $O(N)$. It is also extremely simple.

Other authors of the convex hull algorithm often assume that the input data is stored as a linear array of co-ordinate pairs (x_1,y_1), (x_2,y_2), ..., in arbitrary order. In this case the SPCH algorithm can still be used, but an initial sorting of the data points is necessary. Since the complexity of the sort is $O(N\log N)$, the SPCH algorithm in this case loses its linear-time advantage. However it is worth noting that if the points are already stored in the format of Table 3.1, then the advantage is regained because the additional computation required to find the convex hull has complexity $O(N)$. This was often useful in the object analysis by image processing because the storage scheme of Table 3.1 was already used for other purposes.

Table 3.1   A possible storage scheme for the input data: $x(i) < x(i+1)$, $y(i,j) < y(i,j+1)$. L_k: number of 'black' pixels having $x=x_k$. In applications such as those we consider, data can be stored in this way without increase in computational complexity.

	$x(1)$	$x(2)$	...	$x(k-1)$	$x(k)$	...
$j \setminus i$	1	2	...	$k-1$	k	...
1	$y(1,1)$	$y(2,1)$	...	$y(k-1,1)$	$y(k,1)$	...
2	$y(1,2)$	$y(2,2)$	...	$y(k-1,2)$	$y(k,2)$	...
.	.	.	...	.	.	...
.	.	.	...	.	.	...
L_{k-1}	.	.	...	$y(k-1,L_{k-1})$	.	...
.	.	.	...		.	...
.	.	.	...		.	...
L_1	$y(1,L_1)$	.	...		.	...
L_k		.	...		$y(k, L_k)$	...
.		.	...			...
.		.	...			...
L_2		$y(2, L_2)$	...			...
.			...			...

Chen (1989) presents a generalisation of Sklansky's algorithm; but Toussaint (1991) showed that Chen's method was still not completely general, in other words, it was incapable of correctly finding the convex hull of some polygons in linear time. In contrast, the SPCH approach allows Sklansky's algorithm to be used without generalisation, because of the special properties of $P(S)$.

Figure 3.4 shows two preliminary steps for binary objects and clusters of points respectively. For a cluster of points, the data must be sorted into the order of increasing x increasing y; if necessary, this is a process of $O(N\log N)$. For a binary raster image of an object, the data is already in this required order, and no data collection process is needed. Otherwise, a data collection process might be needed, either to separate objects, or to convert the format of the data supplied. This would probably be a process of $O(N)$, depending on circumstances. In the following, it is assumed that the data has already been sorted into the order of increasing x increasing y as has been done in Table 3.1.

3.2.2.1 Stair-Climbing Method for Simple Polygon Finding

Let S denote a set of N points in a binary image in the plane or in a matrix or an array as shown in Table 3.1. First seek to construct a polygon $P(S)$ satisfying the four conditions: (a) $P(S)$ contains all the points of S; (b) all the vertices V_i of $P(S)$ are points of S; (c) $P(S)$ is non-self-intersecting; (d) $P(S)$ has no externally invisible edges. Obviously there are many ways of constructing such a polygon. Here is presented a method which is referred to as *stair-climbing* (Luo et al. 1992).

In Figure 3.5, let P_l, P_r, P_t, and P_b be the leftmost, rightmost, topmost, and bottommost points of S. Then they $(P_l, P_r, P_t, \text{ and } P_b)$ are also the leftmost, rightmost, topmost, and bottommost points of $P(S)$. Thus the simple polygon $P(S)$ of the planar points S can be regarded as comprising 4 chains C_1 (from P_l to P_b), C_2 (from P_b to P_r), C_3 (from P_r to P_t), and C_4 (from P_t to P_l). Each chain C_i is a polygon path of $P(S)$, and the vertices of C_i are the ones on this path. If the four chains C_1, C_2, C_3, and C_4 are found from the set S, the polygon $P(S)$ can be found by linking the four chains in order.

Let us now construct the chain C_1 as shown in Figure 3.6. Let $x(p)$ and $y(p)$ be the x and y co-ordinates of any point p of S in the plane. Starting from P_l and traversing the chain counter-clockwise, let V_i be the current vertex of C_1. Then the vertex V_{i+1} is chosen as that point p which lies below and to the right of V_i and is nearest to V_i in the x-direction; if there is more than one such point with the same $x(p)$, for example, points p and q, then V_{i+1} is chosen as the one with the smallest $y(p)$, for example, point p. Thus V_{i+1} is chosen so as to satisfy the conditions:

$$x(V_{i+1}) = \min x(p) \qquad p \in S, x(p) > x(V_i), y(p) < y(V_i) \qquad (3.2.1)$$

$$y(V_{i+1}) = \min y(p) \qquad p \in S, x(p) = x(V_{i+1}) . \qquad (3.2.2)$$

This procedure is continued until the point P_b is reached. The equations (3.2.1) and (3.2.2) are actually easy to be achieved while the point p is being found simply by scanning the binary image from left to right and from bottom to top.

The chains C_2, C_3, and C_4, are found similarly (see Appendix 3A). Finally these four chains are linked doubly in series to form the simple polygon $P(S)$. If $P(S)$ is traversed counter-clockwise, the four chains are linked in the order $C_1 \rightarrow C_2 \rightarrow C_3 \rightarrow C_4 \rightarrow C_1$; if $P(S)$ is traversed clockwise, in the order $C_4 \rightarrow C_3 \rightarrow C_2 \rightarrow C_1$

→ C_4.   If the chains of the convex hull are found at the same time as the chains of the simple polygon, then the chains of the convex hull rather than those of the simple polygon are linked.

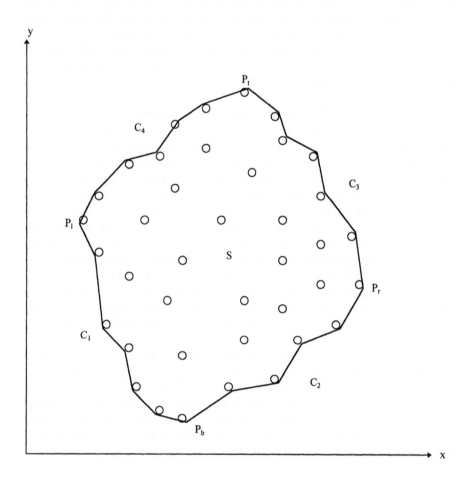

Figure 3.5   Planar points, four most points and four chains.

When this simple polygon finding method is applied on a point set S in an arbitrary order, a suitable storage scheme for the point set S is suggested in Table 3.1: an implementation either as an array or as a list could be used.   In this table, all points with the same value of x are listed in the same column, and these columns are arranged in increasing order of x.   Within each column, the values of y for the points concerned are listed in increasing order of y from top to bottom.   In this scheme, there will, in general, be different numbers of entries in each column; with possibly only one entry in the last row.   This representation can be very simply set up if the points are stored as a matrix of binary pixels or are already sorted in order of their x- and y- co-ordinates; otherwise the preliminary sorting stage mentioned above is necessary.

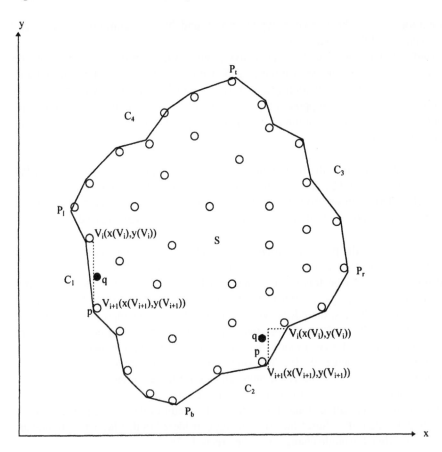

Figure 3.6   Constructing Chain C_1 and C_2 of the simple polygon of point set S.

The stair-climbing approach can still be used even in the following two degenerate cases: (a) when pairs of the four points P_l, P_r, P_t, and P_b are coincident (in this case the number of chains will be two or three); (b) when S has two or more leftmost points with the same x-co-ordinate, two or more bottommost points with the same y-co-ordinate, etc. in this case the polygon will acquire additional edges not associated with any chain, but these are easily dealt with.

The algorithm, *simpoly.cpp*, of the stair-climbing approach for finding the simple polygon of a boundary in a binary image was written in C++ language by the author.   It is listed in Computer Programs at the end of this book.

3.2.2.2 Properties of the Simple Polygon
We now show that the polygon $P(S)$ constructed by this algorithm has the required properties, and we derive some further properties.

Lemma 3.1   The simple polygon $P(S)$ found by stair-climbing for the set S contains all of the planar points S.
Proof   Let V_i and V_j be two successive points on a chain of the simple polygon; thus V_j is V_{i+1}.   Suppose a point $p \in S$, having $x(p) < x(V_j)$,   lies outside $P(S)$ (Figure 3.7); then by equation (3.2.1) p is V_{i+1} and V_j is not V_{i+1}, contradicting our initial assumption.   Suppose now that a point $q \in S$, having $x(q) = x(V_j)$, lies outside $P(S)$; then by equation (3.2.2) q is V V_{i+1} and V_j is not V V_{i+1}, contradicting our initial assumption.

Lemma 3.2   Each of the four chains C_1, C_2, C_3, and C_4 of the simple polygon $P(S)$ of the set S as found by stair-climbing is a single-valued function of x and y.
Proof   This follows from the fact that the x- and y- co-ordinates of successive vertices of each of the four chains C_i are monotonically increasing or decreasing.

Lemma 3.3   If the polygon is traversed counter-clockwise, the angle change of the edges of the simple polygon $P(S)$ found by stair-climbing is 360°.
Proof   Let $P(S)$ be traversed counter-clockwise and consider two consecutive chains C_i and $C_{(i \ module \ 4)+1}$.   Because each chain C_i is a single-valued function of the x- and y-co-ordinates, the edges (viewed as directed edges) adjacent to the starting points ($\in \{P_l, P_r, P_t, P_b\}$) of these two chains will lie in two different but adjacent quadric spaces of the (x,y) plane, and the difference in angle between these edges will be in the range $0° \le \theta \le 180°$ (the equalities corresponding to the above degenerate case b).   Similarly the angle change for three consecutive chains will be in the range $90° \le \theta \le 270°$, for four consecutive chains in the range $180° \le \theta \le 360°$, and for five consecutive chains (i.e. a complete circuit of the simple polygon) in the range $270° \le \theta \le 450°$.   Since the edges being considered in this last case are one and the same edge, the angle change must be precisely 360°.

Lemma 3.4   The simple polygon $P(S)$ found by stair-climbing for the set S has neither externally invisible edges, nor weakly externally visible edges (Toussaint and Avis 1982).
Proof   As shown in Figure 3.8, an externally invisible edge is defined as: Let p be any non-end point on an edge of the simple polygon: from any such point p, if we can draw outwards at least one ray without intersection with the polygon, the point p is called an externally visible point.   If an edge has no externally visible point, it is called an externally invisible edge.   For example, the edges $V_i V_j$, V_{jq} are externally invisible edges.   If some but not all points of an edge are externally visible, then that edge is termed weakly externally visible.   For example, the edge V_{ir} is a weakly externally visible edge.   Because the position of p may vary, it is not shown in Figure 3.8.

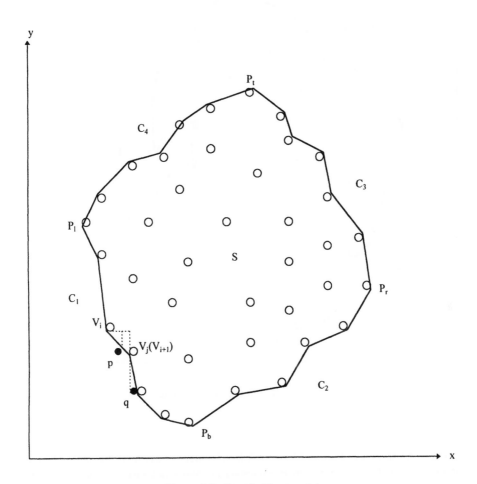

Figure 3.7   Proof of Lemma 3.1.

If $P(S)$ has externally invisible or weakly externally visible edges, then $P(S)$ must be a multi-valued function of the x- and/or y-co-ordinates.   This contradicts Lemma 3.2.

Lemma 3.5   The simple polygon $P(S)$ found by stair-climbing for the set S is non-self-intersecting.

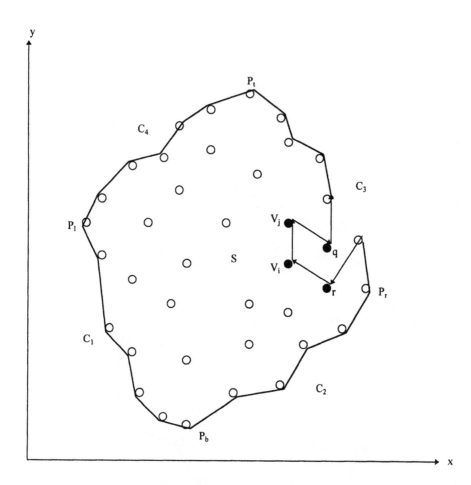

Figure 3.8   Externally invisible edges.

Proof   As shown in Figure 3.9, if $P(S)$ is self-intersecting, then the angle change
of its edges is 720° or more when traversing counter-clockwise.   This contradicts
Lemma 3.3.

Of all points having the same x-co-ordinate, only those points having the largest
and smallest y-co-ordinates have to be queried in constructing a chain (provided
that, as in our application, the points have satisfied the assumption above).   This is
an advantage of the stair-climbing algorithm.   Lemma 3.1 ensures that the simple
polygon $P(S)$ found by stair-climbing for the set S of N points in the plane is
correct.   Lemma 3.4 and 3.5 will make the algorithm for finding the convex hull of
the set S from the simple polygon $P(S)$ very simple and fast (Sklansky 1972,
Toussaint and Avis 1982, Orlowski 1983).

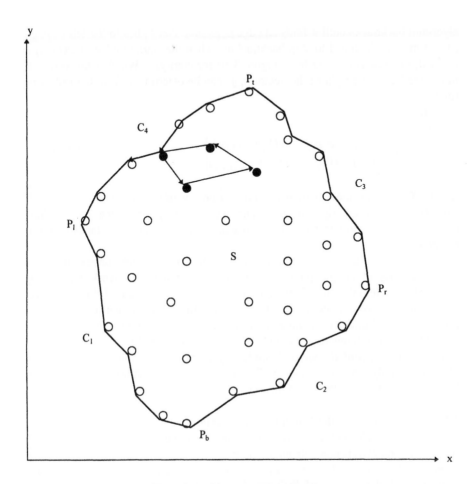

Figure 3.9   Self-intersecting polygon.

3.2.2.3   Sklansky's Algorithm for Convex Hull Finding
In this section Sklansky's original algorithm (1972) is briefly described.

Let $CH(S)$ denote the convex hull of a set S of points, and let $CH(P(S))$ denote the convex hull of a simple polygon $P(S)$, which satisfies the conditions stated in Section 3.2.2. $CH(S)$ is the intersection of all convex sets in the plane containing S, and (for a finite set S) $CH(S)$ is always a convex polygon whose vertices are elements of S, and $CH(S)$ contains all the points of S in the plane (Avis et al. 1985). $CH(P(S))$ is the smallest convex polygon containing $P(S)$ (Shin and Woo, 1986). It is obvious that the convex hull of S is also the convex hull of $P(S)$, i.e. $CH(S) = CH(P(S))$. In our method, a polygon $P(P(S))$ is found from $P(S)$ by Sklansky's algorithm, shown in outline in Figure 3.10. Briefly, assuming $P(S)$ to be traversed counter-clockwise, successive vertices V_j of $P(S)$ are included into $P(P(S))$ as long as $P(S)$ is convex at V_j. If however $P(S)$ is not convex at a vertex V_j, then the algorithm backtracks until it finds an edge $p_{i-1}p_i$ such that V_j lies to the left of $p_{i-1}p_i$. (A test must be included to stop backtracking when the starting edge of $P(P(S))$ is reached; this test is omitted from Figure 3.10 for clarity). Whether the vertex V_j lies to the left or the right of the vector $p_{i-1}p_i$ can be determined from the following rule:

Let:

$$\det|.| = \det\begin{vmatrix} x(V_j) - x(p_i) & y(V_j) - y(p_i) \\ x(p_i) - x(p_{i-1}) & y(p_i) - y(p_{i-1}) \end{vmatrix}.$$

(3.2.3)

If $\det|.|<0$, V_j is on the left of $p_{i-1}p_i$ and is a new vertex of the convex hull. If $\det|.|>0$, V_j is on the right of $p_{i-1}p_i$ and we remove p_i from the convex hull, decrement i by 1, and retest V_j. This procedure continues until the starting point is reached.

In general Sklansky's simple algorithm can compute the convex hull of a restricted class of simple polygons, and it is guaranteed to work for weakly externally visible polygons (Toussaint and Avis 1982, Toussaint 1985). However in the remainder of this section we show that, because of the properties of our $P(S)$ (Section 3.2.3), Sklansky's simple algorithm will always correctly find the convex hull of the original point set S, i.e. $P(P(S)) = CH(P(S)) = CH(S)$.

The algorithm, *conhull.cpp*, of the Sklansky approach for finding the convex hull of a simple polygon was written in C++ language by the author. It is listed in Computer Programs at the end of this book.

3.2.3   The Validity of the Convex Hull Finding
Lemma 3.6   The polygon $P(P(S))$ formed by Sklansky's algorithm from the simple polygon $P(S)$ is non-self-intersecting.
Proof   This follows directly from Lemmas 3.3, 3.4, and 3.5. While $P(P(S))$ is being formed, the vertices of $P(S)$ are checked in succession by equation (3.2.3), and the ones satisfying equation (3.2.3) are included in succession into $P(P(S))$. Therefore from Lemmas 3.3, 3.4, and 3.5, $P(P(S))$ is definitely non-self-intersecting.

Lemma 3.7   The polygon $P(P(S))$ formed by Sklansky's algorithm from the simple polygon $P(S)$ contains all of the planar points of $P(S)$.
Proof   In Figure 3.10, let p_i be a vertex of both $P(P(S))$ and $P(S)$ and suppose the vertex V_j of $P(S)$ is the vertex p_{i+1} of $P(P(S))$. $P(P(S))$ is traversed counter-clockwise. If the following vertex V_{j+1} lies outside $P(P(S))$, it must be on the right of the vector $p_i p_{i+1}$ when $P(P(S))$ is traversed counter-clockwise.   Therefore according to the rule for finding the convex polygon from the simple polygon, p_{i+1} cannot be a vertex of $P(P(S))$. This contradicts the initial assumption.

Lemma 3.8   The polygon $P(P(S))$ formed by Sklansky's algorithm from the simple polygon $P(S)$ is a convex hull.

Proof   According to the algorithm, any vertex V_j of $P(P(S))$ must lie on the left side of the vector $V_{j-1}V_{j-2}$ if $P(P(S))$ is traversed counter-clockwise.   Hence by Lemma 3.7, all points of $P(S)$ are on the left side of any edge of $P(P(S))$, and by Lemma 3.1, all points of S are on the left side of any edge of $P(P(S))$ (the two end points of the edge are excepted).   Therefore $P(P(S))$ is indeed a convex polygon.

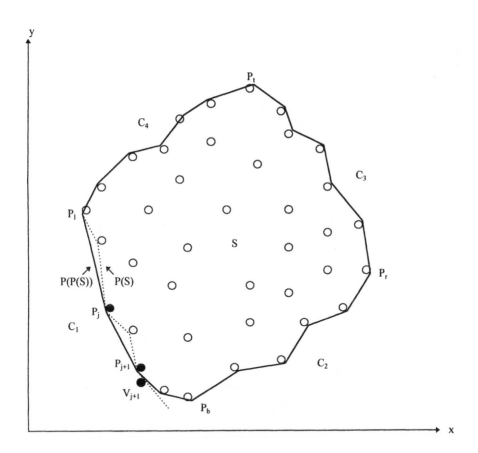

Figure 3.10   Finding convex hull of simple polygon.

Proposition 3.1   The polygon $P(P(S))$ formed by Sklansky's algorithm from the simple polygon $P(S)$ is the convex hull $CH(P(S))$ of the simple polygon $P(S)$, i.e. $CH(P(S)) = P(P(S))$.

Proof   See Figure 3.11.   If $P(P(S))$ is not the convex hull of $P(S)$, then there exists another convex polygon $P'(P(S))$ smaller than $P(P(S))$.   Thus $P'(P(S))$ must have at least one vertex less and at least one edge less than $P(P(S))$.   Consequently $P(P(S))$ possesses at least one vertex p_i (say) lying outside $P'(P(S))$.   Since p_i must also be a vertex of $P(S)$, Lemma 3.7 is contradicted.

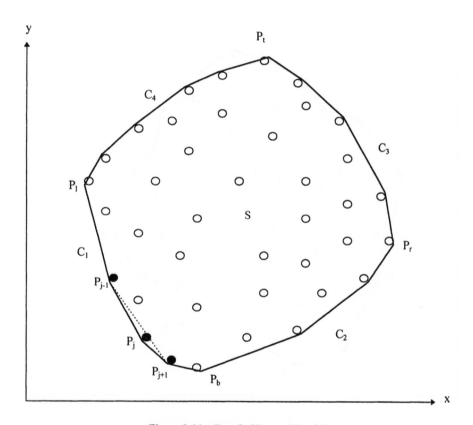

Figure 3.11   Proof of Proposition 3.1.

Proposition 3.2   The above algorithm for finding the convex hull of a finite set of points in the plane is correct.
Proof   This follows directly from Proposition 3.1, using $CH(S) = CH(P(S))$.

Proposition 3.3   The complexity of this algorithm for convex hull finding is $O(N)$ for finding $P(S)$ and O(K) for finding $CH(P(S))$, where N is the number of points in the set S and K is the number of vertices in $P(S)$.   If the data sorting is needed, the complexity is $O(N\log N)$.

Proof

(a) Forming $P(S)$ from S.   Constructing chains C_1 and C_2 by stair-climbing requires at most each of the N points of the set S to be queried (this worst case is the one where no two or more points have the same x-co-ordinate).   Similarly, constructing chains C_3 and C_4 requires at most each of the N points to be queried. Thus the complexity of the of the algorithm for finding $P(S)$ is $O(N)$.

(b) Forming $CH(P(S))$ from $P(S)$.   Sklansky's algorithm is known to be linear in the number of input points.   In our case the number of input points is the number of vertices K in $P(S)$.   Thus the complexity of this stage is $O(K)$.

3.2.4   Conclusions

A simple and fast algorithm (the SPCH algorithm) has been introduced for finding the convex hull of a set S of points in a binary image in a plane.   The algorithm operates in two stages: (a) finding from S a simple polygon $P(S)$ by the stair-climbing algorithm; (b) finding from $P(S)$ the convex hull $CH(P(S))$ by Sklansky's algorithm.   The complexities of the two stages are respectively $O(N)$ and $O(K)$, where N and K are respectively the numbers of points in S and $P(S)$.   In the most general case where the data points are in arbitrary order, a preliminary sorting step of complexity $O(N\log N)$ is necessary and the overall complexity is also $O(N\log N)$. However in two important situations the SPCH algorithm runs in linear time, with complexity $O(N)$: (a) if the data points are already sorted for other purposes, as was often the case in the author's work where the storage scheme of Table 3.1 was used: (b) if the data values are stored as a two-dimensional binary array, as is the case in most image processing applications where a convex hull is required.

3.3   CONVEX HULL BASED SHAPE REPRESENTATION

Many methods of representing the shape of an object, including those utilising the convex hull, have appeared in the literature of image processing and of soils (see Section 3.1.2 and 3.1.3).   In this section, a shape representation is presented which is particularly suitable for objects of random shape such as sand grains, sugar crystals, blood cells, nerve cells, etc., and for the soil particles.

In two dimensional image processing, the image of an object is the projection of the object into two dimensional space.   For example, in the study of soil, a particle is often projected onto a plane in such a way that the projected region is the largest section of the particle.   In soil thin section microscopy, the image of a soil particle is a section of the particle in a certain direction.   In general, the image of an object contains information on the brightness, shadow, projected edge, projected boundary, etc.   However, if we are concerned with the shape of an object in the projection plane, we are just interested in its projected binary image (the projected region or projected boundary) in two dimensional space. From this point of view, an object can be thought of as a set of planar points in the plane of projection, comprising the projected binary image or its boundary. For representation and subsequent recognition and classification of random shaped objects such as the soil particles in this project, because one and only one convex hull can be found from a set of planar points, a shape representation based on the convex hull is likely to be useful. In this approach, the convex hull of the binary image or boundary of an object is found first, then measurements of the convex hull in combination with the object or its boundary are made. Finally, features are extracted from these measurements and used as the components of pattern vectors which represent the shapes of the objects. The author uses a transformed co-ordinate system and normalised features; therefore this method satisfies the requirement of invariance with respect to co-ordinate translation, rotation and scaling.

This section presents the co-ordinate system used and presents a method of representing the boundary and the convex hull of an object by description functions. In Section 3.3.3 this representation is used as the basis of a set of features for shape representation.

3.3.1   Boundary and Convex Hull

In a two dimensional space X, where $X=(x_1, x_2)'$, an object can be described by its boundary. A boundary B is expressed by a sequence of boundary points $p_i(x_1, x_2)$, starting from a point p_1 of the boundary and traversing along the boundary clockwise or counter-clockwise:

$$B = \{p_i(x_1, x_2)\} \qquad (3.3.1)$$

where $i=1,2,...,M$, and M is the number of boundary points. It can also be described as a function in the two dimensional space:

$$x_2 = B(x_1) = f_0(x_1) . \qquad (3.3.2)$$

The discussion below refers to the example in Figure 3.12, which shows a boundary with its convex hull. Like a boundary, a convex hull C can be described by a sequence of its vertices $v_i(x_1, x_2)$, starting from a vertex v_1, traversing along the convex hull clockwise or counter-clockwise:

$$C = \{v_i(x_1, x_2)\} \qquad (3.3.3)$$

where $i=1,2,...,N$, and N is the number of vertices of the convex hull. Thus, $N \leq M$. The convex hull can also be described as a function:

$$x_2 = C(x_1) = g_0(x_1) . \qquad (3.3.4)$$

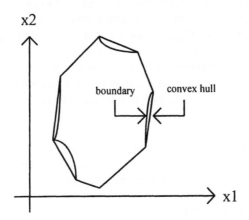

Figure 3.12   The convex hull of a boundary.

In general, equations (3.3.1) and (3.3.3) are not convenient for observation and analysis of the features for object recognition and classification.   Because a boundary may have a complicated shape, equation (3.3.2) cannot be implemented by simple models.   However because the convex hull is just a polygon consisting of straight line segments, equation (3.3.4) can be easily implemented by a set of linear functions.   This is a further reason for choosing to represent the shape of an object by a method based on its convex hull.   Moreover in practice, in many cases, the boundary of an object in a two dimensional image can be approximated by its convex hull.   For example, triangles, rectangles, squares, diamonds, trapezoids, etc., have convex hulls which are the same as themselves.   Circles or ellipses are the limits of their convex hulls.   Soil particles and other random-shaped objects in real digital images can also be approximated by their convex hulls.

3.3.2   Description Function
Direct employment of equation (3.3.4) is unsuitable for shape representation for object recognition and classification, because $g_0(x_1)$ is not invariant with respect to co-ordinate translation, rotation, and scaling.   These problems can be avoided or reduced by using the following co-ordinate system Y.

(1) Coordinate system Y

As shown in Figure 3.13, let $v_l v_r$ be the longest diagonal of the convex hull of an object, having a length D_{max}, with vertices v_l and v_r at its two ends. This diagonal divides the convex hull into two parts: upper part and lower part. Let v_t be the highest vertex with height W_{max1} above $v_l v_r$ in the upper part, v_b the lowest vertex with height W_{max2} above $v_l v_r$ in the lower part, v_t and v_b being so chosen that $W_{max1} \geq W_{max2}$. Then v_l is chosen as the origin of a new co-ordinate system Y, $v_l v_r$ as axis y_1. Axis y_2 is chosen so that v_t lies in the first quadrant assuming right hand axes. In addition, the whole diagram is normalised by the length D_{max} of $v_l v_r$.

(2) Coordinate transform

Obviously, the new co-ordinate system Y, $Y=(y_1, y_2)'$, can be transformed from the original co-ordinate system X, $X=(x_1, x_2)'$ by rotating, translating, and scaling X. This can be done by the following linear transformation:

$$Y = AX + B = \Lambda\Theta X - \Lambda\Theta X_0 \qquad (3.3.5)$$

where

$$A = \Lambda\Theta \qquad (3.3.6)$$

$$B = -\Lambda\Theta X_0 \qquad (3.3.7)$$

$$\Lambda = \begin{bmatrix} 1/D_{max} & 0 \\ 0 & 1/D_{max} \end{bmatrix} \qquad (3.3.8)$$

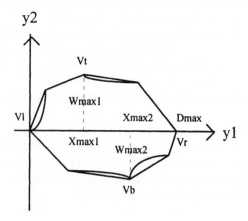

Figure 3.13   Concept and measurement of convex hull.

$$\Theta = \begin{bmatrix} -\cos\theta & \sin\theta \\ \sin\theta & \cos\theta \end{bmatrix} \qquad (3.3.9)$$

$$X_0 = \begin{bmatrix} x_{1I} \\ x_{2I} \end{bmatrix} \qquad (3.3.10)$$

$$\theta = \theta' \quad \text{or} \quad \theta' + \pi \quad \text{so that} \qquad _{\max 1} \geq W_{\max 2} \qquad (3.3.11)$$

$$\theta' = \arctan(\frac{x_{2r} - x_{2I}}{x_{1r} - x_{1I}}) \qquad (3.3.12)$$

$$D_{\max} = d(v_I v_r) = \max\{d(v_i v_j)\} \qquad (3.3.13)$$

$$d(v_i, v_j) = \|x_i - x_j\| = \sqrt{(x_{1i} - x_{1j})^2 + (x_{2i} - x_{2j})^2} . \qquad (3.3.14)$$

Here v_i, v_j are any two vertices of the convex hull, $i,j=1,2,...,N$, and $d(v_i, v_j)$ is the distance between v_i and v_j. Thus, in the co-ordinate system Y, equations (3.3.2) and (3.3.4) become:

$$y_2 = B(y_1) = f_1(y_1) \qquad (3.3.15)$$

$$y_2 = C(y_1) = g_1(y_1) \qquad (3.3.16)$$

where $0 \leq y_1 \leq 1$.

Because the length of each diagonal or edge is not greater than $D_{\max}$, the greatest possible height of the upper part is equal to that of an equilateral triangle; then:

$$y_{2\max} = \sqrt{d^2(v_I, v_r) - (D_{\max}/2)^2} = \sqrt{1 - 1/4} = \sqrt{3}/2 . \qquad (3.3.17)$$

Also the greatest possible height of the lower part is a half of the $D_{\max}$, i.e., the heights of the two halves are equal:

$$y_{2\min} = -D_{\max}/2 = -1/2 . \qquad (3.3.18)$$

Therefore, the limits for y_2 are $-1/2 \leq y_2 \leq +\sqrt{3}/2$.

(3) Description Function
In Y, the axis y_1 divides the convex hull into an upper part and a lower part. Suppose we cut off the lower part, and rotate it -180° about the origin. Then as shown in Figure 3.14 (a), the boundary and the convex hull can be described in a more convenient form than equations (3.3.15) and (3.3.16):

$$y_2 = B(y_1) = f_2(y_1) \tag{3.3.19}$$

$$y_2 = C(y_1) = g_2(y_1) \tag{3.3.20}$$

where $-1 \le y_1 \le 1$ and $0 \le y_2 \le (\sqrt{3})/2$. Equation (3.3.19) and (3.3.20) are easily derived from equations (3.3.15) and (3.3.16) by:

$$f_2(y_1) = f_1(y_1) \qquad\qquad (y_1 > 0, y_2 > 0) \tag{3.3.21}$$

$$f_2(-y_1) = -f_1(y_1) \qquad\qquad (y_1 > 0, y_2 < 0) \tag{3.3.22}$$

$$g_2(y_1) = g_1(y_1) \qquad\qquad (y_1 > 0, y_2 > 0) \tag{3.3.23}$$

$$g_2(-y_1) = -g_1(y_1) \qquad\qquad (y_1 > 0, y_2 < 0) . \tag{3.3.24}$$

$C(y_1)$ in equation (3.3.20) is always a single-valued function of y_1. In equation (3.3.19), $B(y_1)$ either is a single-valued function of y_1 or can be approximated by a single-valued function of y_1 (approximating is necessary in some cases where bays of complicated shape exist in the boundary: methods of approximation are not discussed here). We therefore choose equation (3.3.19) and (3.3.20) rather than equation (3.3.15) and (3.3.16) as the description functions of the objects; and in the following $f_2(y_1)$ is supposed or approximated to be a single-valued function of y_1. Based on these description functions, we define another two useful functions: namely error function $E(y_1)$ and derivative function $D(y_1)$:

$$E(y_1) = C(y_1) - B(y_1) = g_2(y_1) - f_2(y_1) \tag{3.3.25}$$

$$D(y_1) = \frac{d(g_2(y_1))}{dy_1} . \tag{3.3.26}$$

Since the convex hull is composed of straight chords from vertex to vertex, $D(y_1)$ is calculated directly as the slope of these chords. The error function $E(y_1)$ indicates the error caused by approximating the boundary to its convex hull: the derivative function $D(y_1)$ will be used below to find the curvature of the convex hull at a vertex. These two functions are shown in Figure 3.14 (b) and (c) respectively.

3.3.3   Feature Extraction and Shape Classification
The co-ordinate system and description functions presented in Section 3.3 can be used to allow the computation of measurements which are useful for shape representation for purposes such as sorting randomly shaped particles into pattern classes. In this section several such possible measurements are defined, and in Section 3.3.4 examples of their use are given.

Some of the measurements have already been mentioned in passing in Section 3.3. For completeness these measurements are included in this section together with some new ones, and full definitions allowing the values of the measurements to be computed from the description functions in Section 3.3 are given.

The description functions based on the convex hull are simple and convenient for feature measurement, feature extraction, and shape representation.

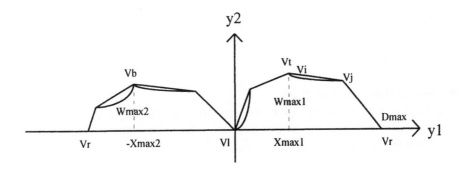

(a)   Function of convex hull and boundary

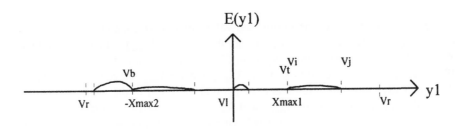

(b)   Error function

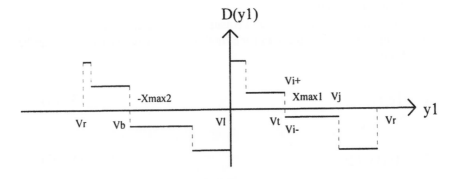

(c)   Derivative function

Figure 3.14   Description function of convex hull.

3.3.3.1 Measurements
From the description functions, we define some measurements as follows:

(a) Half Widths W_{max1} and W_{max2}
Referring to Figure 3.13 and Figure 3.14 (a), the half widths W_{max1} and W_{max2}, are
the height of v_t and v_b respectively. They can be calculated from equation (3.3.20):

$$W_{max\,1} = \max\{g_2(y_1)|_{y_1 > 0}\} \qquad\qquad (3.3.27)$$

$$W_{max\,2} = \max\{g_2(y_1)|_{y_1 < 0}\}. \qquad\qquad (3.3.28)$$

(b) Vertical Half-Symmetry S_{v1}, S_{v2}
The vertical half-symmetry S_{v1} is the symmetry of the upper part about the
perpendicular bisector of the longest diagonal. S_{v2} is the symmetry of the lower
part about the same line as S_{v1}. S_{v1} and S_{v2} are defined by:

$$S_{v1} = X_{max\,1} - 1/2 \qquad\qquad (3.3.29)$$

$$S_{v2} = X_{max\,2} - 1/2 \qquad\qquad (3.3.30)$$

where X_{max1} and X_{max2} are the normalised values of y_1 corresponding to W_{max1} and
W_{max2}, respectively, $W_{max1} = g_2 (X_{max1})$ and $W_{max2} = g_2 (-X_{max2})$ (Figure 3.14 (a)).
X_{max1} and X_{max2} are found from equation (3.3.20) at the same time as W_{max1} and
W_{max2} are found. If two vertices at $y_1 = X_{max11}$ and $y_1 = X_{max12}$ have the same height
W_{max1} (usually corresponding to an edge parallel to axis y_1 in the upper part), then
X_{max1} takes the mean value of X_{max11} and X_{max12}. Two vertices which are at $y_1 = -X_{max21}$ and $y_1 = -X_{max22}$ in the lower part having the same height W_{max2} are processed
similarly.

(c) Area A_c of convex hull
From Figure 3.13, Figure 3.14 (a), and equation (3.3.20), the partial areas A_{c1} and
A_{c2} of the upper and lower parts and the total area A_c of the convex hull can be
obtained from:

$$A_{c1} = \int_0^1 g_2(y_1)dy_1 \qquad\qquad (3.3.31)$$

$$A_{c2} = \int_{-1}^0 g_2(y_1)dy_1 \qquad\qquad (3.3.32)$$

$$A_c = A_{c1} + A_{c2}. \qquad\qquad (3.3.33)$$

If only A_c is required, it may be obtained directly from:

$$A_c = \int_{-1}^{1} g_2(y_1)dy_1 \cdot$$ (3.3.34)

(d) Perimeter P_c of the convex hull
From Figure 3.13, Figure 3.14 (a), and equation (3.3.20), the perimeter P_c of the convex hull can be given by:

$$P_c = \int_{l_c} dl_c$$ (3.3.35)

where dl_c is an element of the boundary of the convex hull.

(e) Area A_p of the original object
Similarly the convex hull, the nominal area A_p of the original object can be calculated from the boundary function (3.3.19):

$$A_{p1} = \int_{0}^{1} f_2(y_1)dy_1$$ (3.3.36)

$$A_{p2} = \int_{-1}^{0} f_2(y_1)dy_1$$ (3.3.37)

$$A_p = A_{p1} + A_{p2}$$ (3.3.38)

or

$$A_p = \int_{-1}^{1} f_2(y_1)dy_1 \cdot$$ (3.3.39)

(f) Perimeter P_p of the original object.
The nominal perimeter, P_p, of the original object can also be derived from equation (3.3.19):

$$P_p = \int_{l_p} dl_p$$ (3.3.40)

where dl_p is an element of the boundary of the original object.

(g) Local Convex Deficiencies $CDLa(v_i, v_j)$ and $CDLp(v_i, v_j)$

The local convex deficiencies $CDLa(v_i, v_j)$ and $CDLp(v_i, v_j)$, for area and perimeter respectively, between the convex hull and the boundary of the object from vertex v_i to vertex v_j, are defined as follows:

$$CDLa(v_i, v_j) = \int_i^j E(y_1) dy_1 \qquad\qquad (3.3.41)$$

$$CDLp(v_i, v_j) = \int_i^j dl_p - \int_i^j dl_c \cdot \qquad\qquad (3.3.42)$$

(h) Curvature $Cur(v_i)$ of convex hull at the vertex v_i

The curvature $Cur(v_i)$ of the convex hull at the vertex v_i is the change in angle at v_i. It can be calculated from equation (3.3.26):

$$Cur(v_i) = \arctan(D(y_1)|_{v_i^+}) - \arctan(D(y_1)|_{v_i^-}) . \qquad\qquad (3.3.43)$$

Care is needed at v_l and v_r.

3.3.3.2   Feature Extraction

For the purpose of pattern recognition and classification, some features can be selected from the measurements and some can be extracted by combining some measurements.   There are a large number of possibilities, some of which might be useful in one case, while some of which might be more useful in another.   For randomly shaped objects, features were extracted as follows:

(a) Width W_s and W_d of object

The width, W_s, of an object is defined as the sum of the half widths W_{max1} and W_{max2}:

$$W_s = W_{max 1} + W_{max 2} \cdot \qquad\qquad (3.3.44)$$

The difference of the half widths, W_d, given by:

$$W_d = W_{max 1} - W_{max 2} \qquad\qquad (3.3.45)$$

may also be useful as an indication of symmetry in some situations.

(b) Horizontal Symmetry S_h

The horizontal symmetry S_h indicates reflectional symmetry of the upper part and the lower part about axis y_1.   It is defined by:

$$S_h = W_{max 2} / W_{max 1} \cdot \qquad\qquad (3.3.46)$$

Correspondingly, S_h' indicates rotational symmetry, where:

$$S_h' = (1 - W_{max2}) / W_{max1} .$$
(3.3.47)

(c) Ratios Rcr_1 and Rcr_2 of convex hull to its convex rectangle.
The relationship of the convex hull to its convex rectangle may be useful. The most promising parameters are thought to be:

$$Rcr_1 = \frac{A_{c1} - (D_{max} \times W_{max1}) / 2}{(D_{max} \times W_{max1}) / 2}$$
(3.3.48)

$$Rcr_2 = \frac{A_{c2} - (D_{max} \times W_{max2}) / 2}{(D_{max} \times W_{max2}) / 2}$$
(3.3.49)

These ratios measure the excesses of the part convex hulls above triangles of the same height.

(d) Area-Perimeter Shape Factor, $Rapc$, of convex hull
The traditional area-perimeter shape factor of the convex hull is given by:

$$Rapc = A_c / P_c^2$$
(3.3.50)

or in normalised form as:

$$Rapc' = 4\pi A_c / P_c^2 .$$
(3.3.51)

(e) Maximal Local Convex Deficiencies $CDMa$ and $CDMp$
The maximal local convex deficiencies $CDMa$ and $CDMp$ are the largest local convex deficiencies among all of the local convex deficiencies (which are measured from vertex to vertex):

$$CDMa = CDLa\,(v_m, v_n) = \max\{CDLa\,(v_i, v_j)\}$$
(3.3.52)

$$CDMp = CDLp(v_m, v_n) = \max\{CDLp(v_i, v_j)\} .$$
(3.3.53)

These give, respectively, the largest and most contorted 'bays along the coastline'. The normalised maximal local convex deficiencies $CDMa'$ and $CDMp'$ are:

$$CDMa' = CDMa / A_c$$
(3.3.54)

$$CDMp' = CDMp / P_c .$$
(3.3.55)

(f) Mean Convex Deficiencies *CDAa* and *CDAp*
The mean convex deficiencies *CDAa* and *CDAp* are the average over all local convex deficiencies:

$$CDAa = (\sum CDLa\,(v_i,v_j))/N \qquad\qquad (3.3.56)$$

$$CDAp = (\sum CDLp(v_i,v_j))/N. \qquad\qquad (3.3.57)$$

(g) Global Convex Deficiencies *CDGa* and *CDGp*
The *CDGa* and *CDGp* between the convex hull and the object are determined by:

$$CDGa = A_c - A_p \qquad\qquad (3.3.58)$$

$$CDGp = P_p - P_c. \qquad\qquad (3.3.59)$$

CDGa may be normalised by dividing by A_c:

$$CDGa' = (A_c - A_p)/A_c \qquad\qquad (3.3.60)$$

and it then gives the 'porosity' of the nominal particle defined by the convex hull. If the original particle contain holes, there is an alternative version of *CDGa'* which may be considered if the holes are considered to be 'unfilled': for soil 'particles', which are often aggregates, the unfilled version has better physical significance.

(h) Maximal Curvature C_{max}
The maximal curvature C_{max} can be obtained by:

$$C_{max} = \max\{Cur(v_i)\} \qquad (i = 1,2,...,N) \qquad\qquad (3.3.61)$$

and normalised:

$$C'_{max} = C_{max}/\pi. \qquad\qquad (3.3.62)$$

The corresponding mean curvature

$$C_{mean} = \frac{1}{N}\sum_{i=1}^{N} Cur(v_i) \qquad\qquad (3.3.63)$$

should always be $2\pi/N$, or the normalised mean curvature

$$C'_{mean} = C_{mean}/\pi \qquad\qquad (3.3.64)$$

should always be $2/N$.

3.3.3.3 Shape Classification

The shape of an object can be represented by a pattern vector, each of whose components is one of the features selected and/or extracted from the measurements. Let R be the vector and r_i be a component of R; then an object can be represented by:

$$R = (\, r_1 \, r_2 \dots r_c \,)^t \tag{3.3.65}$$

where the pattern has c components.   Based on the convex hull of the boundary of an object, all the features, or a selection of the features, can be chosen as the components of R.   As an example, the experiment on pattern recognition below used the following version of R:

$r_1 = W_s$ $r_2 = S_h$ $r_3 = S_{v1}$ $r_4 = S_{v2}$ $r_5 = R_{cr1}$ $r_6 = R_{cr2}$

$r_7 = CDMa'$ $r_8 = CDGa'$ $r_9 = R_{apc}$ $r_{10} = C_{max}'$ $r_{11} = C_{mean}'$.

3.3.4   Examples of Shape Analysis

Five examples were made as a preliminary demonstration of the usefulness of the vector R defined above.   These were (1) an image comprising artificial 'objects' of different geometrical shapes; (2) images of plant leaves of various species of the genus Alchemilia; (3) and (4) two published sets of charts of different shapes of soil particles; (5) the real soil particles in Figure 3.1.   The charts studied in Example 3 were originally intended for use as a reference in visually classifying real soil particles, and the results of Example 3 may be useful in evaluating the charts quantitatively in relation to this purposes.

Example 1

The method used here for convex hull based shape representation was first applied to an artificial image as shown in Figure 3.15.   This input image was first processed to yield the boundary (Luo and Ma, 1989) and the convex hull of each object; and the above features of each object were measured, selected, and extracted.   The algorithm, *edgfoll.cpp*, of the edge following approach for finding the boundary of an object in a binary image was written in C++ language by the author.   It is listed in Computer Programs at the end of this book.   The pattern vectors representing the objects in Figure 3.15 are listed in Table 3.2.   To allow visual examination, these patterns were also transformed and projected onto two dimensional space by the method of principal component transformation.   The projections are shown in Figure 3.16.   From both Table 3.2 and Figure 3.16, we can see that the patterns of similar objects are nearly the same or close to each other, and that the patterns of different objects are clearly different or far away from the others.

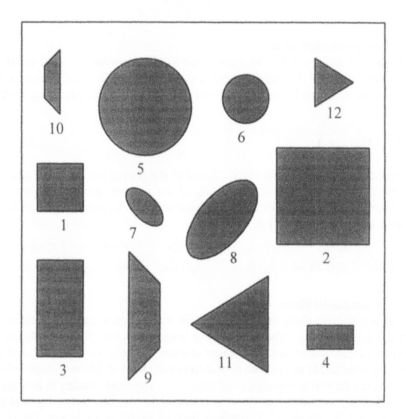

Figure 3.15   Test image.

Table 3.2   Features of Figure 3.15; r_i are defined in the text.

Name		Square		Rectangl		Circle		Ellipse		Trapezoi		Triangle	
No		1	2	3	4	5	6	7	8	9	10	11	12
r_1	W_s	1.00	1.00	0.80	0.78	1.00	1.00	0.50	0.50	0.25	0.24	0.76	0.76
r_2	S_h	1.00	1.00	1.00	1.00	1.00	1.00	1.00	1.00	0.00	0.00	0.00	0.00
r_3	S_{vl}	-0.01	0.00	-0.30	-0.32	0.00	0.00	-0.09	-0.05	0.00	0.00	-0.01	0.00
r_4	S_{vl}	0.01	0.00	0.30	0.32	0.00	0.00	0.09	0.05	-0.50	-0.50	-0.50	-0.50
r_5	R_{cr1}	0.00	0.00	0.00	0.00	0.55	0.53	0.60	0.58	0.51	0.48	0.00	0.00
r_6	R_{cr2}	0.00	0.00	0.00	0.00	0.55	0.53	0.60	0.58	0.00	0.00	0.00	0.00
r_7	$CDMa'$	0.00	0.00	0.00	0.00	0.17	0.07	0.18	0.19	0.00	0.00	0.07	0.05
r_8	$CDGa'$	0.00	0.00	0.00	0.00	0.01	0.02	0.03	0.04	0.01	0.04	0.03	0.05
r_9	R_{apc}	0.62	0.63	0.56	0.55	0.79	0.79	0.66	0.67	0.38	0.37	0.48	0.48
r_{10}	C_{max}'	0.50	0.50	0.50	0.50	0.09	0.08	0.15	0.13	0.75	0.76	0.67	0.69
r_{11}	C_{mean}'	0.50	0.50	0.50	0.50	0.04	0.06	0.08	0.05	0.50	0.50	0.40	0.67

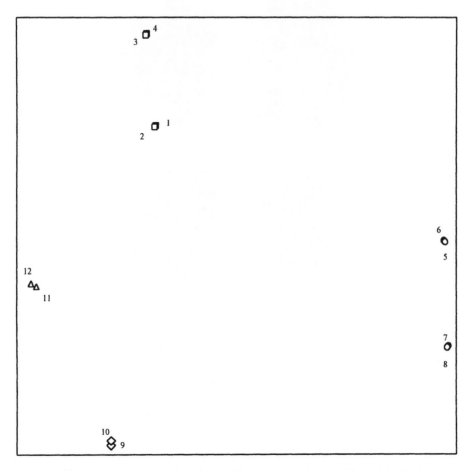

Figure 3.16   Distribution of the testing objects in 2-D space by principal component transform.

Example 2
Figure 3.17 shows the convex hulls of four Alchemilia leaves: A. Mollis, A. Epipsila, A. Venosa, and A. Speciosa.   These were taken from Walters(1991). The original images contained stems which were removed by interactive editing of the images.   Table 3.3 lists the convex deficiency of the leaves as measured by *CDGa'*.   The difference between A. Mollis and A. Speciosa is encouraging, with the other two species lying between these extremes; and this approach should be developed further.

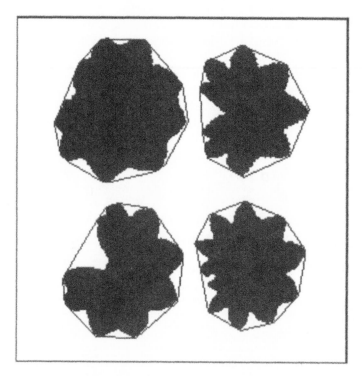

top left: Mollis   top right: Epipsila
Bottom left: Speciosa   bottom right Venosa

Figure 3.17   Convex hull of four leaves.

Table 3.3   Convex deficiency of four Alchemili leaves of Figure 3.17, measured by *CDGa'*.

Mollis		Epipsila	
0.11		0.18	
Speciosa		Venosa	
0.22		0.19	

Example 3

The method of convex hull based shape representation was also applied to the objects in Figure 3.18, which is a chart showing different shapes of soil particles taken from Hodgson (1974). In the original, the columns labelled 'Spherical' and 'Almost spherical' were unnamed, and these two columns had been given the same code number for use on their standard soil description cards. Similarly, the 'Rounded' and 'Almost Rounded' rows had originally both been labelled 'Rounded' and given the same codes. Table 3.4 shows the thinness of the particles measured by the normalised width W_s, which should decrease from left to right. It is seen that there is no overlap between the values for platy, tabular, and almost spherical particles in the three columns on the right, respectively, and that the overlap between the spherical and almost spherical particles is small and possibly in accordance with the shapes as drawn. Table 3.5 shows the roundness of the particles measured by maximal curvature C_{max}' of each particle, which should increase from top to bottom. It can be seen that the values of maximal curvature do increase from top to bottom in accordance with the shapes as drawn, with the exception of the almost rounded almost spherical particle and the almost rounded platy particle. There is also a small increase of maximal curvature, C_{max}', from left to right; this may be an inevitable result of the decrease of sphericity from left to right.

Although the methods of illumination and digitisation will have an effect, these measurements suggest that the chart in Figure 3.18 is not quite as regular as its draughtsman had hoped: this point will be discussed further in Chapter 4 in relation to results obtained from the charts in Figure 3.18 by using the Hough transform.

Example 4

The convex hull based shape representation was also applied to Figure 3.3, which is a similar set of charts published by Bullock (1985). The results of the experiment are listed in Table 3.6.

The Shape Factor, R_{apc}, which would be 1.0 for a circle or lower for less spherical particles, is expected to increase from right to left; and this is the general trend of the results. As in the previous Chart, Maximal Curvature, C_{max}', tends to increase from top to bottom, in the opposite direction to roundness as expected; and it also again tends to increase from left to right. It is expected that Convex Deficiency would increase with Roughness; this does appear to be the general trend, but there is considerable scatter, which probably reflects the difficulty of drawing rough particles accurately.

An interesting point is that, although the smooth section of Figure 3.3 looks very similar to Figure 3.18, slightly different measurements were obtained from corresponding particles, suggesting that the later chart has been redrawn.

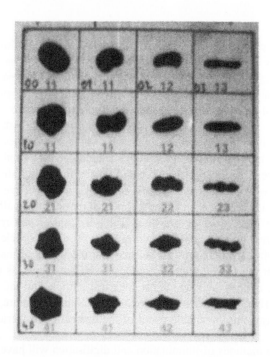

Figure 3.18   Visual Chart of stone (From Hodgson (1974) Soil Survey Field
Handbook, fig. 7, pp. 27).

Table 3.4   Thinness of particle shapes corresponding to the chart of Figure 3.18
measured by normalised width W_s.

	Spherical	Almost Spherical	Tabular	Platy
Rounded	0.749	0.833	0.579	0.255
Almost Rounded	0.946	0.623	0.441	0.293
Subrounded	0.883	0.657	0.450	0.261
Subangular	0.931	0.718	0.505	0.273
Angular	0.826	0.628	0.403	0.291

Table 3.5.   Roundness of particle shapes corresponding to the chart of Figure 3.18
measured by Maximal Curvature C_{max}'.

	Spherical	Almost Spherical	Tabular	Platy
Rounded	0.165	0.148	0.180	0.250
Almost Rounded	0.187	0.250	0.250	0.313
Subrounded	0.187	0.205	0.250	0.250
Subangular	0.250	0.250	0.250	0.352
Angular	0.278	0.353	0.602	0.352

Convex Hull Based Shape Representation

Table 3.6   Features of particle shapes corresponding to the chart of Figure 3.3 but arranged differently.

		Shape Factor $R_{apc} \times 0.001$ ← Sphericity —				Maximal Curvature $C_{max}' \times 0.001$ ← Sphericity —				Convex Deficiency $CDG\alpha \times 0.001$ ← Sphericity —			
Rounded	←Rough	738	731	582	280	275	205	290	455	99	116	150	292
	←Undulating	743	741	580	295	155	187	250	352	53	48	113	179
	←Smooth	744	745	579	265	187	172	250	398	44	52	83	201
Almost rounded	←Rough	756	671	542	329	313	250	352	433	99	143	65	94
	←Undulating	759	671	571	349	205	250	250	398	45	91	46	100
	←Smooth	758	676	559	323	226	148	250	500	30	103	35	78
Sub-rounded	←Rough	750	677	545	313	226	250	264	250	107	122	140	279
	←Undulating	762	686	562	350	241	210	379	585	65	93	116	277
	←Smooth	758	688	567	323	172	165	330	488	65	88	149	299
Sub-angular	←Rough	741	680	573	428	340	250	250	272	138	154	128	319
	←Undulating	742	680	593	430	250	269	250	352	106	128	91	275
	←Smooth	745	678	582	419	280	352	250	500	110	139	96	325
Angular	←Rough	727	661	499	330	250	403	578	656	109	176	203	256
	←Undulating	721	676	515	349	352	398	578	731	63	103	181	240
	←Smooth	720	678	517	346	330	337	358	750	60	103	169	224

Example 5
This method was also applied to the images in Figure 3.1.   The individual soil
particles and voids are obtained by thresholding.   Some attached particles and
voids are separated by the method of Luo (1989).   Some results of the experiment
are shown in Figure 3.19.   From the figure, we can see that the normalised width of
the particles in Figure 3.1 (a) is on average smaller than that of the voids in Figure
3.1(b), i.e., the particles are thinner: there also tends to be a small difference in the
roundness.   These two sets of features have different distributions in this two
dimensional space; and, apart from a few outlets, each of these distributions appears
to form a different cluster.   It will therefore be necessary to discuss automatic
classification of features bearing in mind that more general cases will arise.

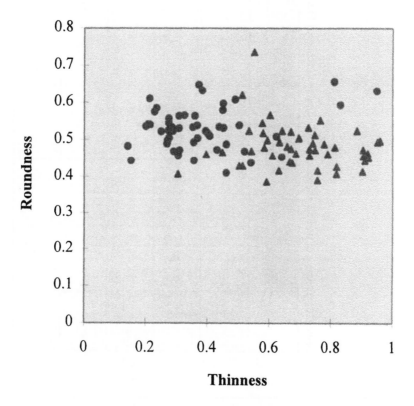

Figure 3.19   Distributions of patterns of particles and voids.   It shows the
Thinness (as measured by W_s) against Roundness (as measured by C_{max}').
Square: Particles in Fig. 3.1 (a); Triangle: Voids in Fig. 3.1 (b).

Example 6

As a guide to choosing an automatic method of classification of shapes of object features, the set of objects shown in outline in Figure 3.20 was analysed. The original was a typical electron micrograph showing soil structure.

To simplify the analysis, the number of measurement was reduced to seven, via:

$$R_1 = W_{max1} \quad R_2 = S_{v1} \quad R_3 = R_{cr1} \quad R_4 = W_{max1} \quad R_5 = S_{v2} \quad R_6 = R_{cr2} \quad R_7 = CDGa' \ .$$

As far as can be seen, the structural (syntactic) method of classification (Young and Fu 1986) is inapplicable here because there is no obvious way of setting up a set of syntax rules by which the pattern structure may be parsed (Fu 1982).

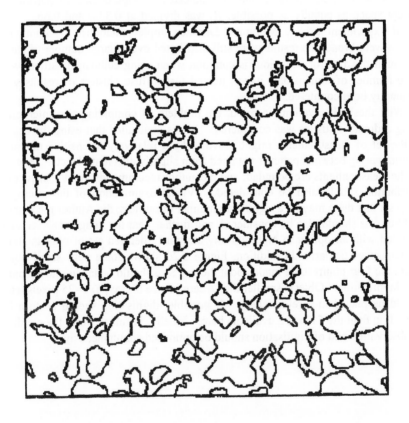

Figure 3.20   Boundaries of particles of a typical electron micrograph.

Ideally, when using a decision theoretic classification method, a Bayesian approach is preferred; but this would require that the class conditional density functions of the patterns be classified either are known or can be estimated a priori. However, this was not the case here. The next choice of method would be cluster analysis (Fu 1980, Spath 1980, Duda and Hart 1973); however, the set of measurements obtained here appeared to fall into a single very diffuse cluster, so that some other method is required here.   This type of behaviour is, in fact, commonly met throughout the whole of soil science when attempting to establish classification schemes; and resort is commonly made to somewhat arbitrary distinctions between the classes.   Therefore, this approach has been tried.

The seven measurements used here have the advantage that each of them has a finite range, being defined to lie within the range 0 to 1, but sometimes being additionally restricted, see Figure 3.21. This was an additional factor leading to the idea of an arbitrary partition of the restricted hypervolume so defined.   In the analysis, 426 classes were defined as indicated in Figure 3.21 to partition the feature space as equally as possible: R_7 was divided at 0.33... and 0.66...   (The actual experiment used a Minimum Distance implementation).   Although the classes were broad, the results were still distributed over a large number of classes. Although this type of behaviour is common when using cellular classifiers with a large number of dimensions, it was judged that diffuse clusters of results would frequently be encountered.

With these observations in mind, the problem of comparing two micrographs using ordinary statistics was considered.   It was concluded that using the centroid of the set of measurements might prove to be a relatively insensitive method of discriminating between patterns obtained from slightly different objects. However, all the measurements are bounded; and the author recommends that the skew of the distribution should also be considered.   Visual examination of the micrograph suggests that there may be a significant number of outliers; the Author recommends that kurtosis should also be considered, and further, that the image analyser should be fitted with an option to highlight any arbitrarily defined set of objects and the outliers in particular.   In addition, Figure 3.20 shows some very small objects. There are four points to be made about these.   Size should be taken into account in the classification.   Objects smaller than a certain size of, say, 5×5=25 pixels length, should be placed in a reject class.   If possible, digitisation should be to a finer resolution than the 512×512 available here.   Finally, in future work, the conditions of observation and of digitisation should be optimised simultaneously.

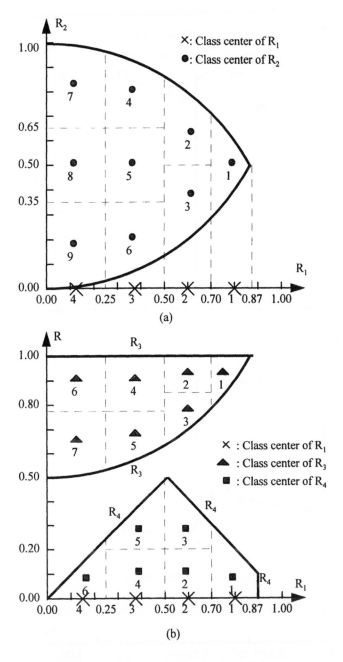

Figure 3.21   Range of features and designed centres of classes.
(a) in R_1-R_2 plane; (b) in R_1-$R_{3,4}$ plane.

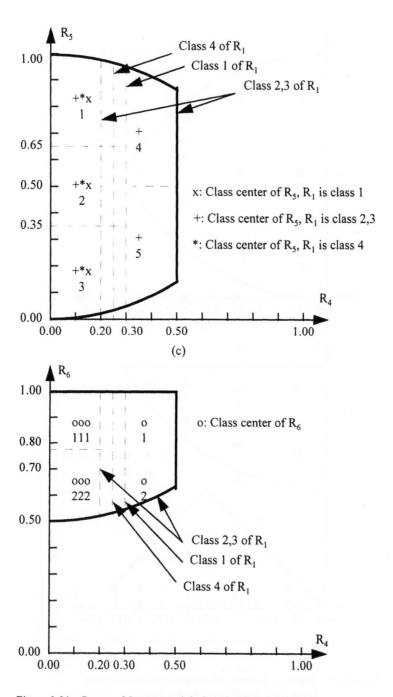

Figure 3.21   Range of features and designed centres of classes.
(c) in R_4-R_5 plane; (d) in R_4-R_6 plane.

3.4 FRACTALS

3.4.1 Introduction

'The name "fractal", from the Latin "fractus", meaning broken, was given to highly irregular sets by Benoit Mandelbrot in his foundational essay in 1975' (Falconer 1997). Sinc Mandelbrot (1975, 1982) introduced fractals, many books have been published on fractals. Some books provide basic mathematical methods (Edgar 1990, Mehaute 1991,and Peitgen et al. 1992). Some books concentrate on the geometric measure theory (Falconer 1985, Mattila 1995). The books witten by Barnsley and Hurd (1993) and Fisher (1995) focus on applications to image compression.

Fractals rose from dealing with the data sets with completely natural or irregular structures. For example, what is the length of a coast line or a river. How the measurements are different in different scales? what is shape of a mountain and the structure of clouds? Since fractal geometry was introduced, it has wide spread into many fields, such as botanics, geograph, medicine, weather study, industry, agriculture, economics, etc. The applications of fractals can be divided into two groups: analyse data sets with completely irregular structures (e.g. decompose clouds or wavelets) and generating data by recursively duplicating certain patterns (e.g. computed fractal images or graphs).

In image processing and analysis, fractal techniques are mainly applied to image compression (Cochran et al 1996) and image coding (Lee and Lee 1998). A few applications are to object modeling, representation and classification (Sato et al. 1996, Li et al. 1997). This section will introduce the idea of using fractal geometry to represent objects for object analysis.

3.4.2 Definition

Various mathematical definition have been given to fractals, but these definitions are not satisfactory in a general context. In object shape analysis using fractal techniques, we will ignore which is the most precise definition. We can say that a fractal shape f of an object is made by recursively duplicating a pattern p of a part of the object:

$$f = f(p) . \tag{3.4.1}$$

When an object is represented by its boundary, the fractal shape f_b (1D dimensional) can be defined as a function:

$$f_b = f(p_b) \tag{3.4.2}$$

where p_b is an irregular detail segment of the boundary at arbitrarily small scales. The irregular segments p_b under different scales may have some sort of self-similarity or self-affinity in a statistical sense.

When an object is represented by its region, the fractal shape f_r (2D) can be defined as a function of an arbitrarily small irregular subregion r:

$$f_r = f(p_r) .\hspace{4cm}(3.4.3)$$

Similarly, the fractal texture t_t (multi-dimentional) can be defined as a funciton of an arbitrarily small subunit of texture c:

$$C_f = f(p_c) .\hspace{4cm}(3.4.4)$$

An example of fractal boundary (curve) is shown in Figure 3.22 (a).   In this figure, the detail segment is a straight line segment with the length equal to 1. From the figure, we can see that the segments under the scale 1/5 is self-similar to the segments under the scale 1/25.   The examples of fractal region and fractal texture are shown in Figure 3.22 (b) and (c).

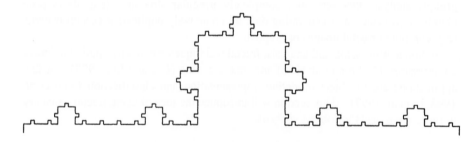

Figure 3.22 (a)   Fractal boundary (curve).

Figure 3.22 (b)   Fractal region.

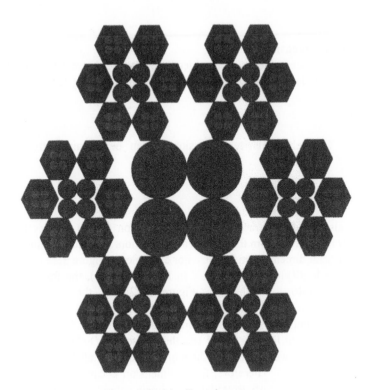

Figure 3.22 (c)   Fractal contexture

3.4.3 Self-similarity

The property of self-similarity or scaling is one of the central condepts of fractal geometry (Peitgen et al 1988).   Self-similarity means the pattern (or some property) of the whole shape is similar to the pattern (or some property) of an arbitrary small part of the shape.   In other words, self-similarity means that the whole shape is recursively composed of (or dicomposed into) an arbitray small part of the object.

An one dimensional objects, for example a segment of line, has self-similarity. It can be divided into N parts with equal length by the scale ratio $r = 1/N$.   A two dimensional object, for instance a square, can be divided into N identical squares by the scale ratio $r = 1/\sqrt{N}$. A three dimensional object, such as a cube can be divide into N identical cubes by $r = 1/\sqrt[3]{N}$.   Thus, we can say these kinds of objects are self-similar objects.   Generally, a D-dimensional self-similar object may be divided into N small copies of itself by $r = 1/\sqrt[D]{N}$.   The fractal boundary in Figure 3.22 (a) is self-similar with scale ratio $r = 1/5$. The fractal region in Figure 3.22 (b) is self-similar with $r = 1/\sqrt{3}$. The fractal texture in Figure 3.22 (c) is self similar with $r=1/\sqrt{3}$.

3.4.4   Fractal Dimension

From the D-dimensional self-similar object, we can see that the number N of the identical parts divided by a scale ratio r can be calculated from (Peitgen et al 1988):

$$N = 1/r^D .$$ (3.4.5)

Conversely, The self-similarity dimension D can be objtained from equation (3.4.5):

$$D = \log(N) / \log(1/r) .$$ (3.4.6)

Here D is also called as fractal dimention. equation (3.4.6) implies that fractal dimension D is different from the Euclidean dimension. Euclidean dimension is an integer, but fractal dimension may not. For example, in Figure 3.22 (a), the fractal dimension $D = \log(7)/\log(5) = 1.209$. In Figure 3.22 (b), the fractal dimension $D=\log(5)/\log(3)=1.46$. While in Figure 3.22 (c), the fractal dimension $D=\log(6)/\log(3)=1.63$. These different non-integer fractal dimensions reflect different fractal (unusual) shapes with different properties. Obviously, they are greater than 1 (straight line $D=1$) and less than 2 (square $D=2$) in 2D space. From the factal dimensions, we can see that the more space a fractal shape fills the greater its fractal dimension is. Therefore, factal dimension D can be used as one of the futures to represent or classify irregular (completely natural) shaped objects.

3.4.5   Multi-fractals

Actually, no irregular shape is completely self-similar to a small part of it. However, it can be divided , by some way, into many subsets, of which each subset has self-similarity. Thus the object can have many fractal demensions D_i corresponding to its subsets s_i. For example, an arch window has a fractal dimension for its rectangle shape and a fractal dimension for its arc shape. Shapes and measures requiring more the one D are known as *multi-fractals* (Peitgen et al 1988).

3.5   FRACTALS BASED SHAPE REPRESENTATION

3.5.1   Boundary and Fractal Dimension

As disscussed in the section of convex hull based shape representation, an object can be described by its boundary or by its region. First, we consider the boundary based. Then extend the boundary based to the region based.

To measure the fractal dimension D of a boundary of an object, we need to know the number N of small segments which form the whole boundary and the scale ratio r. Obviously from equation (3.4.5), $N = N(r)$ is a function of r. The smaller the r, the greater the N. For the purpose of object recognition and classification, the policy of choice of scale ratio r must be the same. Considering the boundary of an object is closed, we can choose the length L_d of the longest diagnal (the radius) of the object as the reference of the scale ratio r:

$$r = 1/L_d . \tag{3.4.7}$$

This is because the objects scaled from the same object by different scale ratio have the same longest diagnal.   Then the number N can be obtained by measuring the "length" of the boundary with the "ruler" r.   In 2D raster image plane, the unit of $1/L_d$ is 1.   The number N is equal to the length L of the boundary.   Hence, the fractal dimension D of the boundary can be measured by:

$$D = \log(L)/\log(2L_d) . \tag{3.4.8}$$

However, the two end points of the longest diagnoal of an object divide the boundary into two parts, as show in Figure 3.13.   In practice, the two parts may not similar to each other.   For this reason, two fractal dimensions D_1 and D_2:

$$D_{1,2} = \log(L_{1,2})/\log(L_d) \tag{3.4.9}$$

are used for the representation of the boundary.   Here D_1 is measured from the upper (longer) boundary. D_2 is measured from the lower (shorter) boundary.

3.5.2   Region and Fractal Dimension
Similarly, the fractal dimension D_1 and D_2 of the region can be measured by:

$$D_{1,2} = \log (A_{1,2})/\log(L_d) \qquad (i{=}1,2) \tag{3.4.10}$$

where A_1 and A_2 are the area of the part A1B and A2B, respectively.

3.5.3   Example of Shape Analysis

Shape representation by the method of fractals/multifractals was tested against the binary image of some industrial spare part models as shown in Figure 3.23.   The image was first processed by edge following to obtain the boundaries of the spare parts.   Then the convex hull of each spare part was found from its boundary. From the convex hull, its length L_d (radius) of the longest diagonal was calculated. The two end points of the diagonal divide the boundary into two parts: upper and lower (see Figure 3.14).   The perimeter L_1 of the upper part and the perimeter L_2 of the lower part are calculated from the boundary.   Thus the fractal dimentionss D_1 and D_2 of the spare part are calculated by:

$$D_1 = \log(L_1)/\log(L_d) \tag{3.5.1}$$

$$D_2 = \log(L_2)/\log(L_d) . \tag{3.5.2}$$

The experimental results of L_d, L_1, L_2, D_1 and D_2 of the 18 spare parts in Figure 3.23 are listed in Table 3.7.   The distribution of the eighteen spare parts in two feature space L_d and D_1 are plotted in Figure 3.24.   In Figure 3.23, we can see that spare part pairs 1 and 17, 2 and 18, 5 and 12, 14 and 15, are identical, respectively. The others are different.   From Figure 3.24, we can see that the identical spare parts are very close, but the different spare parts are far from each other.   This means that fractal/multifractal dimensions can be used as features for object shape representation, recognition, or classification.

Table 3.7   The fractal dimensions of the spare parts

Spare Part	L_d	L_1	L_2	D_1	D_2
1	82.6378	138.3285	138.2055	1.116699	1.116498
2	101.0050	147.6420	147.5190	1.082255	1.082074
3	60.0000	83.1030	82.9800	1.079558	1.079196
4	27.1662	42.2747	42.1517	1.133925	1.133042
5	79.2465	139.4880	139.3650	1.129310	1.129108
6	38.2099	58.9315	58.8085	1.118932	1.118359
7	72.3395	114.9730	114.8500	1.108219	1.107969
8	32.0000	53.5175	53.3945	1.148388	1.147724
9	24.0000	39.8605	39.7375	1.159636	1.158664
10	36.0555	64.0320	63.9090	1.160199	1.159663
11	62.0000	101.9730	101.8500	1.120562	1.120269
12	79.2312	138.1950	138.0720	1.127230	1.127026
13	46.0000	76.8310	76.7080	1.133981	1.133563
14	49.9902	84.2540	84.1310	1.133444	1.133070
15	49.6790	83.9610	83.8380	1.134364	1.133989
16	51.3517	80.8310	80.7080	1.115181	1.114794
17	82.5703	140.3285	140.2055	1.120158	1.119959
18	101.0000	147.9350	147.8120	1.082696	1.082516

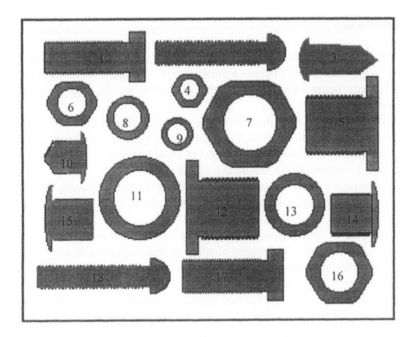

Figure 3.23   Binary Image of Industrial Spare Parts

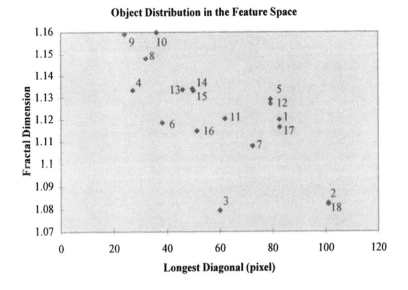

Figure 2.24   Object distribution in two feature pace

3.6 SUMMARY

The chapter starts by presenting an efficient new algorithm, the SPCH algorithm, for finding the convex hull of either a binary image or a cluster of points in a plane, the complexity being O(N) or O(NlogN) depending on the way in which the original data is presented.

The chapter continues to describe a whole family of measurements which are based on the convex hull, and which may be used to describe the shapes of objects. This representation is invariant with respect to co-ordinate rotation, translation, and scaling, and the range of each feature is between 0 and 1.

A preliminary example showed that one of these measurements, the convex deficiency, (or a similar measure), could be developed to assist in the classification of leaves of plants.

An analysis of two popular charts, which are widely used to assist in the subjective classification of the shapes of soil particles, suggested that the regularity of these charts could be improved with a view to making them more reliable.

A preliminary analysis of the shapes of the objects in a typical electron micrograph of a clay soil suggested that the measurements fell into a diffuse cluster, as commonly happens throughout soil science. Therefore, arbitrarily defined class boundaries would probably have to be used in the classification of these objects. However, it was noted that the ranges of the measurements are bounded; and it is suggested that the skew and kurtosis of such populations should be considered as discriminating functions. It is also suggested that an option to highlight outliers from the distributions would be included in computer programs.

Some aspects of the above will be developed further in the following chapters.

References

Akl, S. G. and Toussaint, G. T. (1978) A fast convex hull algorithm. *Information Processing Letters* 7, pp. 219-222.

Arcelli, C., Cordella, L. P., and Levialdi, S. (1981) From local maxima to connected
skeletons. *IEEE Trans. Pattern Analysis Mach. Intell.* PAMI-3, pp. 134-143.

Avis, D. (1980) Comments on a lower bound for convex hull determination. *Information Processing Letters,* 11, pp. 126,.

Avis, D. and Toussaint, G. T. (1981) An efficient algorithm for decomposing a polygon into star shaped polygons. *Pattern Recognition*, Vol. 13, pp. 395-398.

Avis, D., ElGindy, H., and Seidel, R. (1985) Simple On-line Algorithms for Convex Polygons. *Computational Geometry*, Toussaint, G. T. (Editor), Elsevier Science Publishers B.V. (North Holland), pp. 23-42.

Ballard, D. H. (1981) Strip tree: a hierarchical representation for curves. *Communications, ACM*, 24, pp. 310-321.

Barnsley, M. G. and Hurd, L. P. (1993) *Fractal Image Compression.* A. K. Peters.

Bass, L. J. and Schubert, S. R. (1967) On finding the disc of minimum radius containing a given set of points. *Math. Computat.* 21, pp. 712-714.

Bentley, J. L., Faust, G. M., and Preparata, F. P. (1982) Approximation algorithms for convex hulls. *Communications, ACM,* 25, pp. 64-68.

Boas, E. P. V. (1980) On the $\Omega(n\log n)$ lower-bound for convex hull and maximal vector determination. *Information Processing Letters,* 10, pp. 132-136.

Brewer, R. (1964) *Fabric and Mineral Analysis of Soils*, John Wiley.

Bullock, P., Fedoroff, N., Jongerius, A., Stoops, G., and Tursina, T. (1985) *Handbook for Soil Thin Section Description.* Waine Research Publications, Fig. 31, pp. 31.

Bykat, A. (1978) Convex hull of a finite set of points in two dimensions. *Inform. Process. Let*ters, 7, pp. 296-298.

Chen, C. L. (1989) Computing the Convex Hull of a Simple Polygon. *Pattern Recognition*, Vol. 22, No. 5, pp. 561-565.

Cochran, W. O., Hart, J. C. and Flynn. P. J. (1996) Fractal Volume Compression. *IEEE Trans. Visualization and Computer Graphics.* Vol. 2, No. 4, pp. 3113-332.

Dai, M., Baylou, P. (1992) and Najim, M., An efficient algorithm for computation of shape moments from run-length codes or chain codes. *Pattern Recognition*, Vol. 25, No. 10, pp. 1129-1140.

Day, A. M., (1988) Planar convex hull algorithms in theory and practice. *Computer Graphics*, Forum 7, North Holland, pp. 177-193.

Devroye, L. D. and Toussaint, G. T. (1981) A note on linear expected time algorithms for finding convex hulls. *Computing* 26, pp. 361-366.

Duda, R. O., and Hart, P. E. (1973) *Pattern Classification and Scene Analysis*. Wiley.

Eddy, W. F. (1977) A new convex hull algorithm for planar sets. *ACM Trans. Math. Software,* 3, pp. 398-403.

Edgar, G. A. (1990) *Measure, Topology, and Fractal Geometry.* Springer-Verlag.

Falconer, K. (1985) The *Geometry of Fractal Sets.* Cambridge University Press.

Falconer, K. (1997) *Techniques in Fractal Geometry.* John Wiley & Sons.

Ferrari, L., Sankar, P. V., and Sklansky, J. (1980) Minimal rectangular partition of digitized blobs. *Proceedings, 5th International Conference, Pattern Recognition,* pp. 1040-1043.

Fisher, G. (1995) *Fractal Image Compression: Theory and Applications.* Springer-Verlag.

FitzPatrick, E. A. (1984) *Micromorphology of Soils.* Chapman and Hall.

Freeman, H. (1974) Computer processing of line drawing image. *Computer Surveys,* Vol. 6, pp. 57-97.

Fu, K. (1980) *Digital Pattern Recognition.* Springer-Verlag.

Fu, K. (1982) *Applications of Pattern Recognition.* CRC Press, Boca Raton, Florida.

Fu, K. (1987) *Robotics, control, sensing, vision, and intelligence.* McGraw-Hill.

Graham, R. L. (1972) An efficient algorithm for determining the convex hull of a planar set. *Inform. Process. Letters,* 1, pp. 132-133.

Granlund, G. H. (1972) Fourier preprocessing for hand print character recognition. *IEEE Transactions on computers,* Vol. C-22, 195-201.

Hodgson, J. M. (1974) *Soil Survey Field Handbook.* Soil Survey of England and Wales, Harpenden.

Jarvis, R. A. (1973) On the identification of the convex hull of finite set of points in the plane. *Information Processing Letters,* 2, pp. 18-21.

Jeong, C. S. and Lee, D. T. (1988) Parallel convex hull algorithms in 2D and 3D on mech-connected computers. *Int. Conf. Comput. Vision Display,* pp. 64-76.

Kirkpatrick, D. G. and Seidel, R. (1982) The Ultimate Planar Convex Hull algorithm? *Proceeding of the 20th Allerton Conference on Communication, Control and Computing,* Monticello, Illinois, pp. 35-42.

Krumbein, W. C. (1941) Measurement and geological significance of shape and roundness of sedimentary particles. *Journal of Sedimentary Petrology,* vol. 11, pp. 64-72.

Krumbein, W. C. and Sloss, L. L. (1951) *Stratigraphy and Sedimentation.* W. H. Freeman and Company, fig. 4-9, pp. 81.

Lee, C. K. and Lee, W. K. (1998) Fast Fractal Image Block Coding Based on Local Variances. *IEEE Trans. Image Processing,* Vol. 7, No. 6, pp. 888-891.

Li, H., Liu, K. J. R. and Lo, S. C. B. (1997) Fractal Modeling and Segmentation for the Enhancement of Microcalcifications in Ditidal Mammograms. *IEEE Trans. Medical Imaging,* Vol. 16, No. 6, pp. 785-798.

Luo, D. (1989) Core-disdressing-dressing method for automatic image separation. *Journal of Sichuan University,* Natural Science Edition, Vol. 26, No. 3, pp. 309-316.

Luo, D. and Ma, D. X. (1989) Bi-boundary-line method for curve-enclosed area calculation. *J. Sichuan Univ.* (Natural Science Edition) 26, No. 1, pp. 458-65.

Luo, D., Macleod, J. E. S., Leng, X., and Smart, P. (1992) Automatic orientation analysis of particles of soil microstructures. *Geotechnique,* 42, No.1, pp. 97,107.

Mandelbrot, B. B. (1975) *Les Objects Fractals: Forme, Hasard et Dimension.* flammarion.

Mandelbrot, B. B. (1982) *The Fractal Geometry of Nature.* W. H. Freeman.

Mattila, P. (1995a) *Geometry of Sets and Measures in Euclidean Spces.* Canbridge University Press.

Mattila, P. (1995) *Geometry of Sets and Measures in Euclidean Spces.* Canbridge University Press.

McCallum, D. and Avis, D. (1979) A linear time algorithm for finding the convex hull of a simple polygon. *Inform. Process. Letters,* 8, pp. 201-205.

McMillan, N., Fingleton, M., Daly, D., and Townsend, D. (1992) The ACWA, An automatic crystal weight analysis system for laboratory crystal quality control. *Microscopy and Analysis,* May, pp. 23-25.

McQueen, M. M. and Toussaint, G. T. (1985) On the ultimate convex hull algorithm in practice. *Pattern Recognition Letters,* 3, pp. 29-34.

Mehaute, A. (ed.) (1991) *Fractal Geometries: Theory and Applications.* Penton Press.

Melkman, A. A., (1987) On-line construction of the convex hull of a simple polygon. *Inform. Process. Letters,* 25, pp. 11-12.

Miller, R. and Stout, Q. F. (1988) Efficient parallel convex hull algorithms. *IEEE Trans. Comput.* 37(12), pp. 1605-1618.

Orlowski, M. (1983) On the Condition for Success of Sklansky's Convex Hull Algorithm. *Pattern Recognition,* No. 16, pp. 579-586.

Pavlidis, T. (1977) *Structural pattern recognition.* Springer Publication, New York.

Peitgen, H. O., and Saupe, D. (ed. 1988) *The science of Fractal Images.* Springer-Verlag.

Peitgen, H. O., Jurgens, H. and Saupe, D. (1992) *Chaos and Fractals: New Frontiers of Science.* Springer-Verlag.

Pettijohn, F. J. (1949) *Sedimentary Rocks.* Harper & Brothers.

Preparata, F. P. (1979) An optimal real-time algorithm for planar convex hulls. *Communications, ACM,* 22, pp. 402-405.

Preparata, F. P. and Shamos, M. I. (1985) *Computational Geometry, An introduction.* Springer-Verlag.

Rosenfeld, A. (1969) *Picture Processing by Computer.* Academic Press, New York.

Rosenfeld, A. and Johnston, E. (1973) Angle detection on digital curves. *IEEE Transactions on Computers,* 22, pp. 875-878.

Rosenfeld, A. and Kak, A. (1982) *Digital picture processing.* 2nd Edition, Academic Press.

Sato, T., Matsuoka, M. and Takayasu, H. (1996) Fractal Image Analysis of Natural Scenes and Medical Images. *Fractal-An Interdisciplinary Journal on the Compulex Geometry of Nature,* Vol. 4, No. 4, pp. 463-468.

Shamos, M. I. (1978) *Computational Geometry.* Yale University, New Haven, Connecticut, PhD. Thesis.

Shapiro, L. G., and Haralick, R. M. (1979) Decomposition of two-dimensional shapes by graph theoretic clustering. *IEEE Trans. Pattern Analysis Mach Intell.* PAMI-1, pp. 10-20.

Shih, F. Y. and Wu, H. (1992) Decomposition of geometric-shaped structuring elements using morphological transformation on binary images. *Pattern Recognition*, Vol. 25, No. 10, pp. 1097-1118.

Shin, S. Y. and Woo, T. C. (1986) Finding the Convex Hull of a Simple Polygon in Linear Time. *Pattern Recognition*, Vol. 19, No. 6, pp. 453-458.

Sklansky, J. (1972) Measuring Concavity on a Rectangular Mosaic. *IEEE Trans. Computers*, C-21, pp. 1355-1364.

Sklansky, J., (1982) Finding the Convex Hull of a Simple Polygon. *Pattern Recognition Letters,* No. 1, pp. 79-83.

Smart, P. and Tovey, N. K. (1981) *Electron Microscopy of Soils and Sediments: examples*. Oxford University Press.

Smithson, F. (1939) Statistical methods in sedimentary petrology. *Geology Magazine*, Vol. 76, pp. 351.

Sneed, E. D. and Folk, R. L. (1958) Pebbles in the lower Colorado River, Texas - a study in particle morphogenesis. Journal of Geology, Vol. 66, pp. 114-150.

Spath, H. (1980) *Cluster analysis algorithms: for data reduction and classification of objects*. Ellis Horwood..

Toussaint. G. T. (1981) Computational geometric problems in pattern recognition. Kittler, J. (Ed.), *Pattern Recognition Theory and Applications*, NATO Advanced Study Institute, Oxford University, pp. 73-91.

Toussaint, G. T. (1982) Computational geometric problems in pattern recognition. Kittler, Fu, and Pau (eds.), *Pattern Recognition Theory and Applications*, Reidel, pp. 73-91.

Toussaint, G. T. (1985) A historical note on convex hull finding algorithms. *Pattern Recognition Letters.*, Vol. 3, pp. 21-28.

Toussaint. G. T. (1991) A counter-example to a convex hull algorithm for polygons. *Pattern Recognition*, Vol. 24, No. 2, pp. 183-184.

Toussaint, G. T. and Avis, D. (1982) On a convex hull algorithm for polygons and its application to triangulation problems. *Pattern Recognition*, No. 15, pp. 23-29.

Toussaint, G. T. and ElGindy, H. (1983) A counter-example to an algorithm for computing monotone hulls of simple polygons. *Pattern Recognition Letters*, Vol. 1, pp. 219-222.

Tradhanias, P. E. (1992) Binary shape recognition using the morphological skeleton transformation. *Pattern Recognition*, Vol. 25, No. 11, pp. 1277-1288.

Wadell, H. (1932) Volume, shape, and roundness of rock particles. *Journal of Geology*, Vol. 40, pp. 443-451.

Walters, M., A. (1991) *The Garden Journal of the Royal Horticultural Society*, Vol. 116, pp. 62-63.

Young, T. Y. and Fu, K. S. (1986) *Handbook of Pattern recognition and image processing*. Academic Press.

Appendix 3A   Finding the Simple Polygon by Stair-Climbing Method

We can find the chain C_2 from the set S, starting at the point P_r and traversing clockwise as shown in Figure 3.6 in Chapter 3.   The conditions of a point V_{i+1} being a vertex of the simple polygon are:

$$x(V_{i+1}) = \max x(p) \qquad p \in S, x(p) < x(V_i), y(p) < y(V_i) \qquad (3A.1)$$

$$y(V_{i+1}) = \min y(p) \qquad p \in S, x(p) = x(V_{i+1}) \qquad\qquad (3A.2)$$

and the procedure is continued until the point P_b is reached.   In this procedure, the candidate point p is found simply by scanning the binary image from right to left and from bottom to top.

The chains C_3 is constructed starting at P_r and traversing counter-clockwise as shown in Figure 3.5 in Chapter 3.   The conditions for C_3 are:

$$x(V_{i+1}) = \max x(p) \qquad p \in S, x(p) < x(V_i), y(p) > y(V_i) \qquad (3A.3)$$

$$y(V_{i+1}) = \max y(p) \qquad p \in S, x(p) = x(V_{i+1}). \qquad\qquad (3A.4)$$

The candidate point p is found by scanning the binary image from right to left and from top to bottom.

The chains C_4 is constructed starting at P_l and traversing clockwise as shown in Figure 3.5 in Chapter 3.   The conditions for C_4 are:

$$x(V_{i+1}) = \min x(p) \qquad p \in S, x(p) > x(V_i), y(p) > y(V_i) \qquad (3A.5)$$

$$y(V_{i+1}) = \max y(p) \qquad p \in S, x(p) = x(V_{i+1}). \qquad\qquad (3A.6)$$

The candidate point p is found by scanning the binary image from left to right and from top to bottom.

4

Roundness/Sharpness Analysis

4.1 INTRODUCTION

Roundness or sharpness is one of the most used features for description and classification of objects. For example, wherever a soil surveyor describes a sample of soil, the shapes of the particles are often reported with reference to standard charts such as that shown in Figure 4.1. In particular, the roundness or sharpness of the corners of the particles is assessed subjectively by comparison with the charts. The immediate aim here is to place this assessment on an objective basis. For this purpose, the circular Hough Transform was found to be satisfactory. This transform is also useful for other purposes in studying soil microstructure. In summary, it is useful for:

1. measurement of the roundness of the corners of 'standard particles';
2. location of bacteria in electron micrographs of soil;
3. location of other circular groups of particles and similar features in electron micrographs of soil;
4. location of circular bubbles (artefacts) in optical micrographs of soil;
5. location of circular particles in model cement in which spherical ballotini had been used as the aggregate.

When the circular Hough transform was adopted, three factors were considered: memory requirement, time of computation, and programming complexity. However, it was difficult to implement, and the main part of this chapter will start by comparing five methods of implementation, of which, two (the basic method and the directional gradient method) are existing methods, and the other three (the centre method, the centre gradient method, and the radius method) are new. Although the three more efficient programs were about three times more complex to write than the basic simple program, none of the programming was difficult, so no consideration need be given to programming complexity and the consequent cost of development. The second part of the chapter will discuss the Author's method of dealing with corners which are too sharp for the Hough transform to find. Finally, these methods will be used to compare five standard shape description charts. Before any of this, an overview of the Hough transform will be given.

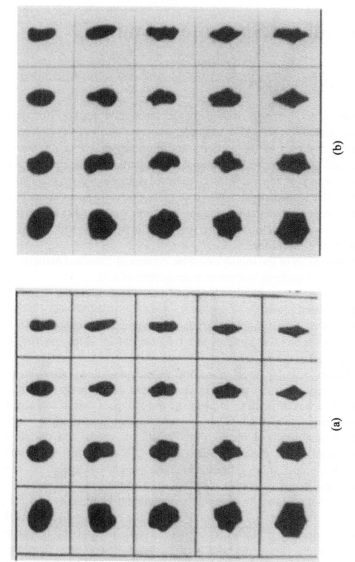

(a)

(b)

Figure 4.1   (a) Visual chart for estimating roundness and sphericity of sand grains (From Krumbein and Sloss (1951) Stratigraphy and Sediments. fig. 4-9, pp. 81); (b) Chart for visual estimation of sphericity and roundness (From Brewer (1964) Fabric and Mineral Analysis of Soils, fig. 1, pp. 21).

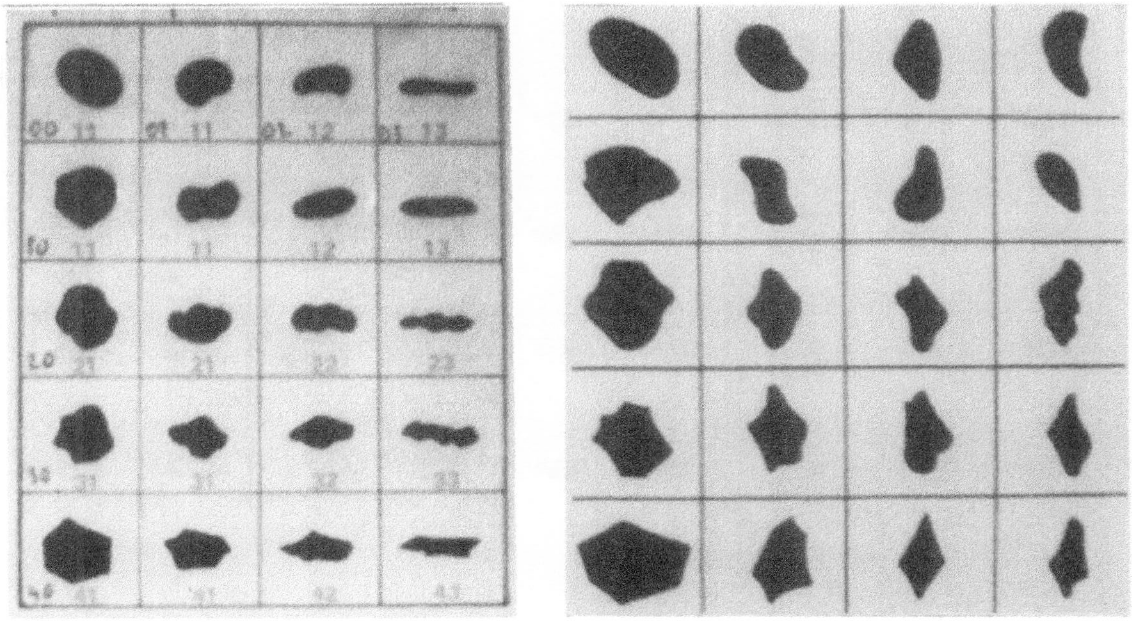

Introduction

87

(d)

(c)

Figure 4.1   (c) Stone shape (From Hodgson (1974) Soil survey field Handbook, fig. 7, pp. 27);   (d) Roundness and sphericity classes (From FitzPatrick (1984) Micromorphology of Soil, fig. 5.9, pp. 117).

Roundness/Sharpness Analysis

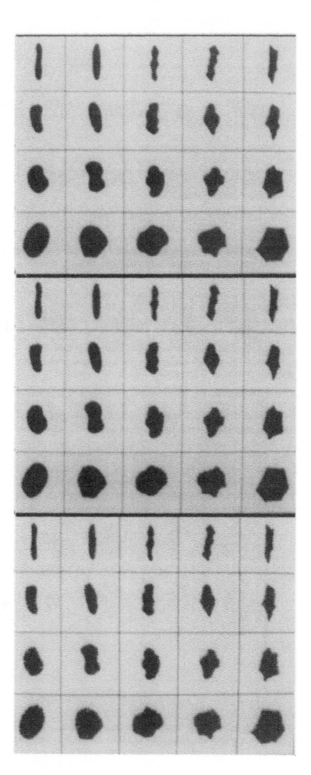

Figure 4.1 (e) Sphericity and roundness charts combined with roughness/smoothness grades (From Bullock (1985) Handbook for Soil Thin Section Description, fig. 31, pp. 31).

4.1.1 The Problem of Roundness Analysis

Sharpness/roundness is often an important feature for shape description and subsequent pattern recognition of an object.

Considering the *sharpness* of an object, the *curvature* analysis can be used. Many methods for curvature analysis have been proposed. One simple version of the methods, so-called k-curvature algorithm, was proposed by Rosenfeld and Johnston (1973), and improved by Rosenfeld and Weszka (1975) (see also Anderson and Bezdek 1984). Their method is taking the dot product of the two unit vectors joining a point (x_i, y_i) to (x_{i+k}, y_{i+k}) and to (x_{i-k}, y_{i-k}) to estimate the curvature at a contour point. The more popular methods are to find the curvature by the ratio of the angle change $d\theta(s)$ with respect to the arc length ds along a curve or the contour of the object (Duda and Hart 1973, Haralick and Shapiro 1992, Schalkoff 1989, Seeger and Seeger 1994). The sharpness of the object, therefore, can be expressed by a function of the curvature along the contour of the object.

Considering the roundness of an object, the *circle fitting* can be used. The circle fitting is to find the best circles which fit a curve or the contour of the object. Two types of circle fitting were proposed: one was based on the least square error, such as (Ballard and Brown 1982); another was based on the Circular Hough transform as described below. The roundness of the object, therefore, can be described by a function of the radii of a set of circles fitting the corners along the contour of the object.

In soil microstructure study, the latter approach has been more usually followed. Krumbein (1940) (see also Pettijohn 1957) gave the definition of the roundness as shown in Figure 4.2, and calculated the roundness *Round* of a particle by:

$$Round = \frac{1}{NR_I} \sum_{i=1}^{N} r_i \qquad (4.1.1)$$

where N is the number of the circles fitting the corners, and R_I is the radius of the inscribing circle of the particle. Several years later, Krumbein and Sloss (1951) and then some other scientists (Brewer 1964, Hodgson 1974, FitzPatrick 1984, and Bullock 1985) made standard visual charts, as shown in Figure 4.1, for particle shape classification, in which 5 levels of roundness are distinguished. Based on Krumbein's definition of roundness, in our study, the problem concerned is how to detect the circles fitting the corners by image processing theory and techniques.

4.1.2 The Problem of Circle and Arc Detection

In roundness measurement by circle fitting, the problem is how to estimate or determine the parameters a, b, and r of a circle from a set of observations of a curve, where (a,b) are the coordinates of the centre of the circle, and r is its radius. This circle must fit the curve in some sense. One of the methods for circle or circular arc detection is the circular Hough transform, which is an extension of the original Hough transform.

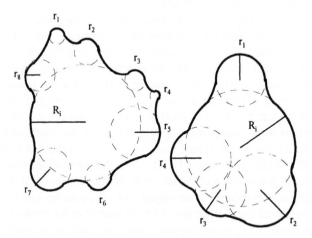

Figure 4.2   Diagram of Pebbles, showing geometrical nature of roundness (see
Krumbein (1940) Bulletin Geology Society of America, vol. 51, fig. 11, pp. 670).

    This chapter will present a use of the circular Hough transform in finding the
'Roundness of the corners' of a curve in a plane.   The basic method is
computationally intensive in both time and memory.   A method based on the
direction gradient is faster but still requires a large amount of computer memory.
In this chapter an implementation that requires much less memory is suggested.
Extensions to find the digital forms of the intrinsic equation of a curve and the
evolute of a curve will also be indicated.

4.2   THE HOUGH TRANSFORM

4.2.1   Introduction
The earliest Hough transform was proposed by Hough (1962) for straight line
detection.   Subsequently, this method was developed to detect circles (Duda and
Hart 1972) and arbitrary curves (Ballard 1981).   The Hough transform was also
applied to solve multivariable functions, especially in cases where the number of
variables is less than the number of equations (Schalkoff 1989).   Some examples of
the successful use of Hough transforms are the detection of human haemoglobin
'fingerprints' (Ballard et al. 1975), detection of tumours (Kimme et al. 1975) and
ribs (Wechsler and Sklansky 1977) in chest radiographs, detection of storage tanks
in aerial images (Lantz et al. 1978), etc.   Illingworth and Kittler (1988) gave a

survey of the wide applications of Hough transforms.   Although the method is a
very powerful one for determining the parameters of an analytic function, its
computation time is too long in many applications, especially in real time
applications, so many scientists focused on the reduction of the complexity of
Hough transform algorithms: see, for example, Ibrahim et al. (1985), Silberberg
(1985), Fisher and Highnam (1989), Cypher et al. (1990), Kannan and Chuang
(1990), Guerra et al. (1989), Kao et al. (1993), Princen et.al. (1992, 1994), etc.
Some other scientists have developed Hough transform algorithms using cache
techniques (for instance Brown 1986).

4.2.2   Definition of Hough Transform

Let $f(X,P)$ be an analytical function of a set X of n variables, $X=\{x_1, x_2, ..., x_n\}$, with
a set P of m parameters, $P=\{p_1, p_2, ..., p_m\}$ (In our application X will be $\{x,y\}$,
where x and y are the co-ordinates of a point in the plane of an image, and P will be
$\{a,b,r\}$, where a, b, and r are the centre co-ordinates and the radius of a circle to be
fitted).   The general Hough transform, HT, is a transform which maps the function
$f(X,P)$ in the variable space X into $A(P)$ in the parameter space p:

$$A(P) = HT(f(X,P)) \, . \tag{4.2.1}$$

Referring to Princen (1992), the Hough transform can be expressed or
implemented by the transform function:

$$A(P) = HT(f(X,P)) = \sum_X W(f(X,P),X,P) \tag{4.2.2}$$

where $W(.)$ is the Hough transform kernel function defined as follows: if $f(X,P)=0$
for an observation of X at P, $W(.)=1$; otherwise, $W(.)=0$.

4.2.3   Algorithm of Hough Transform

From equation (4.2.2), an accumulator $A(P)=A(p_1, p_2, ..., p_m)$ is needed in
implementing the Hough transform.   The number of dimensions of the accumulator
is equal to the number, m, of the parameters, P, of the analytical function $f(X,P)$.
The size of each dimension is equal to the range of the corresponding parameter.
One way to implement a Hough transform algorithm is: for an observation X of
$f(X,P)$, find out all possible values of P which satisfy the equation:

$$f(X,P) = 0 \, . \tag{4.2.3}$$

Accumulate $A(P)$ with respect to each P:

$$\tag{4.2.4}$$
$$A(P) := A(P) + 1$$

and continue this procedure for all of the observations X of $f(X,P)$. Another way is: for a set of observations of X, determine the value of the kernel function $W(.)$ at P; accumulate $A(P)$ at each P:

$$A(P) = \sum_X W(.) \qquad\qquad (4.2.5)$$

and continue this procedure for all of the possible parameters P of $f(X,P)$.

The result of a Hough transform is a statistical distribution of the number of the observations X of $f(X,P)$ in parameter space. Then, for the purpose of line detection, circle detection, or arbitrary curve detection, the parameters P are determined by finding the co-ordinates of the points in accumulator space, at which the accumulator $A(P)$ has local maximal values.

4.2.4   Circular Hough Transform
The Circular Hough transform is used to detect circles or circular arcs (Duda and Hart 1972, O'Gorman and Clowes 1976, Rosenfeld and Kak 1982, Ballard and Brown 1982, Schalkoff 1989, Haralick and Shapiro 1992, etc.) or find a set of circles to fit a curve (Luo et al 1995). The Circular Hough transform maps a circle C:

$$(x-a)^2 + (y-b)^2 = r^2 \qquad\qquad (4.2.6)$$

in variable space $X=\{x,y\}$ into parameter space $P=\{a,b,r\}$, where x, y, a, b and r are as defined in Section 4.2.1. By the circular Hough transform, a point (x,y) of C in the variable space becomes the side surface of a cone in parameter space, of which the vertex is at point (a,b), $a=x$, $b=y$, and the axis is parallel to the r-axis. If n is the number of pixels on C, then there will be n cones in accumulator space, and the centre of C is given by the intersection point of the side surfaces of the n cones. Similarly the radius of C is the height of the intersection point above the plane $r=0$.

In summary, for circle detection or circle fitting, the parameters (a,b,r) are the co-ordinates of the point where the accumulator $A(a,b,r)$ has a local maximal value. Two simple common algorithms of Hough transform and three algorithms developed by the Author are introduced below.

4.3   ALGORITHMS FOR CIRCULAR HOUGH TRANSFORM

This Section will discuss five methods of implementing the circular Hough transform. These differ in: the amount of memory required; the time required for calculation; and , conversely, the scope and accuracy of the results obtained.

4.3.1   Curve Detection
All the examples in this chapter refer to boundary curves of particles; but the methods could also be applied to unclosed curves such as the centre lines of rivers.

Any reliable method of obtaining these curves may be used; and in the following it is usually assumed that this has already been done.

4.3.2 Basic Method

A simple implementation of the Circular Hough Transform (Duda and Hart, 1972) uses the basic method.

For a given parameter (a,b,r), a set of points $\{(x_i,y_i)\}$ which satisfy the circle function (4.2.6), must all lie on the circumference defined by (a,b,r). Inversely, if a set of points $\{(x_i,y_i)\}$ all lie on the same circumference, they must satisfy the same circle function (4.2.6) with the same parameters (a,b,r). This means that from finite sets of parameters (a_j,b_j,r_j) of each point (x_i,y_i), we can find a common set of parameters (a,b,r) for all points $\{(x_i,y_i)\}$, defined by which the circumference includes all the points $\{(x_i,y_i)\}$. From this point of view, the basic method can be applied for circular Hough transform.

(1) Algorithm

The basic algorithm for circular Hough transform needs an accumulator $A(a,b,r)$. The algorithm for an object or a curve is in brief as follows. As indicated above, it is assumed that pre-processing has already been done to identify the set of n points $\{(x_i,y_i)\}$ of the object which is to be analysed using the Hough transform.

Step 1   An accumulator array $A(a,b,r)$ is set to zero.

Step 2   For each point in the set, a set of m possible pairs of parameters $\{(a_j,b_j)\}$ are chosen, and the other set of parameters $\{r_{ij}\}$ are calculated from equation (4.2.6):

$$r_{ij}^2 = (a_j - x_i)^2 + (b_j - y_i)^2 . \tag{4.3.1}$$

For each (a_j,b_j,r_{ij}) thus found, a vote of 1 is added to the corresponding cell of the accumulator array of equation (4.2.4):

$$A(a_j,b_j,r_{ij}) := A(a_j,b_j,r_{ij}) + 1. \tag{4.3.2}$$

Step 3   The accumulator array $A(a,b,r)$ is searched for local maxima, each of which indicates a circular arc which fits part of the curve more or less exactly. Hence, the parameters of the circle being detected are (a_k,b_k,r_k), at which the distribution of $A(a_k,b_k,r_k)$ satisfies:

$$A(a_k,b_k,r_k) = \max_j \{A(a_j,b_j,r_j)\} . \tag{4.3.3}$$

Crudely, the height of a maximum indicates the size of the arc over which agreement is obtained, and the breadth of the peak indicates how good the agreement is. Due to the effect of digitisation, values of r less than 2 should be excluded both here and in the following methods.

Actually, when a curve is fitted by a set of circles, the contributions to the accumulator of a small arc of a large circle may be larger than that of a large arc of a small circle. Therefore, the accumulator should be normalised so that the circles best fitting the curve could be found. The normalisation can be achieved by multiplying the accumulator array $A(a,b,r)$ preceding Step 3 by a scale factor:

$$S(r) = \frac{1}{2\pi r} .$$ (4.3.4)

If this is done, the height of a maximum approximates to the angle subtended at the centre of the circle by the arc of agreement. This additional step, however, is only required if circles of varying size are involved.

(2) Discussion

In this method, the computational time and the size of memory required for the accumulator depend upon the range of a, b, and r. Obviously this method is slow because it involves a four-fold loop over each of x, y, a, and b. It also requires sufficient memory to hold the three-dimensional accumulator array. For example, if the ranges of a, b, and r were each 512 pixels, the accumulator array would require $512^3 = 134{,}217{,}728$ cells if programmed conventionally. Usually, this method is too big and too slow to run for a practical image. In the Author's experiments, the size of the array had to be reduced to $256 \times 256 \times 128 = 8{,}388{,}608$; and, even then, only one computer in the university was large enough to run the program. On the other hand, the author found this to be a comparatively exact circle detection method.

If the image contains only one curve, and if it is continuous, then the loop over x and y can be replaced by edge-following, which is faster; but there is still the loop over a and b, so the memory requirement is unchanged.

4.3.3   Directional Gradient Method

A faster implementation of the Circular Hough Transform was obtained by using a directional gradient method to analyse the boundaries of black-and-white images, as had been done by Kimme et al. (1975) and Haralick and Shapiro (1992). As shown in Figure 4.3, the centre of a circle is the point where all the radii of the circle intersect. Now, the direction of a radius is given by the direction of the intensity gradient of the circumference at the intersection point of the radius and the circumference (or the reverse of this direction). Thus, only the parameters (a,b) in that direction through that intersection point are of concern.

(1) Algorithm

The procedure for circular Hough transform by the gradient method was as follows:

Step 1   An accumulator array $A(a,b,r)$ is set to zero.

Step 2   The image is scanned as before, but now the direction of the intensity gradient, θ_i, is found at each point on the curve to give the direction of the radius.

Step 3   For each of the points found above, a set of m possible parameters $\{r_j\}$ is chosen, and the other set of parameters $\{(a_j, b_j)\}$ is   calculated from:

$$\begin{cases} a_j = x_i + r_j \cos\theta_i, \\ b_j = y_i + r_j \sin\theta_i, \end{cases}$$
(4.3.5)

then the accumulator array $A(a_j, b_j, r_j)$ is incremented as before:

$$A(a_j, b_j, r_j) := A(a_j, b_j, r_j) + 1.$$
(4.3.6)

Step 4   Point (x_i, y_i) and direction θ_i are updated and the algorithm is repeated from Step 2 for all the points on the curve.

Step 5   The accumulator $A(a,b,r)$ is searched for local maxima, from which the parameters (a,b,r) of the fitting circles are determined.

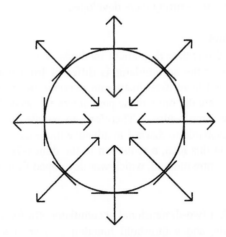

Figure 4.3   the directions of the gradient at the points of a circle.

(2)   *Discussion*

Experiments were made using both grey images and thresholded binary images; but it was decided to concentrate on pre-thresholded binary images in the present study. In finding the intensity gradients, the positive sides of the filters should all be positive to avoid accidentally reversing the direction of the intensity gradient; such reversal can occur with some of the larger filters discussed by Smart and Tovey

(1988). In addition, 5×5 filters give better smoothing of the digitisation steps along boundaries than do 3×3 filters.   Otherwise, the choice of filter for finding the intensity gradient was thought to be not critical.   Therefore, the 20U formula of Smart and Leng (1991, 1993), which is a 'wholly positive' 5×5 filter, was chosen here for its simplicity.

Although this method is faster than the basic method, the experiments showed it to be less accurate than the basic method, and it does not give any reduction in memory requirement.

In passing, it may be noted that this method could be extended to give the intrinsic equation of a continuous curve.   The direction, ψ, of the tangent to the curve is perpendicular to the normal, and the distance, s, along the curve can be estimated by any of the conventional methods.   Thus, the digital version of:

$$\frac{d\psi}{ds} = f(s) \tag{4.3.7}$$

could be calculated.

In order to reduce the memory requirement to a size which would run on commonly available computers, the following methods of circular Hough transform for circle detection or circle fitting were developed.

4.3.4   Centre Method

In both the basic and directional gradient methods, we can see that in parameter space, the histogram of the accumulator is different from point to point.   Only those parameters which have local histogram maxima are needed.   In roundness analysis of an object, actually only those parameters are needed of which the radius is the smallest at the same centre.   Therefore, to reduce the memory size of the accumulator, it is reasonable to discard in advance those parameters which will not be needed.   Based on this idea, a reduction in the dimensions of the accumulator was achieved by the centre method, which was developed from the basic method.

(1)   Algorithm

In the centre method, a two-dimensional accumulator $A(a,b)$, a sequential memory with four components, and a threshold function $T(r)$ are needed. Details of the threshold will be given in Section 4.4.   The main procedure of the centre method for circular Hough transform is as follows:

Step 1   The accumulator array $A(a,b)$ is set to zero.

Step 2   The set of n points of the curve $\{x_i, y_i\}$ is obtained as before.

Step 3   A trial value of the parameter r_j is chosen.

Step 4   As shown in Figure 4.4 (a) and (c), for each of the points on the curve, using the chosen value of the parameter r_j, then for every possible value of b_k, the corresponding value of a_k is calculated from:

$$a_k = x_i \pm \sqrt{r_j^2 - (y_i - b_k)^2} \; . \tag{4.3.8}$$

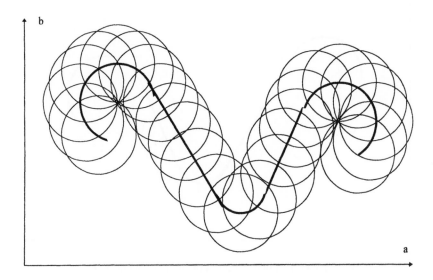

Figure 4.4 (a)   Locii of centres of circles of radius, $r=r_1$, Centre method.

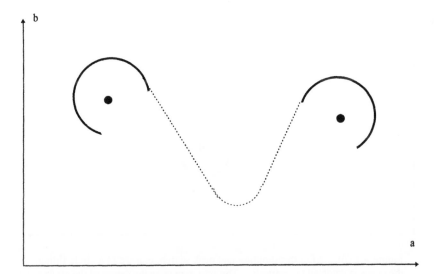

Figure 4.4 (b)   After thresholding and peak search, two arcs of circles fitting the curve are detected temporarily.   The two spots express the centres of the circles.

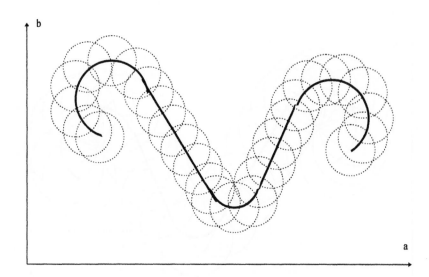

Figure 4.4 (c)   Locii of centres of circles of radius, $r=r_2$.

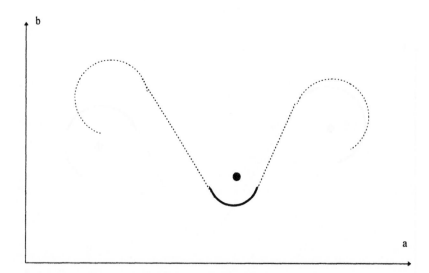

Figure 4.4 (d)   After thresholding and peak search, one arc of a circle fitting
the curve is detected temporarily.   The spot expresses the centre of the circle.

Note that (a_k, b_k) is a point on the circle centred at (x_i, y_i). For each of these pairs of values (a_k, b_k), the accumulator $A(a,b)$ is incremented:

$$A(a_k, b_k) := A(a_k, b_k) + 1 . \tag{4.3.9}$$

Step 5 The accumulator $A(a,b)$ is thresholded by a function $T(r)$, (which will be explained in Section 4.4):

$$A(a_k, b_k) := \begin{cases} A(a_k, b_k) & \text{if} \quad A(a_k, b_k) \geq T(r_j) \\ 0 & \text{otherwise} \end{cases} . \tag{4.3.10}$$

Step 6 The accumulator array $A(a,b)$ is searched for local maxima, and the corresponding parameters a_j, b_j, r_j, and the value in the accumulator array, $A(a_j, b_j)$, are stored in a list in sequential memory. Figure 4.4 (b) and (d) show arcs of circles located by this step.

Step 7 The accumulator is re-set to zero, the parameter r_j is updated, and the algorithm is resumed from Step 4 for all possible parameters r.

Step 8 The list of parameters (a,b,r) is itself searched for local maxima.

(2) Quick Version
When only the circles fitting the corners along the contour of the object are needed for the roundness measurement, only the parameters (a,b,r) with smallest r at (a,b) need be stored. As shown in Figure 4.5, if there are two radii r_1 and r_2 $(r_2>r_1)$ detected at the same point (a,b), the arc corresponding to r_2 is not considered as a corner. Therefore, in this particular problem, a two-dimensional array was used to store the value of r at (a,b) instead of using a list in sequential memory. In each iterative step 4, this two-dimensional array was overwritten under the rule of smallest r. To find the circles fitting corners, the two-dimensional array is searched for small radii. This quick version may sometimes be inappropriate, so care is needed before accepting it.

(3) Discussion
In this method, the number of dimensions of the accumulator is reduced from 3 dimensions to 2 dimensions. Therefore, the size of the accumulator plus the size of the sequential memory is much less than the 3 dimensional accumulator in the basic method. The accuracy of the transform is the same as the basic method. However, the run time is now greater than that of the basic method.

If the image contains only one curve, and if it is continuous, then the loop over x and y can be replaced by edge-following, but there is still the loop over a and b. In the present work, use of the centre method was limited to a preliminary trial, which led to the development of both of the methods following.

4.3.5 Gradient Centre Method

As mentioned when discussing the directional gradient method, the centre of a circle is the intersecting point of the radii of the circle, and the direction of each radius is the same as that of the gradient at the point where the radius intersects the circumference. Clearly, combining the directional gradient method and the centre method, called gradient centre method, can achieve the reduction of both the memory size and the run time.

(1) Algorithm

Like the centre method, the gradient centre method needs a two dimensional accumulator $A(a,b)$ and a sequential memory with four components. Combining the algorithms of the directional gradient method and the centre method, the procedure for the gradient centre method is in brief:

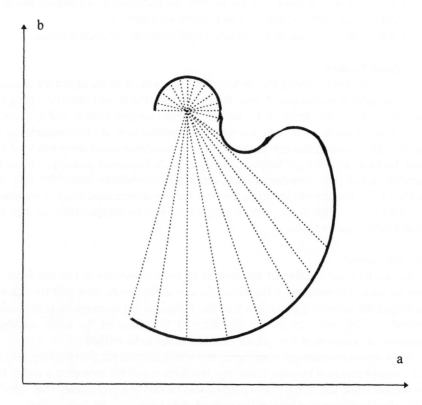

Figure 4.5   Here two arcs of circles have been detected at the same centre point. The arc with smaller radius is kept as a corner feature. The other arc is discarded, because it is not considered as a corner.

Step 1   The accumulator $A(a,b)$ is set to zero.

Step 2   The set of n points $\{(x_i,y_i)\}$ and the corresponding direction θ_i of each point (x_i,y_i) are obtained as before.

Step 3   A trial value of the parameter r_j is chosen.

Step 4   As shown in Figure 4.6, for each of the points on the curve, the other pair of parameters (a_j, b_j) is calculated by:

$$\begin{cases} a_j = x_i + r_j \cos\theta_i, \\ b_j = y_i + r_j \sin\theta_i, \end{cases}$$

(4.3.11)

and the accumulator $A(a,b)$ is incremented at each parameter (a_j, b_j):

$$A(a_j, b_j) := A(a_j, b_j) + 1.$$

(4.3.12)

Here (a_j, b_j) is a point lying on the line at angle θ_i intersecting the curve at (x_i,y_i) and distant r_j from the curve.

Step 5   The accumulator $A(a,b)$ is thresholded by a function $T(r)$:

$$A(a_j, b_j) = \begin{cases} A(a_j, b_j) & \text{if} \quad A(a_j, b_j) \geq T(r_j) \\ 0 & \text{otherwise} \end{cases}.$$

(4.3.13)

Step 6   If $A(a_j, b_j)$ is a local maximum, the corresponding parameters a_j, b_j, r_j, and $A(a_j, b_j)$ are stored in a list in sequential memory.

Step 7   The accumulator is re-set to zero, the parameter r_j is updated and the algorithm is resumed from Step 4 for all possible parameters r.

Step 8   The list of parameters (a,b,r) can be searched for local maxima.

As in Section 4.3.5.3, a similar quick version of the gradient centre method is applied for finding the circles fitting corners.

(2)   Discussion

Obviously, in this method, both the size of the memory and the run time are reduced.   However, the accuracy might be less than the centre method. This is because, like the directional gradient method, the accuracy depends on that of the directions of the gradient.   Therefore, the following method was also considered.

4.3.6   Radius Method

In considering the accuracy of the circular Hough transform, in some cases, the results by the directional gradient method and the gradient centre method are not as good as they should be.   At the price of increased run time, another development of the basic method, similar to the centre method, called radius method, can be used to reduce further the size of the memory.

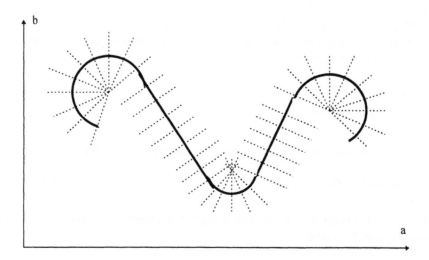

Figure 4.6   Locii of centres of circles of radius, Direction gradient method.

(1)   Algorithm

Unlike the centre method and the gradient centre method, the radius method needs a one dimensional accumulator $A(r)$.   Similarly, it also requires a sequential memory with four components.   The procedure of this method is slightly different from the centre method.   It can be explained as follows:

Step 1   The accumulator array $A(r)$ is set to zero.
Step 2   The set of n points $\{x_i, y_i\}$ is obtained as before.
Step 3   A trial pair of values of the parameters (a_j, b_j) is chosen.
Step 4   As shown in Figure 4.7 , for each of the points on the curve, the parameter r_{ij} is calculated from:

$$r_{ij}^2 = (x_i - a_j)^2 + (y_i - b_j)^2 \qquad\qquad (4.3.14)$$

and the accumulator $A(r)$ is incremented:

$$A(r_{ij}) := A(r_{ij}) + 1. \qquad\qquad (4.3.15)$$

Step 5 The accumulator $A(r)$ is thresholded by a function $T(r)$:

$$A(r_{ij}) = \begin{cases} A(r_{ij}) & \text{if} \quad A(r_{ij}) \geq T(r_{ij}) \\ 0 & \text{otherwise} \end{cases} \tag{4.3.16}$$

Step 6 The accumulator array $A(r)$ is searched for local maxima, and the corresponding parameters a_j, b_j, r_k, and value $A(r_k)$ are stored in a list in sequential memory.

Step 7 The accumulator $A(r)$ is re-set to zero, the parameters (a_j, b_j) are updated, and the algorithm is resumed from Step 4 for all possible parameters (a, b).

Step 8 The list of parameters (a, b, r) is searched for local maxima.

Similarly, a quick version of the radius method for finding circles fitting corners is that: in each iterative Step 6, only the parameters a_j, b_j, r_k, and $A(r_k)$ with the smallest value of r are stored in the sequential memory.

(2) Discussion
In this method, much less memory is required than in the methods mentioned above, and the accuracy is as the same as the basic method. However, the run time is still similar to the basic method and higher than the directional gradient method.

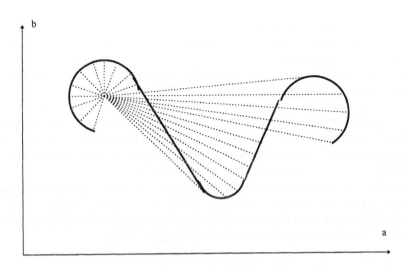

Figure 4.7   Radii from centre (a_1, b_1) to various points on the curve.

The computer program *cirhft.cpp* of the algorithm by radius method for circular Hough transform, written in language C++ by the author, was listed in Computer Programs at the end of this book.

4.4   THRESHOLD FUNCTION *T*(*r*)

In circle detection and circle fitting, usually, the criterion of circle fitting is that the best circle fitting to a curve is the one of which the intersecting arc with the curve is the largest among all the circles fitting to the curve. However, as explained in Section 4.3.3.2, a small intersecting arc of a very large circle fitting to a curve may be larger than a large arc of a very small circle. In this case, we might not think the very large circle is the best circle fitting the curve.   Therefore the criterion of the circle fitting should be a function of or normalised by the radius of the circle.   On the other hand, because of noise, digitisation, and edge detection operation, a straight line segment may be thick and rough.   From this consideration, a straight line segment should be discriminated from a curve.   Therefore, a lower boundary of the criterion of circle fitting should be set.   For these reason, a threshold function *T*(*r*) for circular Hough transform is designed to meet the needs of the criterion and the lower boundary.

The threshold function *T*(*r*) can be specified by users to suit different purposes. The simplest formula is:

$$T(r) = \alpha \cdot 2\pi r \qquad\qquad (\alpha_0 < \alpha < 1) \qquad\qquad\qquad (4.4.1)$$

where α_0 is the lower boundary.   If both the accumulator $A(.)$ and the threshold function $T(r)$ are normalised by $S(r)$, then the threshold function $T(r)$ would be a constant, α.   equation (4.4.1) implies that if $A(.)$ is greater than $T(r)$, the circle may be considered to fit the curve over a proportion α of the circumference of the circle, and the quality of fit using $A(.)$ is independent of the radius.

However a correction of $T(r)$ may be needed because $T(r)$ should be greater than the least value which can discriminate an arc of a circle with radius r from a segment of a straight line.   The noise and the thickness of the curve should be taken into account as mentioned above.   From this point of view, another formula for the threshold function, $T(r)$, is determined as follows.

As shown in Figure 4.8, let T_n be the thickness of a curve produced by edge detection operation, and R_n the roughness of the curve caused by noise.   Then, to discriminate an arc of a circle from an imperfect segment of a straight line, the threshold $T(r)$ should be greater than the least length of the arc:

$$T(r) > 2r\theta = 2r \cdot \arccos\frac{r - (T_n + R_n)}{r} = 2r \cdot \arccos(1 - \frac{T_n + R_n}{r}). \qquad (4.4.2)$$

The normalised threshold by r, $T(r)/r$, from this formula, is actually the angle subtended by the intersecting arc at the centre of the circle. Therefore, detected by this threshold function, the quality of fit using $A(.)/r$ is independent of the radius.

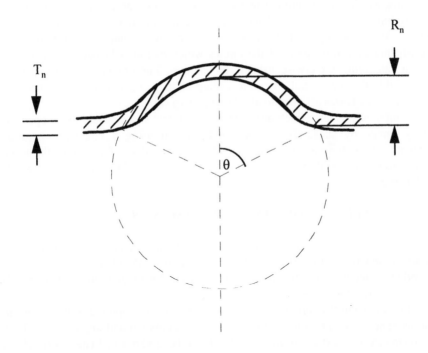

Figure 4.8   Determination of least threshold $T(r)$; a thick line is shown shaded.

The use of $T(r)$ is illustrated in Figure 4.9. $A(r)$ was calculated for one centre (a,b) using the Radius method; and $T(r)$ was calculated from equation (4.4.2) using $T_n=1$ and $R_n=1$.   After thresholding, only the peaks of $A(r)$ remain, see the black solid part of $A(r)$ in Figure 4.9.   It is the final curve, $A'(r)$, which is then scanned to find the circles.   In this example, only one circle was found, with radius 12.

4.5   SHARP CORNERS

In digitised images, the resolution is at best 2 pixels; and this imposes a lower limit on the size of the circles which can be found by the Hough transform.   In the problems which are of immediate interest here, only corners which are on the convex hull are of interest.   Therefore, the convex hull was scanned vertex by vertex.   Whenever a pair of closely spaced vertices were found, they were tested is see whether they were parts of the circles which had already been found by the Hough transform.   Otherwise, using a run length of 5 or 7 pixels, a pair of tangents was fitted to the convex hull to define a sharp corner.   As an expedient, a nominal radius of 2 pixels was ascribed to all of these sharp corners.

An alternative idea, which occurred at a very late stage, would be to open the binary image by successive erosion and dilation using a circular structuring element.   It is expected that this would have the effect of rounding the sharp corners to the radius of the structuring element, so that the Hough transform would find them.

4.6   EXAMPLES OF ROUNDNESS/SHARPNESS ANALYSES

As seen in Section 4.1, the roundness of an object is defined as a function of the radius of the circles fitting the corners of the contour of the object. The first step is to find the contour or the edge of the object.   Then the circular Hough transform is applied to detect the circles.

Often after digitisation, a circular low pass filter was applied to the image in Fourier space to suppress the noise caused by illumination and digitisation.   Then the boundary was extracted and the 20U-formula (Smart and Leng, 1991, 1993) was used to find the direction of the intensity gradient along the boundary.   The output comprised the co-ordinates X and the directions θ of the edge.   The diagram of the system is as shown in Figure 4.10.

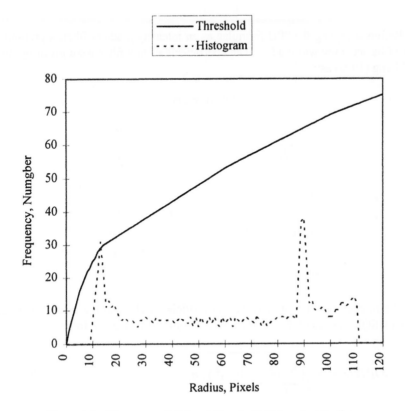

Figure 4.9   Histogram of $A(r)$ and Threshold $T(r)$ against Radius r.

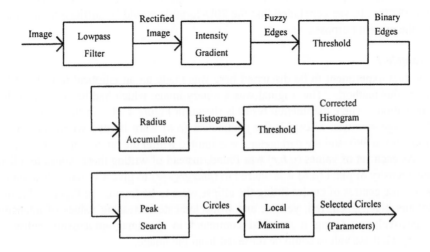

Figure 4.10   Flow chart of circular Hough Transform system.

Before accepting the 20U formulae as an intensity gradient filter, a preliminary test of its accuracy was made.   The coefficients of this filter were given by Smart and Leng (1993) as:

20U formulae

$$\frac{dI}{dx} \qquad\qquad\qquad\qquad \frac{dI}{dy}$$

	−1		1			1	1	1	
−1	−1		1	1	1	1	1	1	1
−1	−1	x,y	1	1			x,y		
−1	−1		1	1	−1	−1	−1	−1	−1
	−1		1			−1	−1	−1	

The image used for this test was an artificial circle; and the mean square root error (MSQRT error) of the direction of the radii was calculated from:

$$MSQRTerror = \sqrt{(\sum_{i=1}^{n}(\theta_{gi} - \theta_{ci})^2)/n} \qquad\qquad (4.6.1)$$

where θ_{gi} is the angle calculated by gradient filter at an edge point, θ_{ci} is the theoretical angle calculated from an edge point to the centre of the circle, and n is the number of points concerned.   The MSQRT error of the filter 20U was 6.828977°.   It was concluded that the 20U-formula would be sufficiently accurate for the present purposes.

Example 1
The first experiment to be discussed here was made on an elliptical test object by the radius method.   The original was a binary image which had been obtained by calculation.   The experimental result is shown in Figure 4.11.   In this experiment, the image size was 512×512, the parameters (a,b) were limited within the range from 190 to 390, and the parameter r was limited within the range from 2 to 128.
    As each set of values (a,b,r) was found, instead of writing these values to a list, the intensity of pixel (a,b) was altered to (*maxgrey* -r) to give a visual indication of where the centres of circles fitting the ellipse were to be found.   In Figure 4.11, the colours blue, green, red, yellow, and white indicate increasing values of intensity respectively.   Using a standard command in the image-processing software (Semper), these values could be retrieved from the image.

In Figure 4.11, some centres have appeared along the major axis of the ellipse. These are centres of inscribed circles, which are not circles of curvature, and which should be disregarded here.

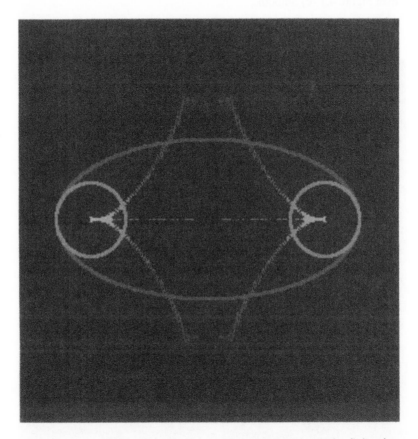

Figure 4.11   A boundary of an ellipse, some centres of the circles fitting the ellipse, and two circles fitted at the ends of the major axis.

The pair of bright cusp-like curves are the locii of the centres of curvature of the ellipse; these have been truncated at $b = \pm390$.   Since the evolute of a curve is defined as the locus of the centres of curvature of the curve, these cusp-like curves form the evolute of the ellipse.

By inspection of the calculated results, the centres and radii of the circles of curvature at the ends of the major axis of the ellipse have been found; and these circles have been superimposed on the figure.

Example 2

Figure 4.12 illustrates the radius method applied to the measurement of the roundness of particles.   In Figure 4.12, the outer boundary is the boundary of a particle taken from a standard chart given by Bullock (1985) for soil particles see Figure 4.1 (e) Smooth; however, Figure 4.12 was digitised individually at a larger scale than Figure 4.1 (e) Smooth.

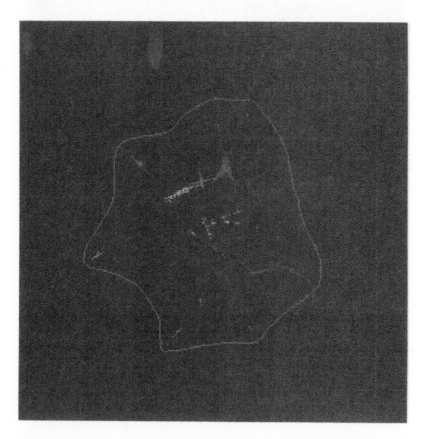

Figure 4.12 (a)   The boundary of a particle in Figure 4.1 (e-Smooth) and some centres of circles fitting the boundary.

The immediate problem was to measure the roundness of the corners.   This was achieved by fitting circles to the boundary using the radius method and the threshold function $T(r)$ as indicated above.   Only those circles centred within the particle are of interest, thus defining the region over which (a,b) was varied and reducing the run time.   (This point is discussed further in Section 4.6.6 below).

The results were stored in the image as explained in the previous Section.   Also, only the smallest circles were required; if two or more values of r were obtained for the same centre (a,b) only the smallest value of r was retained.   Then, because the intensity was reset to (*maxgrey - r*), the centres of the smaller circles showed more brightly.   These reset pixels are visible in Figure 4.12 (a), where red, yellow, and white indicate increasing values of intensity.   Next, the reset pixels were scanned to find the smallest circle at each of the corners; these circles are shown in Figures 4.12 (b) and (c).

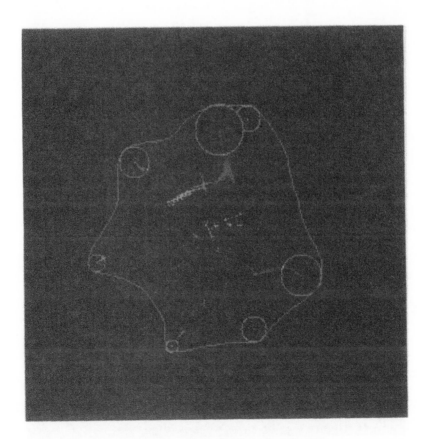

Figure 4.12 (b)   Circles fitted at selected centres.

Example 3

The radius method was also applied to the five visual charts of particles as shown in Figures 4.1 (a) - (e-Smooth). Each of the five charts was digitised into a 512×512 image. After image preprocessing, the particles were segmented to produce individual boundaries. Then the circles r_i which fit the corners of each particle were detected by the radius method. In addition, the inscribing circle R_I of a particle, defined as the largest circle among all the smallest circles fitting inside the boundary of the particle, was found. Thus, the roundness *Round* of the particle was calculated by Krumbein's equation, i.e. equation (4.1.1), where the sum is taken to include all circles with radii $r_i \leq R_I$. The results are shown in Tables 4.1 - 4.6.

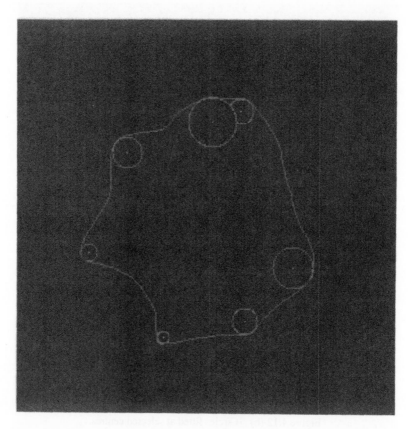

Figure 4.12 (c)   Final set of circles fitting the corners of the boundary

Table 4.1   Roundness/sharpness of the Chart in Figure 4.1 (a) measured by the radius method and equation (4.1.1).

| | ← Sphericity — | | | | Average |
	Round				
Rounded	0.632	0.600	0.636	0.556	0.606
Almost Rounded	0.461	0.615	0.500	0.500	0.519
Subrounded	0.390	0.517	0.460	0.524	0.473
Subangular	0.264	0.414	0.545	0.314	0.384
Angular	0.284	0.357	0.300	0.250	0.298
Average	0.406	0.501	0.488	0.429	

Table 4.2   Roundness/sharpness of the Chart in Figure 4.1 (b) measured by the radius method and equation (4.1.1).

| | ← Sphericity — | | | | Average |
	Round				
Rounded	0.579	0.567	0.545	0.556	0.562
Almost Rounded	0.381	0.637	0.538	0.556	0.528
Subrounded	0.470	0.385	0.500	0.444	0.450
Subangular	0.263	0.415	0.513	0.250	0.360
Angular	0.235	0.393	0.250	0.333	0 303
Average	0.386	0.479	0.469	0.428	

Table 4.3   Roundness/sharpness of the Chart in Figure 4.1 (c) measured by the radius method and equation (4.1.1).

| | ← Sphericity — | | | | Average |
	Round				
Rounded	0.675	0.625	0.633	0.714	0.662
Almost Rounded	0.405	0.564	0.700	0.571	0.560
Subrounded	0.400	0.476	0.630	0.429	0.484
Subangular	0.356	0.482	0.333	0.429	0.400
Angular	0.190	0.200	0.333	0.286	0.252
Average	0.405	0.469	0.526	0.486	

Table 4.4   Roundness/sharpness of the Chart in Figure 4.1 (d) measured by the radius method and equation (4.1.1).

	← Sphericity —				Average
	Round				
Rounded	0.522	0.526	0.569	0.267	0.471
Almost Rounded	0.359	0.515	0.441	0.308	0.406
Subrounded	0.356	0.294	0.429	0.436	0.379
Subangular	0.324	0.329	0.438	0.231	0.331
Angular	0.276	0.315	0.244	0.282	0.279
Average	0.367	0.396	0.327	0.305	

Table 4.5   Roundness/sharpness of the Chart in Figure 4.1 (e-Smooth) measured by the radius method and equation (4.1.1).

	← Sphericity —				Average
	Round				
Rounded	0.509	0.549	0.392	0.455	0.476
Almost Rounded	0.346	0.476	0.363	0.208	0.348
Subrounded	0.419	0.365	0.410	0.280	0.369
Subangular	0.161	0.256	0.393	0.493	0.326
Angular	0.064	0.189	0.355	0.240	0.212
Average	0.300	0.367	0.383	0.335	

Table 4.6   Average values and proposed values of roundness *Round*.

	Average of *Round*	Proposed value
Rounded	0.555	0.550
Almost Rounded	0.472	0.480
Subrounded	0.431	0.410
Subangular	0.360	0.340
Angular	0.269	0.270

From the tables, we can see that, the values in each column of each table increase from bottom to top with a few exceptions. This is roughly in agreement with the original design. However, some overlaps among rows can be found. This is not so good as the original intention. The values appear to be reasonably constant from column to column, although there does seem to be a slight tendency for *Round* to decrease with sphericity.

These problems might be caused by the following reasons. First of all, drawing a corner to a specified sharpness appears to be exceedingly difficult. Secondly, the digitisation and the quantisation may roughen some portions of smooth edges and round off some sharp corners. Third, the resolution of the digitisation may cause some inaccuracy at very sharp corners. To a certain extent, the second and third of these problems can be minimised by increasing the resolution when digitising the images; but the first problem is inherent in the charts themselves.

Left-hand column of Table 4.6 shows the average roundness for each class based on all the results in Tables 4.1-4.5. From the original presentation of the charts, there had been some doubt as to whether the Rounded and Almost Rounded classes had been intended to be the same or different. It seems from Table 4.6 that they are intended to be different; the results from the individual charts also being consistent with this conclusion. The differences between the values of *Round* for the classes are respectively: 0.083, 0.041, 0.071, and 0.091. Apart from 'experimental variability', these differences appear to be equal, suggesting that *Round* should vary linearly from class to class. On this basis, a set of equally spaced central values for the classification of particles is proposed in the right-hand column of Table 4.6.

Further Points

When studying the roundness of objects, the centre of curvature of the sharpest corner in any local region must lie within the particle, because the boundary at that corner cannot double back between the circumference and the centre of curvature without reducing the radius of curvature further. It follows that only the interior of a particle need be scanned for centres of curvature.

Further if only corners whose radii of curvature are less than an agreed threshold value, s, are required, then these centres must lie within s of the boundary. Therefore, a mask could be constructed by: eroding the particles by s; and subtracting the eroded particles from the original particles. Then only the inner rim area defined by the mask need be scanned.

In all of the tests made here, maxima were extracted from the histograms by simple scanning. However, in more complicated cases, a maximum may fragment into a set of local maxima. A possible approach to this case would be to use cluster analysis to group the maxima, and then to find the circle with the highest number of votes in each group. Based on experience with a similar problem, the Author's tentative opinion is that cluster analysis would be more likely to succeed than would smoothing the histogram.

All of the analyses discussed in this chapter have been for binary images, for which votes of either 0 or 1 were added to the accumulator arrays. There are possible extensions to grey level images, based on the concept that the votes should be proportional to the intensity or to the modulus of the intensity gradient, depending on the circumstance of the case.

4.7 CONCLUSIONS

Five methods of using the Circular Hough Transform to find approximately circular portions of curves and hence measure the roundness of particles have been implemented and tested.

The basic method was found to be accurate but slow and excessively demanding in memory (3-D accumulator).

The direction gradient method was fast but inaccurate and excessively demanding in memory (3-D accumulator).

The centre method was accurate and less demanding in memory (2-D accumulator) but slow.

The gradient centre method was fast and less demanding in memory (2-D accumulator) but inaccurate.

The radius method was accurate and much less demanding in memory (1-D accumulator) but slow.

If the region in which the centres of curvature might fall can be restricted at the outset, then the run time can always be improved, and the sizes of all the accumulator arrays except that for the radius method can be reduced. In particular, when measuring the roundness of particles, only the interior of the particle need be scanned; and if the radius of curvature can be restricted, only an inner rim need be scanned.

If only the smallest radius of curvature at any given centre of curvature is required, then the memory requirement may be reduced.

A method of thresholding which compensates for the radius of curvature of arcs of circles has been established; and this has been extended to incorporate an empirical adjustment for imperfections in the curves.

A method of finding corners which are too sharp to be found by the circular Hough transform has been implemented.

Extensions to find the evolute of a curve and the intrinsic equation of a curve have been indicated (Section 4.3.4 and Section 4.6.3).

The new methods have indicated some irregularities in the draughtsmanship of five standard charts which are used for classification of the shapes of particles.

A set of values of the roundness parameter, *Round*, has been proposed for automatic classification of the shapes of particles.

References

Anderson, I. M. and Bezdek, J. C. (1984) Curvature and tangential deflection of discrete arcs: A theory based on the commutator of scatter matrix pairs and its application to vertex detection in planar shape data. *IEEE Trans. Pattern Analysis Mach. Intel.*, Vol. 6, pp. 27-40.

Ballard, D. H. (1981) Generalising the Hough transform to detect arbitrary shapes. *Pattern Recognition*, Vol. 13, pp. 111-122.

Ballard, D. H. and Brown, C. M. (1982) *Computer Vision*. Prentice-Hall Inc.

Ballard, D. H., Marinucci, M., Proietti-Orlandi, F., Rossi-Mari, A., and Tentari, L. (1975) Automatic analysis of human haemoglobin finger prints. *Proc. 3rd Meeting, International Society of Haematology*.

Brewer, R. (1964) *Fabric and Mineral Analysis of Soils*. John Wiley.

Brown, C. M. (1986) A space-efficient Hough transform implementation for object detection. Wegman, E. J. and DePriest, D. J. (Eds.), *Statistical Image Processing and Graphics*. Marcel Dekker, Inc., pp. 145-166.

Bullock, P., Fedoroff, N., Jongerius, A., Stoops, G., and Tursina, T. (1985) *Handbook for Soil Thin Section Description*. Waine Research Publications, Fig. 31, pp. 31..

Cypher, R. E., Sanz, J. L. C. and Snyder, L. (1990) The Hough transform has O(N) complexity on N×N mesh connected computers. *SIAM J. Comput.*, Vol. 19, pp. 805-820.

Duda, R. O., and Hart, P. E. (1972) Use of Hough transformation to detect lines and curves in pictures. *Communications of the ACM*, Vol. 15, pp 11-15.

Duda, R. O., and Hart, P. E. (1973) *Pattern Classification and Scene Analysis*. John Wiley & Sons, pp. 363.

Fisher, A. L. and Highnam, P. T. (1989) Computing the Hough transform on a scan line array processor. *IEEE Trans. Pattern Analysis Mach. Intel.* Vol. 11, pp. 262-265.

FitzPatrick, E. A. (1984) *Micromorphology of Soils*. Chapman and Hall.

Guerra, C. and Hambrusch, S. (1989) Parallel algorithms for line detection on a mech. *J. Parallel Distrib. Comput.* Vol. 6, pp. 1-19.

Haralick, R. M. and Shapiro, L. G. (1992) *Computer and robot Vision*. Addison-Wesley, pp. 575-577, 602-627.

Hodgson, J. M. (1974) *Soil Survey Field Handbook. Soil Survey of England and Wales*. Harpenden.

Hough, P. V. C. (1962) *A method and means for recognising complex patterns*. US. Patent, No. 3,069,654.

Ibrahim, H. A. H., Kender, J. R., and Shaw, D. E. (1985) The analysis and performance of two middle-level vision tasks on a fine-grained SIMD tree machine. *Proc. IEEE Comput. Soc. Conf. Comput. Vision Pattern Recognition*, pp. 248-256.

Illingworth, J. and Kittler, J. (1988) A survey of the Hough transform. *Comput. Vision, Graphics, Image Processing*, Vol. 44, pp. 87-116.

Kannan, C. S. and Chuang, Y. H. (1990) Fast Hough transform on a mesh connected processor array. *Inform. Process. Lett.* Vol. 33, pp. 243-248.

Kao, T. W., Horng, S. J., Wang, Y. L., and Chung, K. L. (1993) A constant time algorithm for computing Hough transform. *Pattern Recognition*, Vol. 26, pp. 277-286.

Kimme, C., Ballard, D. H., and Sklansky, J. (1975) Finding circles by an array of accumulators. *Communications of the ACM*, Vol. 18, pp. 120-122.

Krumbein, W. C. (1940) Flood gravel of San Gabriel Canyon. *California, Bull. Geol. Soc. Am.*, vol. 51, Fig. 11, pp. 670.

Krumbein, W. C. and Sloss, L. L. (1951) *Stratigraphy and Sedimentation*. W. H. Freeman & Co., Fig. 4-9, pp. 81.

Krumbein, W. C. and Sloss, L. L. (1955) *Stradigraphy and Sedimentation*. W. H. Freeman & Co.

Lantz, K. A., Brown, C. M., and Ballard, D. H. (1978) Model-driven vision using procedure description motivation and application to photointerpretation and medical diagnosis. *Proc. 22nd International Symp., Society of Photo-optical Instrumentation Engineers.*

Luo, D., MacLeod, J. E. S., and Smart, P. (1995) Circular Hough transform for automatic analysis of roundness of soil particles. *Pattern Recognition*, Vol 28, No. 11, pp. 1745-1749.

O'Gorman, F. and Clowes, M. B. (1976) Finding picture edges through collinearity of feature points. *IEEE Transactions on Computers*, Vol. C-25, pp. 449-454.

Pettijhon, F. J. (1957) *Sedimentary Rocks*. Harper & Row, pp. 57-59.

Princen, J., Illingworth, J. and Kittler, J. (1992) A formal definition of the Hough transform: Properties and relationships. *J. Math, Imaging Vision*, Vol. 1, pp. 153-168.

Princen, J., Illingworth, J., and Kittler, J. (1994) Hypothesis testing: A framework for analysing and optimising Hough transform performance. *IEEE Trans. Pattern Analysis Mach. Intel.* Vol. 16, No. 4, pp. 329-341.

Rosenfeld, A. and Johnston, E. (1973) Angle detection on digital curves. *IEEE Trans. Computers*, Vol. 22, pp. 875-878.

Rosenfeld, A. and Kak, A. C. (1982) *Digital Picture Processing*. Academic Press.

Rosenfeld, A. and Weszka, J. S. (1975) An improved method of angle detection on digital curves. *IEEE Trans. Computer*, Vol. 24, pp. 940-941.

Schalkoff, R. J. (1989) *Digital Image Processing and Computer Vision*. John Wiley & Sons Inc.

Seeger, U. and Seeger, R. (1994) Fast corner detection in grey-level images. *Pattern Recognition Letters*. Vol. 15, No. 7, pp. 669-675.

Silberberg, T. M. (1985) The Hough transform on geometric arithmetic parallel processor. *IEEE Comput. Soc. Wk shop, Comput. Architecture Pattern Analysis Image Database Management*, pp. 387-393.

Smart, P. and Leng, X. (1991) Textural analysis by transputer - Report on SERC Transputer Loan TR1/099. *SERC/DTI Transputer Loan Initiative Reports, SERC, Rutherford Appleton Laboratory*, Didcot. No. 10, pp. 1-15.

Smart, P. and Leng, X. (1993) Present developments in image analysis. *Scanning Microscopy*, Vol. 7, No. 1, p. 5-16.

Smart, P. and Tovey, N. K. (1988) Theoretical aspects of intensity gradient analysis. *Scanning*, Vol. 10, pp. 115-121.

Wechsler, H. and Sklansky, J. (1977) Finding the rib cage in chest radiographs. *Pattern Recognition*, Vol. 9, pp. 21-30.

5

Orientation Analysis

5.1 INTRODUCTION

This chapter will present a new method of measuring the orientation of objects, the Directed Vein method; and it will compare this method with (a) a method based on the author's convex hull algorithm, which was discussed in Chapter 3; (b) the Principal Components Transform method; and (c) the method of Moments.   To anticipate the results, the last three methods appear to give comparable estimates of an "elongation direction", whilst the Directed Vein method will discover an "internal preferred orientation" if this is present and strongly marked.

In image processing and pattern recognition, orientation analysis is used for feature measurement of objects.   The orientation features of objects can be used for describing, recognising, and classifying objects, or for some other relevant study with respect to orientations of objects.   For example, in remote sensing, one can measure the orientation of a ship in the sea to predict where the ship is going towards; in fishing, one can detect the direction of the movement of a shoal of fish to trace and fish the shoal; in raising livestock on a plain, one can identify the direction in which a herd is moving, in order to control the herd; in meteorological observations, one can analyse the directions of the pressure gradients in a meteorological map to forecast weather, and so on.   Therefore, orientation analysis has been attached importance in image processing and pattern recognition.

5.1.1 Problem of Orientation Analysis
In the study of soil micro-structure, much interest has been focused on the orientation analysis of electron or optical micrographs of soil specimens.   The orientation analysis is used for such purposes as investigating the relationships between soils and geological and geochemical conditions.   This is because the orientation of these soil particles, voids, domains, plates, and so on, is related to the geological and geochemical conditions, natural conditions such as temperature, pressure, water flow, ice movements, snow melting, etc., as well as to the qualitative classification of soil (Smart 1966 (a) and (b); Smart 1972; Dickson and Smart 1978; Smart and Dickson 1979; Smart and Tovey 1982).   This type of orientation analysis is often considered to be particularly important in clay soils, where the particles are flat plates.   For example, one of the most important aspects is the relationship between on the one hand the orientation of soil particles and of the voids between them, and on the other hand the pressure on the surface of the soil (Dickson and Smart, 1978) and the speed of water drainage through the soil

(Smart, 1972).   Usually, the pressure on the surface can be easily applied and measured, and the speed of water drainage can also easily be detected. However, it is not easy to measure the orientations of soil particles automatically.   Hence, orientation analysis has been thought to be important in studying soil microstructure.

In soil micro-structure study, various methods have been proposed to obtain quantitative parameters describing micro-structure of the degree of orientation. The earlier methods used hand mapping (Smart 1966 (a) and (b), McConnochie 1974).   Smart and Tovey (1982) mention some early attempts to use optical techniques for analysing electron micrographs.

In recent years, digital techniques of image processing and image analysis have become more and more interesting. True two dimensional derivative signals of the secondary electron image were produced by digitally computing the changes in intensity between neighbouring pixels in two orthogonal directions, and the intensity gradient method was provided for measuring the preferred orientation of soil structure within a micrograph.   The method is attributed to Unitt (1975) (see Smart and Tovey, 1982). Tovey (1980) and Tovey and Sokolov (1981) developed the technique to obtain indices of anisotropy of the fabric for a number of different soils.   More recently, Smart (1981) and Tovey and Smart (1986) suggested an approximate method to refine this technique. Smart and Tovey (1988) gave a new idea, based on the two dimensional form of Taylor's expansion, for finding the best formulae for intensity gradient analysis depending on the amount of noise present in the micrographs. Smart and Leng (1993) suggested alternative formulae, which were based on weighted averages, although this was not explained in the paper. Automatic mapping methods based on intensity gradient analysis were then developed (see Leng et al. 1993). Some alternative methods, which appear to have been less useful, were summarised by Smart and Leng (1994).   The emphasis on almost all this previous work was on field measurements; the methods considered in this chapter are feature measurements.

5.1.2   Development of Orientation Analysis
The above methods analyse the anisotropy of the micro-structure on a point by point basis.   This chapter will consider four other methods, called the Directed Vein method (Luo et al. 1992), the Convex Hull method (Luo et al. 1992), the Principal Components Transformation method, and the method of Moments, for the automatic orientation analysis of the soil micro-structure on a particle by particle basis. In the Directed Vein method, (1) an image we refer to as the directed vein image is obtained by transforming from the boundaries of particles in the original image as represented as a chain code of direction, and (2) the orientation of each vein is found by calculating the expectation of the directions of vectors of a vein. This expectation is taken as the orientation of the particle.   In the Convex Hull method, (1) the convex hull of the boundary of each particle is constructed by the method described in Chapter 3, and (2) the maximal diagonal of the convex hull is picked up and its direction is taken as the orientation of the particle.   In the

Principal Components Transformation method, (1) the scatter matrix of the boundary (or area) points of an object (particle in our study) is found, (2) the eigenvalues and eigenvectors of the scatter matrix are found, and (3) the boundary points are mapped into a new vector space with the eigenvectors as its basis vectors. The eigenvector corresponding to the largest eigenvalue is the principal component, and the direction of this basis vector is taken as the orientation of the object. In the method of Moments, (1) the moments of the boundary (or area) of an object (particle in our study) are found, (2) the direction of the principal axis of the boundary is found from the moments, and (3) the direction of the principal axis is taken as the orientation of the object. Some experimental results and comparisons of the four methods are given at the end of this chapter.

The Principal Components method and the method of Moments are in fact mathematically equivalent in the sense that they lead to the same equations and hence are expected to lead to identical results. However they are treated here as different methods because they are conceptually different and reach the same result by different algebraically routes. A further difference, a practical one, is that the two methods tend to be implemented in different software library routines or packages.

5.2 DIRECTED VEIN METHOD

A veins is defined as a curve on the surface of an object. Examples of veins include curves in finger prints, leaf fibres, wood circles, etc. A vein in a two dimensional space is a planar curve, and the orientation of the vein is the direction of the curve defined as below for a given traverse direction. When analysing orientation, the boundary of each soil particle (or void) is considered as a vein.

To find the direction of the curve, the approach is: first construct the directed image, then compute the orientation.

5.2.1 Directed Vein Image
Let C be a vein or a curve with two end points A and B in two dimensional space, as shown in Figure 5.1. Let D be the directed curve, i.e. the directed version of the undirected curve C, and the traverse direction is from A to B. On the curve D, any point p, between A and B, traverses the direction of the slope line $S(p)$ passing through p. If the curve C is described by

$$y = f(x) \tag{5.3.1}$$

then the slope $k(p)$ of $S(p)$ is

$$k(p) = \frac{dy}{dx}\Big|p = \tan\phi(p) \tag{5.3.2}$$

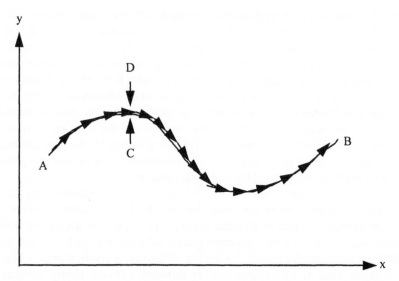

Figure 5.1   Undirected and directed vein. To see it clearly, C and D are separated slightly.

where $\phi(p)$ is the angle between $S(p)$ at p and the x-axis.   Thus a small directed segment curve $d(p)$ of D at p can be replaced by a small directed segment line, a vector $s(p)$, of $S(p)$.   Clearly the summation

$$S = \sum s(p) \tag{5.3.3}$$

of the vectors $s(p)$ is an approximation of D.   Therefore, $s(p)$ is called as the directed image of C.

   In the discrete case, a curve is actually a polysegment, as shown in Figure 5.2, and equations (5.3.1) and (5.3.2) will become respectively

$$m = f(n) \tag{5.3.4}$$

$$k(p) = \frac{\Delta m}{\Delta n}\Big|p = \tan \phi(p). \tag{5.3.5}$$

When Δm and Δn are units of the discrete grid, equations (5.3.3) and (5.3.4) describe the same polysegment, the only difference between them being that the former is directed but the latter not.   An example of the directed image of a discrete curve is shown in Figure 5.2.

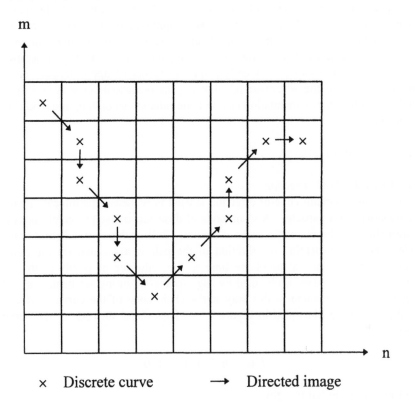

×   Discrete curve   →   Directed image

Figure 5.2   Discrete curve and its directed image.

5.2.2 Orientation of a Vein

From equation (5.3.3) and Figure 5.2, we can see that a directed vein consists of many elemental vectors. Therefore, the direction of a directed vein is defined as follows.

Definition 1. Let $\phi(i)$ be the angle of the *ith* element vector on a curve, $prob(\phi(i))$ be the probability of the angle $\phi(i)$. Then the orientation Φ of the curve C is defined as the expected mean $E(\phi)$ of $\phi(i)$:

$$\Phi = E(\phi) = \sum \phi(i)\,prob(\phi(i)).$$

(5.3.6)

Clearly each $\phi(i)$, and therefore also Φ, will be affected by noise (measurement and quantisation noise as well as noise due to the nature of the particles themselves).   Hence if equation (5.3.6) were applied directly, a large error would be produced.   Some further processing is therefore necessary before the orientation of a particle is calculated.   The method adopted was based on partitioning the directed vein representing a boundary into segments of approximately constant direction: this has the advantage of allowing the processed curve to be displayed legibly.   Before the segmentation can be done reliably, smoothing must be used to reduce the noise.

5.2.3   Algorithm

(1)   Chain Code of Direction
As a first step, a chain code of direction is used to represent the directed image of the boundary of a particle.   A chain code of direction is a sequence of codes each representing the direction of a curve at a point.   With each pair of adjacent points, a code number representing the dirction of the pair is associated (in the author's programs this is done at the same time as the sequence of points or the curve representing a boundary is obtained by edge following during segmentation).   The sequential code obtained in this way is the chain code of the curve.   The code numbers used are illustrated in Figure 5.3.   Thus the chain code of the curve in Figure 5.2 is:

$$7\ 6\ 7\ 6\ 7\ 1\ 1\ 2\ 1\ 0$$

if it traverses from left to right.

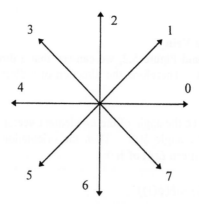

Figure 5.3 Code of directions.

However for the subsequent analysis the direction change between two adjacent elements of the curve must lie between -180° and +180°, and correspondingly the change in code number must lie in the range -3 to +3 inclusive; therefore, the chain code is modified as follows. Let n_i and n_{i+1} denote two adjacent code numbers of a chain code defined as above, and N_i and N_{i+1} be the corresponding two adjacent code numbers of the modified chain code. N_i is determined from n_i as follows:

$$N_1 = n_1;$$
$$for\ (i = 1;\ \ i <= end\_of\_chain;\ \ i++)$$
$$\{$$
$$\qquad k = INT(N_i / 8);$$
$$\qquad r = N_i - k * 8;$$
$$\qquad d = n_{i+1} - r;$$
$$\qquad N_{i+1} = \begin{cases} n_{i+1} + (k+1)*8; & if\ \ d < -3 \\ n_{i+1} + (k-1)*8; & else\ \ if\ \ d > +3 \\ n_{i+1} + k*8; & else \end{cases}$$
$$\}$$

where $INT(x)$ denotes the integer part of x. For example, the modified chain code for the curve in Figure 5.2 is:

$$7\ 6\ 7\ 6\ 7\ 9\ 9\ 10\ 9\ 8$$

(2) Smoothing
Common methods of smoothing include low-pass filtering, neighbourhood mean filtering, etc. In our case, simple two point mean filtering was found to yield adequately smooth curves: if N_i and N_{i+1} are two adjacent code numbers, L_i and L_{i+1} are the corresponding lengths (or inter-pixel distances), then the code number N_i' of the smoothed chain code is determined from $N_i'=(N_iL_i+N_{i+1}L_{i+1})/(L_i+L_{i+1})$. In the example, this yields the smoothed chain code:

$$6.586\ \ 6.586\ \ 6.586\ \ 6.586\ \ 8.000\ \ 9.000\ \ 9.414\ \ 9.414\ \ 8.586$$

In order to obtain a smoother chain code, the above smoothing operation can be done two or three times. After a total of three smoothing operations, the code in the example becomes:

$$6.586\ \ 6.586\ \ 6.983\ \ 7.946\ \ 8.832\ \ 9.300\ \ 9.207$$

which on rounding back to integers becomes:

$$7\ 7\ 7\ 8\ 9\ 9\ 9$$

(3) Piecewise Segmentation

The problem of segmentation is how to choose the division points. One of the very effective methods is to choose the vertices of a polygon, or the turning points of a segment piecewise curve formed by the chain code of the curve, as the division points. For instance, the chain code in the above example has a division point at 8, and splits into two segments:

$$7\ 7\ 7 \text{ and } 9\ 9\ 9$$

on discarding the break point itself at value 8.

(4) Modulo-4 Chain Code.

The distinction between opposite directions has no physical meaning in interpreting the micrographs used here. Therefore the direction of a curve k in the plane may always be specified as an angle Φ_k in the range $0 \leq \Phi_k < 180°$, corresponding to code number N_i'' of the segments of the curve in the range $0 \leq N_i'' < 4$. From the discussion above we can see that our existing code number may be outside this range. Therefore the code number must be changed to a modulo-4 chain code.

Suppose N_i' is a code number in a chain code and N_i'' is N_i' modulo 4. Then if each N_i' is replace by N_i'', the chain code:

$$7\ 7\ 7 \text{ and } 9\ 9\ 9$$

will become:

$$3\ 3\ 3 \text{ and } 1\ 1\ 1.$$

Note that the change to modulo-4 code cannot be made until after segmentation, otherwise again changes in direction would be wrongly interpreted.

(5) Orientation Analysis Proper

When the pre-processing has been done, the final stage is the orientation analysis itself.

To obtain the orientation of a curve in an image, the code numbers N_i'' of a chain code should be transformed into angles $\phi(i)$, $\phi(i)=N_i''*45°$. The probability $prob(\phi(i))$ of the angle $\phi(i)$ can be obtained from the length of the code in a chain. So equation (5.3.6) can be used directly to calculate the orientation Φ_k of the curve k, representing particle k:

$$\Phi_k = \sum \phi_k(i) prob(\phi_k(i)). \qquad (5.3.7)$$

The orientation given by the above is the mathematical expectation of the vector angles of a curve. In practice, it is correct for curves consisting of a few segments with acute angles between their directions, but if there are obtuse angles between their directions the orientation calculated may be quite different from what would be estimated intuitively.   Figure 5.4 shows an instance of this problem.   Clearly it is necessary to rotate the orientation counter-clockwise.   In order to solve this problem the following definition is given:

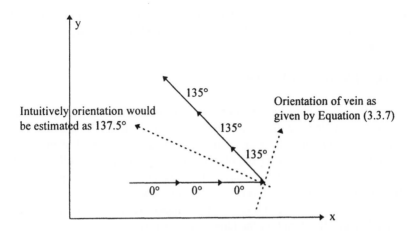

Figure 5.4   Case where angle between the directions of the two segments is obtuse.

Definition 2.   Suppose $\phi(i)$ and $\phi(j)$ $(i \neq j)$ are respectively the angles of two adjacent segments i and j, joining at point p.   Suppose $\phi(j) > \phi(i)$.   Then (compare equation (5.3.7) the angle $\phi(ij)$ between segments i and j is defined as

$$\phi(ij) = \begin{cases} \phi(i)\,prob(\phi(i)) + \phi(j)\,prob(\phi(j)) & for \quad (\phi(j) - \phi(i)) \leq 90° \\ (\phi(i) + 180°)\,prob(\phi(i)) + \phi(j)\,prob(\phi(j)) & for \quad (\phi(j) - \phi(i)) > 90° \end{cases}$$

$$(5.3.8)$$

If $\phi(ij)$ is greater than or equal to 180°, then $\phi(ij)$ should be rotated by 180° clockwise:

$$\phi(ij) := \phi(ij) - 180° \qquad if \quad \phi(ij) \geq 180°. \qquad\qquad (5.3.9)$$

To apply this definition when calculating the orientation of a polygon, an iterative method must be used.   The n edges of the polygon are first taken in adjacent pairs and an orientation is calculated for each pair.   In effect, this step replaces the n original edge directions with $m=n/2$ directions.   In the next step these m directions are similarly taken in adjacent pairs and replaced by $m/2$ directions, and so on until only one direction remains.   This direction is taken as the orientation of the polygon.   If at any stage there is an odd number of directions, the last one is not processed but is carried forward as it stands to the next stage. As this is a new method, some useful theory is summarised in *Appendix 5A.1* and 5A.2; in particular, this algorithm would produce an orientation of 90° if applied to a circle, so a trap is needed.

The computer program *dv.cpp* of the algorithm for the directed vein method, written in language C++ by the author, was listed in Computer Programs at the end of this book.

5.3   CONVEX HULL METHOD

The orientation of an object can be defined as the direction of the longest diagonal of the object.   The longest diagonal of the object can be found by the Convex Hull method.   This is because the longest diagonal of the convex hull of the object is actually the longest diagonal of the object.   Finding the convex hull of an object and the longest diagonal of the convex hull are discussed in Chapter 3.   The direction of the longest diagonal is calculated as follows.

Let v_l and v_r be the two end points of the longest diagonal of the convex hull of an object, then the direction θ of the longest diagonal is:

$$\theta = \arctan\frac{y(v_r) - y(v_l)}{x(v_r) - x(v_l)} \qquad\qquad -90° < \theta \leq 90° \qquad\qquad (5.4.1)$$

where $x(v_l)$, $x(v_r)$, and $y(v_l)$, $y(v_r)$ are the x and y coordinates of v_l and v_r, respectively.

Hence, in the Convex Hull method, the procedures of measuring the orientation of an object are:

Step 1. Finding the convex hull of an object.
Step 2. Finding the longest diagonal of the convex hull.
Step 3. Calculating the orientation of the object by equation (5.4.1).

However in some cases a polygon may have an edge which is longer than any diagonal (Figure 5.5).   To allow for such cases all edges are regarded as diagonals when determining which diagonal is longest.

If a particle is circular or nearly circular, its orientation does not exist.   A rule such as the following must be used to detect such cases: If the convex hull has more than one longest diagonal and if all the longest diagonals lie within a 45° sector, then the length of the longest diagonal is accepted and the mean orientation of the longest diagonals is taken as the orientation of the particle; otherwise the particle is classified as (almost) circular and unoriented.

Figure 5.5 Convex hull with edge longer than any diagonal.

5.4 PRINCIPAL COMPONENTS TRANSFORMATION

In the author's work on soil microstructure, the Principal Components Transformation was used both for orientation analysis and for dimensionality reduction of feature sets for pattern recognition. This section is primarily concerned with its use in orientation analysis: however a general introduction to the transformation encompassing both uses is first given.

In the Principal Components Transformation, a set S of N points (or, equivalently, of vectors drawn from the origin to the points) in a high dimensional h space can be projected into a low dimensional d space, $d \leq h$. In the low dimensional d space, the principal transform has a number of optimal properties. First of all, the components of the transformed vector (the *principal components*) are uncorrelated, i.e. the scatter matrix of the vectors is diagonalized. Second, the first component provides the greatest variance from the d components, the second component provides the second greatest variance from the d components, and so on. This implies that the information contained in the d components is compressed into a small number of d axes. Third, it maximises the sum of squares of interpoint distances and has the best preservation of spatial relation of points to the centre of gravity, or the total variance from the d principal components is the largest among all possible choice of d orthonormal vectors. Therefore, the Principal Components Transformation is widely used for dimensionality reduction and information compressing. It is also used for principal axis detection of a set of data, i.e. principal axis transformation. Especially, in pattern recognition, it is used for visual examination of the N points, to see whether the N points can be classified into groups or clusters, where d is usually taken as 2.

In pattern recognition, the first work that introduced the method of principal components into the field of pattern recognition was by Watanabe (1965). Webster (1977) used Principal Components Transformation in soil classification, to analyse, display, and interpret relationships in multivariate soil populations with 15 components of features. Later Watanabe (1985) used the principal axis transformation in pattern recognition as the entropy minimisation and in pattern recognition as the covariance diagonalization.

In using Principal Components Transformation for orientation analysis, the author's method was based on taking the set S as comprising the boundary points of the particle; this was faster than using the interior points of the particle. The direction of the first principal component of S was then taken as the orientation of the particle.

5.4.1 Theory of Principal Component Transformation

For the mathematical realisations of Principal Components Transformation, a few basic methods have been reviewed by Webster (1977), Chien (1978), Watanabe (1985), Kittler et al. (1991), Fionn (1991), etc. Here a brief strategy of the Principal Components Transformation is given as follows.

For a given set X of N points (vectors) in high dimensional h space x, we try to find a transform matrix C to map the given set X into Y in a new low dimensional d space y, such that the d components of Y_i are uncorrelated, even though in many practical cases, some of the components of X_i are correlated to a greater or lessen extent. In greater detail, the procedure in the previous paragraph is as follows.

The given set of points is

$$X = \begin{bmatrix} x_{11} & x_{21} & \cdots & x_{N1} \\ x_{12} & x_{22} & \cdots & x_{N2} \\ \cdots & \cdots & & \cdots \\ x_{1h} & x_{2h} & \cdots & x_{Nh} \end{bmatrix} = \begin{bmatrix} X_1 & X_2 & \cdots & X_N \end{bmatrix} \qquad (5.5.1)$$

where the components for the ith individual are:

$$X_i = \begin{bmatrix} x_{i1} & x_{i2} & \cdots & x_{ih} \end{bmatrix}' \qquad (i = 1, 2, ..., N) \qquad (5.5.2)$$

and it is these which may be correlated. We require

$$Y = \begin{bmatrix} y_{11} & y_{21} & \cdots & y_{N1} \\ y_{12} & y_{22} & \cdots & y_{N2} \\ \cdots & \cdots & & \cdots \\ y_{1d} & y_{2d} & \cdots & y_{Nd} \end{bmatrix} = \begin{bmatrix} Y_1 & Y_2 & \cdots & Y_N \end{bmatrix} \qquad (5.5.3)$$

where $d \leq h$, and where the components of the *ith* individual are now:

$$Y_i = \begin{bmatrix} y_{i1} & y_{i2} & \cdots & y_{id} \end{bmatrix}' \qquad (i = 1, 2, ..., N) \qquad (5.5.4)$$

and it is these which must be uncorrelated.

For convenience, the origin is usually moved to the centre of gravity of the N points, i.e. to

$$\overline{X} = \frac{1}{N} \sum_{i=1}^{N} X_i \quad \text{or} \quad \overline{X}_k = \frac{1}{N} \sum_{i=1}^{N} X_{ik} \quad (k=1, 2, ..., h). \qquad (5.5.5)$$

Then the coordinate system is transformed according to:

$$Y = C(X - \overline{X}) \qquad (5.5.6)$$

where

$$C = \begin{bmatrix} c_{11} & c_{12} & \cdots & c_{1h} \\ c_{21} & c_{22} & \cdots & c_{2h} \\ \cdots & \cdots & & \cdots \\ c_{d1} & c_{d2} & \cdots & c_{dh} \end{bmatrix} = \begin{bmatrix} C_1 \\ C_2 \\ \cdots \\ C_d \end{bmatrix} \qquad (5.5.7)$$

$$C_i = \begin{bmatrix} c_{i1} & c_{i2} & \cdots & c_{ih} \end{bmatrix} \qquad (i = 1, 2, ..., d). \qquad (5.5.8)$$

Then, the condition that the components of Y_i should be uncorrelated is:

$$\frac{1}{n-1} YY' = \begin{bmatrix} \lambda_{11} & & & 0 \\ & \lambda_{22} & & \\ & & \cdots & \\ 0 & & & \lambda_{dd} \end{bmatrix} = \Lambda \qquad (5.5.9)$$

where Λ is a diagonal matrix and Y' is the transpose matrix of Y, λ_{ii} is the component of Λ, $\lambda_{ii} \neq 0$.

Once the transform matrix C has been found, the component of Y corresponding to the largest λ_{ii} is the principal component of X.

First it is necessary to eliminate Y from equation (5.5.9) using equation (5.5.6):

$$\frac{1}{n-1} YY' = \frac{1}{n-1}(C(X - \overline{X}))(C(X - \overline{X}))' = \frac{1}{n-1}C(X - \overline{X})(X - \overline{X})'C' = CAC'$$

where

$$A = \frac{1}{n-1}(X - \overline{X})(X - \overline{X})' \cdot$$ (5.5.10)

Therefore

$$CAC' = \Lambda \ .$$ (5.5.11)

Next, because the transform matrix should be a normal transform, i.e.

$$C'C = I$$ (5.5.12)

where I is the unit matrix, post-multiplying equation (5.5.11) by C gives

$$CA = \Lambda C$$

or

$$CA - \Lambda C = 0.$$ (5.5.13)

Here C is not equal to 0, so the characteristic equation of equation (5.5.13) is:

$$|A - \lambda I| = 0.$$ (5.5.14)

Solving equation (5.5.14), d eigenvalues, λ_i (i=1, 2, ..., d; $d \le h$), can be found. Arrange the d eigenvalues in descending order, i.e.

$$\lambda_1 \ge \lambda_2 \ge ... \lambda_d$$ (5.5.15)

and replace them in equation (5.5.13), the ith eigenvectors, C_i, of the transform matrix C can be found, satisfying the condition:

$$AC_i = \lambda_i C_i \ .$$ (5.5.16)

Then the N points X in h dimensional space x, can be transformed into N 'new' points Y in d dimensional space y:

$$Y = \begin{bmatrix} C_1 \\ C_2 \\ ... \\ C_d \end{bmatrix} [X - \overline{X}] = \begin{bmatrix} Y^1 \\ Y^2 \\ ... \\ Y^2 \end{bmatrix}$$ (5.5.17)

$$Y^i = \left[C_i(X_1 - \overline{X}) \quad C_i(X_2 - \overline{X}) \quad \cdots \quad C_i(X_N - \overline{X}) \right] \tag{5.5.18}$$

the first component Y^1 is the first principal component of the set X, and the vector C_1 is the first principal axis of X.

5.4.2 Orientation by Principal Component Transformation

The Principal Components Transformation described above is equivalent to a translation and a pure rotation. In two-dimensional space, let X be a set of boundary points of an object in coordinate system x. Now first the origin of x is translated to the centre of gravity of the boundary, and then the coordinate system x is rotated by angle θ to a new coordinate system y, the transform matrix C being given by:

$$C = \begin{bmatrix} \cos\theta & \sin\theta \\ -\sin\theta & \cos\theta \end{bmatrix} = \begin{bmatrix} C_1 \\ C_2 \end{bmatrix} \tag{5.5.19}$$

$$C_1 = \begin{bmatrix} \cos\theta & \sin\theta \end{bmatrix} \tag{5.5.20}$$

$$C_2 = \begin{bmatrix} -\sin\theta & \cos\theta \end{bmatrix}. \tag{5.5.21}$$

Then, the new set Y of the boundary points in coordinate system y is expressed by:

$$Y = C(X - \overline{X}) = \begin{bmatrix} C_1 \\ C_2 \end{bmatrix} \begin{bmatrix} X - \overline{X} \end{bmatrix} = \begin{bmatrix} Y^1 \\ Y^2 \end{bmatrix} \tag{5.5.22}$$

$$Y^i = C_i \begin{bmatrix} X_1 - \overline{X} & X_2 - \overline{X} & \cdots & X_N - \overline{X} \end{bmatrix}. \tag{5.5.23}$$

We require that the first component Y^1 is the principal component of X, and the vector C_1 is the principal axis of X. If X is transformed to Y by Principal Components Transformation, the transform matrix C is

$$C = \begin{bmatrix} c_{11} & c_{12} \\ c_{21} & c_{22} \end{bmatrix} = \begin{bmatrix} C_1 \\ C_2 \end{bmatrix} \tag{5.5.24}$$

$$C_1 = \begin{bmatrix} c_{11} & c_{12} \end{bmatrix} \tag{5.5.25}$$

$$C_2 = \begin{bmatrix} c_{21} & c_{22} \end{bmatrix}. \tag{5.5.26}$$

Therefore, the two transform matrices should be the same, i.e.

$$\begin{bmatrix} \cos\theta & \sin\theta \\ -\sin\theta & \cos\theta \end{bmatrix} = \begin{bmatrix} c_{11} & c_{12} \\ c_{21} & c_{22} \end{bmatrix}.$$ (5.5.27)

Thus, the angle θ of the principal axis is

$$\theta = \arccos c_{11} \quad \text{or} \quad \theta = \arctan(c_{12}/c_{11}).$$ (5.5.28)

Because the length of the principal axis reflects the longest diagonal of the boundary of the object, the direction θ of the principal axis is taken as the orientation of the object.

Therefore, the procedures of the orientation analysis by Principal Components Transformation are:

Step 1. Calculating the scatter matrix A of the set of the boundary points X of an object by equation (5.5.10).

Step 2. Solving the characteristic equation (5.5.14) of A to find the eigenvalues λ_i, and arranging λ_i in a descending order.

Step 3. Finding the eigenvectors C_i by equation (5.5.16), and pick up C_1 corresponding to λ_1.

Step 4. Calculating the orientation θ of the object according to equation (5.5.28).

The computer program *pct.cpp* of the algorithm for the principal component transform method, written in language C++ by the author, was listed in Computer Programs at the end of this book.

5.5   METHOD OF MOMENTS

In physics and engineering, moments are a very useful toolkit for measurement, analysis, and design.   For example, moments can be used to find the centre of gravity of an object, to determine the conditions of the balance of levers, to analyse the motion of rigid objects, etc.   Since Hu (1962) proposed the moment invariant, moments have been widely used in image processing and pattern recognition, e.g. in object recognition, scene matching, and image classification.   Moments are especially useful for edge detection, feature measurement, feature extraction, and shape description of data or objects, and also in 3-D image processing and recognition.   This is because moments reflect some characteristics of data or objects such as centre of gravity, centrality, diagonality, divergence, imbalance, etc. Among the moment-based edge detection techniques, Machuca and Gilbert (1981) used the moments found in a region to determine the edge location.   Tabatabai and Mitchell (1984) determined edge location by fitting first three grey level moments to the edge data.   Lyvers et al. (1989) proposed an efficient geometric moment-based method for subpixel edge detection.   Ghosal and Mehrotro (1993) used orthogonal moment operators for the same purpose.   In pattern feature measurement, extraction, and orientation invariant recognition of shapes, Teague (1980), and Teh and Chin (1988) gave a general overview of the applications of moments. Wen and Lozzi (1993) used line moments of an object's boundary for recognition and inspection of manufactured parts. In 3-D image processing and recognition, use of 3-D moment invariants was first proposed by Sadjadi and Hall (1980). Galvez and Canton (1993) used 3-D moments for normalisation and shape recognition of 3-D objects. In this section, a method using moments of the boundary of an object was presented for orientation analysis of soil particles in the study of soil micro-structure.

5.5.1 Theory of the Moments

Let X be a set of h variables in an h dimensional space, $X = (x_1, x_2, ..., x_h)$. Let $f(X)$ be a function of X. Then, the $p+q+...+r$ order moment is defined as follows

$$M_{pq...r} = \int ... \int f(x_1, x_2, ..., x_h) x_1^p x_2^q ... x_h^r dx_1 dx_2 ... dx_h .\qquad (5.6.1)$$

The moment for the discrete case becomes:

$$M_{pq...r} = \sum ... \sum f(x_{1i}, x_{2j}, ..., x_{hk}) x_{1i}^p x_{2j}^q ... x_{hk}^r \qquad (5.6.2)$$

where $p, q, ..., r, = 0, 1, ..., h$. Let $L=p+q+...+r$. If $L=0$, the moment is called 0 order moment, and it is the volume determined by the function $f(X)$. If $L=1$, the moment is called 1st order moment, and it indicates the gravity centre if it is normalised by 0 order moment. Similarly, if $L=2$, the moment is called 2nd order moment, and it reflects the symmetrical axis. The 3rd order moment, ("Skew"), and the 4th order moment ("Kurtosis"), are useful in some cases. The moments higher than 4th order are more complicated to calculate, and because they have less physical meaning, therefore, they are relatively rarely used.

However the moment defined as above is variant with respect to coordinate translation, rotation, and scaling. This is not convenient in practice. Therefore, the popular way is to use central moments, which are invariant with respect to coordinate translation.

5.5.2 Central Moments

Let Y be a set of h variables of a new coordinate system y, which is transformed from coordinate system x by translation as follows:

$$Y = X - \overline{X} \quad or \quad y_i = x_i - \overline{x}_i \qquad (5.6.3)$$

where

$$Y = (y_1, y_2, ..., y_h)$$

$$\overline{X} = (\overline{x}_1, \overline{x}_2, \ldots, \overline{x}_h)$$

and

$$\overline{x}_i = \int f(x_1, x_2, \ldots, x_h) x_i dx_i \ / \int f(x_1, x_2, \ldots, x_h) dx_i \ . \qquad (5.6.4)$$

Then the central moments are given as the same form as equations (5.6.1) and (5.6.2):

$$M^c_{pq \ldots r} = \int f(y_1, y_2, \ldots, y_h) y_1^p y_2^q \ldots y_h^r dy_1 dy_2 \ldots dy_h \qquad (5.6.5)$$

$$M^c_{pq \ldots r} = \sum \ldots \sum f(y_{1i}, y_{2j}, \ldots, y_{hk}) y_{1i}^p y_{2j}^q \ldots y_{hk}^r \ . \qquad (5.6.6)$$

Because the coordinate system y is translated from the coordinate system x, the central moments are invariant with respect to coordinate translation.

5.5.3 Orientation by Moments

The boundary of an object in a two dimensional plane can be represented by a function $f(x_1,x_2)$ of n points in two dimensional space x_1 and x_2. $f(x_1,x_2)$ has the value 1 on the boundary and 0 elsewhere. If the coordinates x_1 and x_2 are translated to coordinates y_1 and y_2 by:

$$y_i = x_i - \overline{x}_i \qquad (i = 1, 2) \qquad (5.6.7)$$

and the coordinate axes of y_1 and y_2 are rotated by angle θ so that y_1 lies along the principal axis of the boundary, the new coordinates z_1 and z_2 are respectively:

$$z_1 = y_1 \cos\theta + y_2 \sin\theta \qquad (5.6.8)$$

$$z_2 = -y_1 \sin\theta + y_2 \cos\theta \ . \qquad (5.6.9)$$

After the rotation to the principal axis, there is no correlation between z_1 and z_2. This means that the summation of the products $z_1 z_2$ for all points in the plane should be zero:

$$\sum_{j=1}^{n} z_{1j} z_{2j} = 0. \qquad (5.6.10)$$

That is

$$\sum_{j=1}^{n} [y_1 y_2 (\cos^2\theta - \sin^2\theta) - \sin\theta \cos\theta \, (y_1^2 - y_2^2)] = 0 \ . \qquad (5.6.11)$$

From equation (5.6.11), θ can be found as:

$$\tan 2\theta = \frac{2 \sum_{j=1}^{n} y_{1j} y_{2j}}{\sum_{j=1}^{n} y_{1j}^2 - \sum_{j=1}^{n} y_{2j}^2} \cdot \qquad (5.6.12)$$

Comparing equation (5.6.12) with equation (5.6.6), it is clear that the numerator of equation (5.6.12) is the moment M'_{11} of the boundary, the first term of the denominator of equation (5.6.12) is the moment M'_{20}, and the second term is the moment M'_{02}. Therefore, the direction of the principal axis of the boundary is taken as the orientation of the boundary, it is given by :

$$\tan 2\theta = \frac{2 M_{11}^c}{M_{20}^c - M_{02}^c} \qquad (5.6.13)$$

where

$$M_{11}^c = \sum_{j=1}^{n} y_{1j} y_{2j} \qquad M_{20}^c = \sum_{j=1}^{n} y_{1j}^2 \qquad M_{02}^c = \sum_{j=1}^{n} y_{2j}^2 \cdot \qquad (5.6.14)$$

Replace equation (5.6.7) in (5.6.14),

$$M_{11}^c = \sum_{j=1}^{n} (x_{1j} - \bar{x}_1)(x_{2j} - \bar{x}_2) = \sum_{j=1}^{n} (x_{1j} x_{2j} - x_{1j} \bar{x}_2 - x_{2j} \bar{x}_1 + \bar{x}_1 \bar{x}_2)$$

$$= M_{11} - M_{10} M_{01}/n - M_{01} M_{10}/n + M_{10} M_{01}/$$

$$= M_{11} - M_{10} M_{01}/n \qquad (5.6.15)$$

$$M_{20}^c = \sum_{j=1}^{n} (x_{1j} - \bar{x}_1)^2 = \sum_{j=1}^{n} (x_{1j}^2 - 2 x_{1j} \bar{x}_1 + \bar{x}_1^2)$$

$$= M_{20} - 2 M_{10}^2/n + M_{10}^2/n$$

$$= M_{20} - M_{10}^2/n \qquad (5.6.16)$$

$$M_{02}^c = \sum_{j=1}^{n} (x_{2j} - \bar{x}_2)^2 = \sum_{j=1}^{n} (x_{2j}^2 - 2 x_{2j} \bar{x}_2 + \bar{x}_2^2)$$

$$= M_{02} - 2 M_{01}^2/n + M_{01}^2/n$$

$$= M_{02} - M_{01}^2/n \cdot \qquad (5.6.17)$$

Then (5.6.13) becomes:

$$\tan 2\theta = \frac{2(nM_{11} - M_{10}M_{01})}{n(M_{20} - M_{02}) - (M_{10}^2 - M_{01}^2)} \, . \tag{5.6.18}$$

Because $M_{00} = n$, therefore, the orientation θ of the boundary is given:

$$\tan 2\theta = \frac{2(M_{00}M_{11} - M_{10}M_{01})}{M_{00}(M_{20} - M_{02}) - (M_{10}^2 - M_{01}^2)} \, . \tag{5.6.19}$$

Let

$$M' = 2(M_{00}M_{11} - M_{10}M_{01})$$
$$M'' = M_{00}(M_{20} - M_{02}) - (M_{10}^2 - M_{01}^2)$$

and

$$\theta' = \frac{1}{2}\arctan \frac{2(M_{00}M_{11} - M_{10}M_{01})}{M_{00}(M_{20} - M_{02}) - (M_{10}^2 - M_{01}^2)} \, . \tag{5.6.20}$$

Then, the orientation of the boundary of the object is:

$$\theta = \begin{cases} \theta' + 90^\circ & \textit{if } M' \geq 0, \ M'' < 0 \\ + 45^\circ & \textit{if } M' > 0, \ M'' = 0 \\ \theta' - 90^\circ & \textit{if } M' < 0, \ M'' < 0 \\ - 45^\circ & \textit{if } M' < 0, \ M'' = 0 \\ \theta' & \textit{otherwise} \end{cases} \tag{5.6.21}$$

5.6 EXAMPLES OF ORIENTATION ANALYSIS

To illustrate the operations, the four methods proposed above: Directed Vein, Convex Hull, Principal Components Transformation, and Moments, were implemented in three experiments.   The system of the automatic orientation analysis is shown in Figure 5.6.

Example 1
The four methods were first tested by an ellipse, as shown in Figure 5.7.   The orientation of the ellipse was set to 30°.   The orientations measured by the four methods are listed in Table 5.1.   The experimental results indicate that the four methods yield nearly the same result for some objects with some special shape.

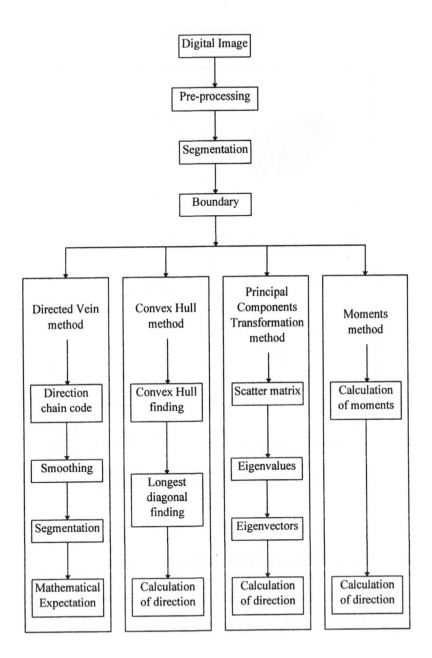

Figure 5.6   Flow chart of orientation analysis.

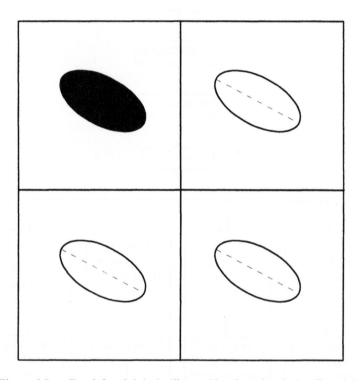

Figure 5.7   Top left: Original ellipse with orientation 30.°   Top right:
Boundary and orientation 29° measured by Directed Vein method.   Bottom
left: Boundary and orientation 28° measured by Convex Hull method.
Bottom right: boundary and orientation 27° measured by Principal
Components.   Transformation method and method of Moments.

Table 5.1   The orientations of an ellipse measured by four methods.

Methods	Directed Vein	Convex Hull	Principal Components Transformation	Moments
Orientations	29°	28°	27°	27°

Example 2

The four methods were then applied to an artificial image as shown in Figure 5.8. In Figure 5.8, the orientation of the snail should be in the direction of the line which passes through both the head and the tail. On one basis, the orientation of the joining leaves should be the common direction of each leaf, i.e. the direction of internal preferred orientation; on another basis, the orientation should be in the orthogonal direction, i.e. the elongation direction of the aggregate of leaves. The orientations of the three objects measured by the four methods are listed in Table 5.2, and drawn by straight lines in Figure 5.8.

The experimental results indicate that, the orientations measured by the Principal Components Transformation method and the method of Moments are exactly the same, as expected. For the single leaf, which is a simple object, the other two methods give an almost identical result. For the snail, the Convex Hull is in general agreement with the first two methods, and, to judge from Figure 5.8, the Directed Vein result is approximately the same. For the joining leaves, the Convex Hull gives a somewhat similar result to the first two methods; but the Directed Vein result is almost 90° different. This is probably because the Directed Vein method, by its nature, will lead to emphasise internal edges (in contrast, for example, to the convex Hull method where the orientation found is a global one based on the principal diagonal of the complete object). The somewhat different orientation found by the Directed Vein method in the snail image may have similar explanation. These results suggest that it might be possible to use the Directed Vein method in parallel with one of the other methods to distinguish between different types of objects.

Example 3

The four methods were finally applied to a micrograph image, as shown in Figure 5.9, on which the particles were clearly distinguishable after thresholding. The experimental results of the orientations measured by the four methods are listed in Table 5.3 and plotted in Figure 5.10 respectively: From Table 5.3 and the Figure 5.10, we can see that all the methods appear to have operated correctly. The orientations measured by the methods of Directed Vein and Convex Hull are slightly different from each other and also different from the Principal Components Transformation method and the method of Moments. This is because they are different in both concept and calculation. The orientations measured by the methods of Principal Components Transformation and Moments are exactly the same. This is because the principle of both of them is the same, but the calculations are different. The Directed Vein method is simple and fast, but sensitive to the boundary of an object. It is particularly useful for the cases where the orientation of an object is determined by the boundary. The Convex Hull method is a little more complicated than the Directed Vein method. It is especially useful for the cases where the orientation is determined by the longest diagonal of an object. The Principal Components Transformation method and the method of Moments are both slow, but both of them can be called from standard software libraries.   Therefore it is convenient to use the latter two methods for general purpose orientation analysis.

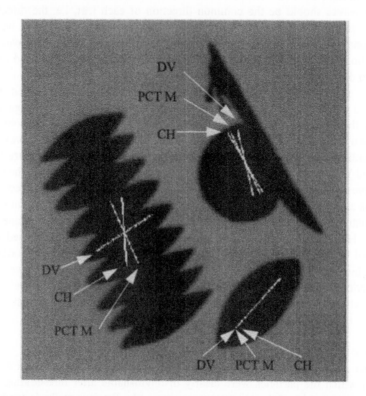

Figure 5.8   Snail (top right), Joining leaves(left), leaf (bottom right), and their orientations expressed by straight lines.   DV: Directed Vein; CH: Convex Hull; PCT: Principal Components Transformation; M: Moments.

Table 5.2   The orientations of three objects measured by four methods.

Methods	Directed Vein	Convex Hull	Principal Components Transformation	Moments
Leaf	47°	48°	47°	47°
Snail	-76°	-58°	-63°	-63°
Joining Leaves	32°	-86°	-65°	-65°

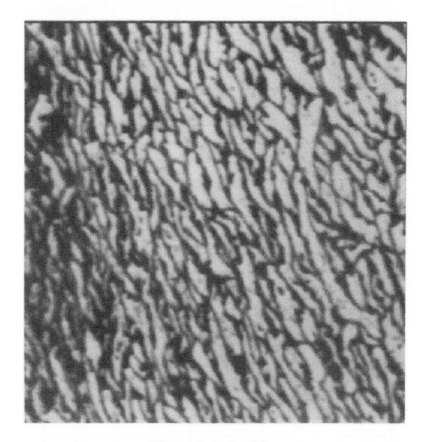

Figure 5.9   Soil particles.

Table 5.3   The orientations (in degrees) measured by four methods: DV: Directed Vein; CH: Convex Hull; PCT: Principal Component Transformation; and M: Moments.

Object No.	Orientation by DV	Orientation by CH	Orientation by PCT	Orientation by M
1	14	47	49	49
2	-82	-81	-72	-72
3	63	68	68	68
4	12	18	16	16
5	67	68	68	68
6	72	72	70	70

Table 5.3 (cont.)

Object No.	Orientation by DV	Orientation by CH	Orientation by PCT	Orientation by M
7	82	79	83	83
8	69	74	78	78
9	61	62	66	66
10	57	59	57	57
11	63	65	69	69
12	69	68	69	69
13	77	75	75	75
14	65	70	72	72
15	73	74	78	78
16	59	63	67	67
17	79	76	80	80
18	76	79	88	88
19	59	58	60	60
20	63	72	71	71
21	60	55	55	55
22	76	79	86	86
23	60	68	71	71
24	53	53	55	55
25	61	82	89	89
26	78	94	86	86
27	-95	-88	-83	-83
28	89	85	90	90
29	58	67	67	67
30	49	53	50	50
31	61	66	67	67
32	63	73	75	75
33	87	82	85	85
34	67	67	66	66
35	56	56	58	58
36	-84	-86	-92	-92
37	-75	-76	-77	-77
38	63	65	63	63
39	56	57	59	59
40	-89	-85	-83	-83

Table 5.3 (cont.)

Object No.	Orientation by DV	Orientation by CH	Orientation by PCT	Orientation by M
41	-73	-99	-89	-89
42	63	64	64	64
43	66	61	66	66
44	68	66	68	68
45	59	67	66	66
46	61	72	69	69
47	69	56	60	60
48	33	35	37	37
49	55	53	52	52
50	64	65	69	69
51	54	60	63	63
52	58	60	67	67
53	47	46	47	47
54	71	75	86	86
55	51	55	57	57
56	52	57	60	60
57	65	71	72	72
58	72	62	59	59
59	75	68	67	67
60	70	57	55	55
61	66	61	59	59
62	67	63	69	69
63	67	70	70	70
64	56	58	65	65
65	76	72	72	72
66	69	70	69	69
67	62	64	64	64
68	54	58	57	57
69	63	64	64	64
70	72	70	73	73
71	39	44	45	45
72	63	62	58	58
73	41	48	50	50
74	64	69	71	71

Table 5.3 (cont.)

Object No.	Orientation by DV	Orientation by CH	Orientation by PCT	Orientation by M
75	57	59	59	59
76	61	72	64	64
77	69	75	76	76
78	57	58	57	57
79	56	58	58	58
80	65	72	69	69
81	86	80	83	83
82	66	63	60	60
83	69	70	72	72
84	69	71	72	72
85	60	64	71	71
86	40	56	50	50
87	-92	-88	-90	-90
88	58	65	68	68
89	49	58	60	60
90	37	42	53	53
91	62	58	55	55
92	68	67	68	68
93	83	74	70	70
94	59	65	66	66
95	58	59	60	60
96	60	82	78	78
97	74	61	65	65
98	48	62	63	63
99	55	62	63	63
100	53	59	58	58
101	46	50	54	54
102	83	81	88	88
103	61	66	71	71
104	88	75	77	77
105	24	29	26	26
106	67	60	65	65
107	69	65	66	66
108	67	64	62	62

Table 5.3 (cont.)

Object No.	Orientation by DV	Orientation by CH	Orientation by PCT	Orientation by M
109	50	44	45	45
110	57	58	59	59
111	56	61	67	67
112	40	44	46	46
113	41	50	44	44
114	48	52	48	48
115	-70	-64	-66	-66
116	54	70	69	69
117	51	61	62	62
118	-9	-9	-26	-26
119	58	63	63	63
120	62	63	67	67
121	61	62	64	64
122	43	39	40	40
123	85	74	72	72
124	64	66	66	66
125	32	37	40	40
126	51	59	54	54
127	56	53	40	40
128	12	41	38	38
129	54	69	65	65
130	59	70	64	64
131	61	77	79	79
132	87	78	76	76
133	43	48	44	44
134	71	72	67	67
135	-74	-87	-76	-76
136	-81	-87	-85	-85

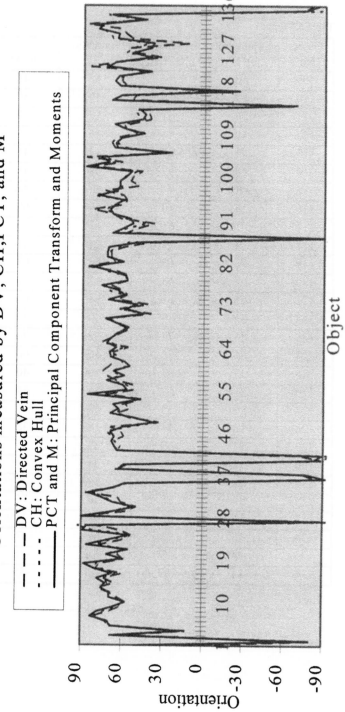

Figure 5.10   Experimental results of orientations measured by the four methods. DV: Directed Vein; CH: Convex Hull; PCT: Principal Components Transformation; and M: Moments.

5.7   Discussion and Summary

There are a few problems which have not been brought out in the above. Both the method of Moments and the Principal Components Transformation method can become unstable for a few rare objects, for example, if equation (5.6.13) attempts to divide zero by zero; the implementation, therefore, need traps to deal with these rare cases safely. The Convex Hull method needs a trap to deal with objects for which two or more instances of the longest diagonal occur; the Author's method of implementing this was explained in Section 5.4. A practical problem might arise with the Directed Vein method in that it is not immediately obvious which orientation is being reported, particularly if a large number of moderately contorted objects have to be analysed at high speed. General points arising from the body of the chapter are summarised below.

The Directed Vein method proposed here is a simple and fast approach for the automatic orientation analysis of microstructures of soil specimens. This method would appear to be suitable for the orientation analysis not only of veins, curves, and boundaries, but also of any objects which can be described by curves. For simple objects, the orientations obtained by this method accord basically with the 'elongation direction'; otherwise, with the 'internal preferred orientation'.

The Convex Hull method discussed above is also simple and is the fastest of all the four methods. This is because it is easier to get the boundary of a soil particle or of an inter-particle void (by area thresholding or edge detection) than to get, say, a directed vein. Moreover the algorithm to establish the simple polygon of a boundary using the stair-climbing approach, to construct the convex hull from the simple polygon by the Author's method of Chapter 3, and to find the longest diagonal from the convex hull, are fast as well as simple. The orientations of particles also accorded basically with the elongation direction as judged by a human observer (Figure 5.8).

The orientation of an object found by Principal Components Transformation method is not as sensitive to the noise of the boundary as the Directed Vein method; this is because most of the information of the boundary is compressed into the principal components. Although, the basic computation is more complicated in calculation than are the Directed Vein method and Convex Hull method (because it is necessary to solve the characteristic function to find eigenvalues and eigenvectors), there is a quick and easy formula for the 2-D case.

The orientation of an object calculated by the method of Moments, as for the Principal Components Transformation, is not sensitive to the noise of the boundary of an object. Unlike the Principal Components Transformation, the method of Moments does not solve any complicated equations. Therefore, it is in general simpler for calculation of orientations. Compared with the Convex Hull method, it is simpler in programming, but slower in calculation. This is because it needs many more square calculations.

The last two methods, method of Moments and Principal Components Transformation method, are different algebraical routes to produce the orientation of the Principal Axis.   Although the concept of the orientation of the longest diagonal of the convex hull is different from the concept of the principal axis, it appears that the Convex Hull method tends to produce an orientation which is in general agreement with the first two methods.   In general, therefore, the choice between these three methods of estimating the elongation direction will depend on the speed and availability of software (unless the user has special requirements). For simple objects, the Directed Vein method appears to be the fastest method of estimating the elongation direction; but it is based on an entirely different concept, so it will be necessary to consider whether it would be the correct choice for less simple objects.   In some cases, the Directed Vein method might be used in parallel with one of the other methods to distinguish between different types of objects.

References

Chien, Y. (1978) *Interactive Pattern Recognition*. Marcel Dekker Inc.

Dickson, J. W., and Smart, P. (1978) Some interactions between stress and microstructure of kaolin. *Emerson, W. W., et al. (Eds.)*, *Modification of Soil Structure*. Chichester, Wiley, pp. 53-57.

Fionn, M., *Multivariate analysis methods*. Vaughan, R. A. (Ed.), Pattern Recognition and Image Processing in Physics. (1991) *Scottish Universities Summer School in Physics & Adam Higher, Bristol, Philadelphia and New York*.

Galves, J. M. and Canton, M. (1993) Normalisation and shape recognition of three-dimensional objects by 3-D moments. *Pattern Recognition*, Vol. 26, No. 5, pp 667-681.

Ghosal, S. and Mehrotro, R. (1993) Orthogonal moment operators for subpixel edge detection. *Pattern Recognition*, Vol. 26, No. 2, pp 295-306.

Haralick, R. M. (1984) Digital step edge from zero crossing of second direction derivatives. *IEEE Trans. Pattern Analysis Mach. Intell.*, Vol. 6, pp. 58-68.

Hu, M. K. (1962) Visual pattern recognition by moment invariants. *IRE, Trans., Inf. Theory*, Vol. 8, pp 179-187.

Kittler, J., Etemadi, A. and Choakjarernwanit, N. (1991) Feature selection and extraction in pattern recognition. *Vaughan, R. A. (Ed.), Pattern Recognition and Image Processing in Physics. Scottish Universities Summer School in Physics & Adam Higher, Bristol, Philadelphia and New York*.

Leng, X., Hounslow, M. W., Bai, X., Luo, D., Costa, L. da F., Xue, X., Tovey, N. K., and Smart, P. (1993) Image analysis of clay microstructure. *Proc. Conf. Image Processing: Applications in Civil Engineering, Hawaii, National Engineering Federation*, pp. 77-86.

Luo, D. and Ma, D. (1989) Bi-boundary-line method for curve-enclosed area calculation. *Journal of Sichuan University (Natural Science Edition)*, Vol. 26, No. 1, pp. 58-65.

Luo, D., Macleod, J. E. S., Leng, X., and Smart, P. (1992) Orientation analyses of particles in soil microstructures. *Geotechnique*, Vol. 42, pp. 97-107.

Lyvers, E. P., Mitchell, O. R., Akey, M. L., and Reeves, A. P. (1989) Subpixel measurements using a moment based edge operator. *IEEE Trans. Pattern Analysis Mach. Intell.*, Vol. 11, No. 2, pp 1293-1308.

McConnochie, I. (1974) Fabric changes in consolidated kaolin. *Geotechnique*, Vol. 24, pp. 207-222.

Machuca, R. and Gilbert, A. L. (1981) Finding edges in noisy scenes. *IEEE Trans. Pattern Analysis Mach. Intell.*, Vol. 3, No. 1, pp 103-111.

Marr, D., and Hildreth, E. (1980) Theory of edge detection. *Proc. Roy. Soc. London*, Vol. B207, pp. 187-217.

Nevatia, R. (1977) A colour edge detector and its use in scene segmentation. *IEEE Trans. Systems Man Cybernetics*, Vol. SMC-7, pp. 820-826.

Nevatia, R., and Babu, K. R. (1980) Linear feature extraction and description. *Computer Graphics Image Processing*, Vol. 13, pp. 257-269.

Sadjadi, F. A. and Hall, E. L. (1980) Three-dimensional moment invariants. *IEEE Trans. Pattern Analysis Mach. Intell.*, Vol. 2, pp. 127-136.

Smart, P. (1966a) *Soil Structure Mechanical Properties and Electron Microscopy.* PhD Thesis, Cambridge University.

Smart, P. (1966b) Particle arrangements in kaolin. *Proc. 15th National Conference on clays and clay minerals*, Vol. 15, pp. 241-245.

Smart, P. (1972) A microstructural view of the mechanical properties of saturated clay. *Geotechnique*, Vol. 22, pp. 368-371.

Smart, P. (1981) Quantitative SEM methods for soil fabric analysis (discussion of paper by Tovey and Sokolov, 1981). *Scanning Electron Microscopy*, Vol. 1, pp. 551-553.

Smart, P., and Dickson, J. W. (1979) Deformation and shear of normally flocculated kaolin. *Easterling K. E. (Ed.), Mechanisms of Deformation and Fracture.* Pergamon, pp. 129-136.

Smart, P. and Leng, X. (1993) Present developments in image analysis. *Scanning Microscopy*, Vol. 7, No. 1, pp. 5-16.

Smart, P. and Leng, X. (1994) *Orientation mapping.* Report, CE-GE94-49, University of Glasgow.

Smart, P., and Tovey, N. K. (1982) *Electron Microscopy of Soils and Sediments: Techniques.* Clarendon Press.

Smart, P., and Tovey, N. K. (1988) Theoretical aspects of intensity gradient analysis. *Scanning*, Vol. 10, pp. 115-121.

Tabatabai, A. J., and Mitchell, O. R. (1984) Edge location to subpixel values in digital imagery. *IEEE Trans. Pattern Analysis Mach. Intell.*, Vol. 6, No. 2, pp 188-201.

Teague, M. R. (1980) Image analysis via the general theory of moments. *Jour. Opt. Soc. Amer.*, Vol. 70, No. 8, pp 920-930.

Teh, C. and Chin, R. T. (1988) On image analysis by the methods of moments. *IEEE Trans. Pattern Analysis Mach. Intell.*, Vol. 10, No. 4, pp 496-513.

Tovey, N. K. (1980) A digital computer technique for orientation analysis of micrographs of soil fabric. *J. Micrographs*, Vol. 120, pp. 303-317.

Tovey, N. K. and Sokolov, V. N. (1981) Quantitative SEM methods for soil fabric analysis. *Scanning Electron Microscopy*, Vol. 1, pp. 537-554.

Tovey, N. K. and Smart, P. (1986) Intensity gradient techniques for orientation analysis of electron micrographs. *Scanning*, Vol. 8, pp. 75-90.

Unitt, B. M. (1975) A digital computer method for revealing directional information in images. *J. Physics*, E Series 2, Vol. 8, pp. 423-425.

Watanabe, S. (1967) Karhunen-Loeve expansion and factor analysis--Theoretical remarks and applications. *Transactions of the Fourth Prague Conference on Information Theory, Statistical Decision, Functions & Random Processes, 1965.* Publishing House of the Czechoslovakk Academy of Sciences, pp. 635.

Watanabe, S. (1985) *Pattern Recognition: Human and Mechanical.* John Wiley & Sons.

Webster, R. (1977) *Quantitative and Numerical Methods in Soil Classification and Survey.* Clarendon Press.

Wen, W. and Lozzi, A. (1993) Recognition and inspection of manufactured parts using line moments of their boundaries. *Pattern Recognition*, Vol. 26, No. 10, pp 1461-1471.

Young, T. Y., and Fu, K. S. (1986) *Handbook of Pattern Recognition and Image Processing.* Academic Press.

Appendix 5A.1 The Double-boundary Method

The method proposed by Luo and Ma (1989) is summarised here.

Select any group of pixels with value 1 and use track following to build up the double boundary of this area. Traverse clockwise (or counter clockwise) along its boundary as follows:

Step 1. Stand at a point with value 1 on the edge of the area with value 1 on the right (w.r.t. the proposed direction of traverse round the object) and value 0 on the left.

Step 2. Turn left and go straight ahead one pixel. If this pixel has value 1, go to Step 2.

Step 3. Turn right and go straight ahead one pixel. If this pixel has value 1, go to Step 2.

Step 4. Turn right and go straight ahead for 1, or 2, or 3 pixels. On encountering the first of these pixels having value 1, go to Step 2.

Step 5. If none of these 3 pixels has value 1, turn right and go to Step 4.

Step 6. Stop if the point with value 1 at Step 2 is the starting point.

When the algorithm is going to jump from Step 3 or Step 4 to Step 2, set the point to a value BL if the current value was 0, and to a value BR if the current value was 1. After Step 6, the set of points with value BL forms the outer boundary, and the set of points with value BR forms the inner boundary. These two boundaries are called the double boundary of the area. Then the double boundary can be used to separate objects from each other.

Let P_i denote the set of points belonging to the *ith* object, and let BR_i and BL_i be the double boundary of the *ith* object. Then, a point p can be classified into P_i, if it satisfies the following condition:

$$P_i = \{p: p \text{ lies within boundary } BR_i\} \tag{5A.1.1}$$

or it is classified into background BG if it satisfies:

$$BG = \{p: p \text{ lies outside any boundary } BL_i\}. \tag{5A.1.2}$$

After the object separation procedure is completed one keeps one boundary of the double boundary as the edge of the particle, and discards the other one.

Appendix 5A.2   Lemmas and Propositions

The following lemmas and propositions relate to the Directed Vein method of orientation analysis described in the main text.

Lemma 1.   The orientation found for a closed smooth curve will tend to be near the orientation of its longest diagonal.

Proof: The probability is greater for code number nearer to that of the longest diagonal than for those far away from that of the longest diagonal. Therefore from equation (5.3.6) in Section 5.3, the orientation will be near the direction of the longest diagonal.

Lemma 2.   The orientation found for a regular polygon with n edges is between $(90° - 180°/n)$ and $(90° + 180°/n)$.

Proof: Let an edge of a regular polygon lie parallel to the x-axis (Figure 5A.1). As a result of the changes to the modulo-4 chain code and Lemma 1, the orientation of the polygon is near the direction of L, see Figure 5A.1. Hence angle α is

$$\alpha = 90° - \alpha/2 = 90° - (360°/n/2) = 90° - 180°/n . \qquad (5A.2.1)$$

The other extreme occurs when the polygon is rotated by γ counter-clockwise. In this case the orientation α' will be

$$\alpha' = \alpha + \gamma = \alpha + 360°/n . \qquad (5A.2.2)$$

Substitute (5A.2.1) into (5A.2.2):

$$\alpha' = 90° - 180°/n + 360°/n = 90° + 180°/n . \qquad (5A.2.3)$$

Proposition 1.   The orientation found for a long-shaped closed curve is approximately in the direction of its length.

Proof: This is directly from Lemma 1, or is a special case of Lemma 1.

Proposition 2.   The orientation found for a circle is $90°$.

Proof: A circle can be considered as a regular polygon with an infinite number of sides. Therefore in equation (5A.2.1) and (5A.2.3), in letting n approach infinity, we obtain $\alpha \approx \alpha' \approx 90°$.

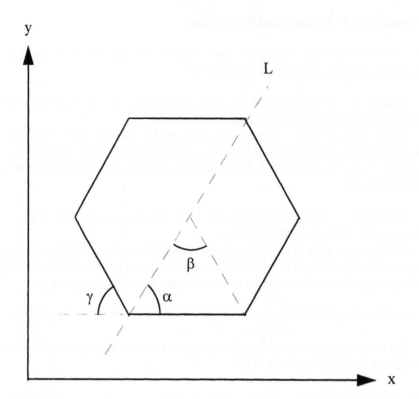

Figure 5A.1   Example on orientation of a regular polygon.

6

Arrangement Analysis

6.1 INTRODUCTION

Automatic analysis of relationships among objects in an aggregate is important within image processing and pattern recognition. For example, cars running on a motorway are in a parallel arrangement, cars running on a roundabout are in a circumferential arrangement, cars entering or leaving a roundabout are in a radial arrangement, and cars in a car park are in a different parallel arrangement. From the arrangement of the cars, we can distinguish the motorway, the roundabout, and the car park from each other. In the study of soil microstructure, the arrangement of clay particles is one of the three most important factors: size, shape, and arrangements (Brewer 1964). Baver (1948), a soil physicist, defined structure as the arrangement of soil particles. Kubiena's concept (1938, 1953) dealt with arrangement only. Some work of Krumbein and Sloss (1955) and Pettijohn (1957) dealt with specific arrangements. The analysis of the arrangement of linear or tabular particles within aggregates or the arrangement of aggregates within regions is also one of the very meaningful subjects. For instance, one of our research topics is the analysis of how elongated particles fit together: random, parallel, radiating, rings, loosely, etc., or the analysis of what aggregates of particles are: bundles, domains, random clusters, radial clusters, spherical aggregates, etc. Smart (1971) reviewed the structure of fine-grained soils as seen in the electron microscope with particular reference to the mechanical properties of the soils. The concepts reviewed were concerned with inter-particle behaviour and particle arrangements, such as cross-section packet, cross-section domain, etc. Van Olphen (1963) suggested that there are seven different clay particle arrangements (see also Burnham 1970). FitzPatrick (1984) gave a more detailed descriptions of aggregates. Smart and Tovey (1981) presented a collection of selected aggregates as examples of soil microstructure. Because different arrangements of particles within aggregates reflect some natural conditions, such as pressure, water flow, ice melting, shrinking and swelling, etc. (Brewer 1964), we may use the features of the arrangements of the particles within aggregates to recognise some special aggregates which imply that some related changes happened while the aggregates were being formed. Therefore, automatic analysis, recognition, or classification of the arrangement of objects within aggregates is significant in study of soil microstructure.

As a step towards the automatic achievement of these goals, this chapter will concentrate on distinguishing between the six arrangements of elongated objects described below. The method proposed is based on estimates of the differences of measurements of the orientations and positions of the particles. This method arose from a proposed extension of the linear Hough transform; however, it was found possible to use a fast simplified method based on feature measurements. These two aspects of the work will be discussed in turn, preceded by a discussion of the characteristics of the six arrangements concerned, and followed by some further suggestions.

6.1.1   Aggregates
There are many different relationships between objects within an aggregate. Some relationships are not easy to describe, but some are simple. The simple relationships are such as: parallel, cross, triangle, rectangular, ring, radial, random, etc. Here, we focus our study on six simple arrangements in 2-D dimensional space: three kinds of parallel arrangements namely parallel vertical-section, parallel cross-section, and parallel region arrangement, and three sorts of non-parallel arrangements: radial region, circumferential region, and random region arrangements. These are discussed in turn below.

6.1.2   Examples of Arrangements

(1)   Parallel Vertical-Section Arrangement
An example of parallel vertical-section arrangement is shown in Figure 6.1. The aggregate is elongated, and the objects within the aggregate have the same orientation as that of the aggregate. This type of feature is seen in cross-sections of failure zones in clay soil (e.g. Smart 1966), In the common direction, the objects are co-linear in groups to form a few columns, i.e. vertical-section arrangement. Each column contains many objects. These columns are close to each other to form a narrow strip or band. The long axis of the strip is parallel to the direction of the objects. The distribution of the distances between objects in the direction of the objects is much wider than in the direction perpendicular to that of the objects

(2)   Parallel Cross-Section Arrangement
Figure 6.2 shows an example of parallel cross-section arrangement. This is somewhat similar but not quite the same as Smart's (1971) stack. Like the parallel vertical-section arrangement, the objects within the aggregate lie in the same direction. In the common direction, the objects are co-linear in groups to form many rows, i.e. cross-section arrangement. Each row contains quite a few objects. These rows are close to each other to form a narrow strip or band. Unlike the parallel vertical-section arrangement, the long axis of the strip is perpendicular to the direction of the objects. The distribution of the distances between objects in the direction of the objects is much narrower than in the direction perpendicular to that of the objects.

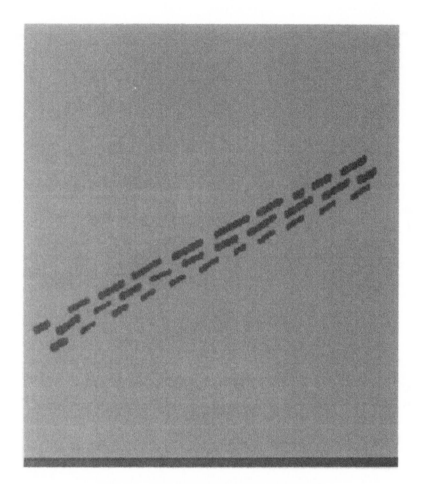

Figure 6.1   Parallel vertical-section arrangement.

(3) Parallel Region Arrangement

Figure 6.3 shows an example of the parallel region arrangements. This is sometimes named as "cross-section domain" (see Smart 1971). Like the parallel vertical-section arrangement and the parallel cross-section arrangement, the orientations of the objects within the aggregate are the same. In the common direction, the objects are co-linear in groups to yield many columns. Each column includes many objects. The difference from the previous two arrangements is that the objects in the parallel region arrangement scatter in a wider region but not in a strip or a band. The distributions of the distances between objects are not greatly different in the direction parallel and the direction perpendicular to that of the objects.

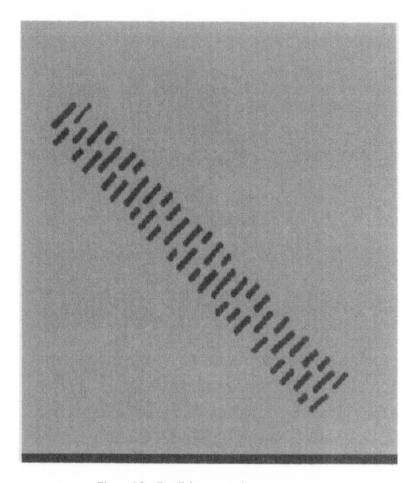

Figure 6.2   Parallel cross-section arrangement.

(4)   Radial Region Arrangement

Figure 6.4 shows an example of radial region arrangement.   In this arrangement, the orientations of the objects are not the same.   The objects are co-linear in groups to yield many rays.   Each ray includes many objects.   The rays intersect at or near the same point, so that the arrangement looks like the rays originating from a point source.   Radial region arrangements can be subdivided into a complete class, in which the orientations are distributed through a complete 360° range, and an incomplete class, in which the orientations are restricted to a narrower range.   The present treatment is aimed at complete radial region arrangements.   Complete radial region arrangements of clay plates are occasionally found around micro-organisms in soils; in this case, the central objects of Figure 6.4 are replaced by the micro-organism.

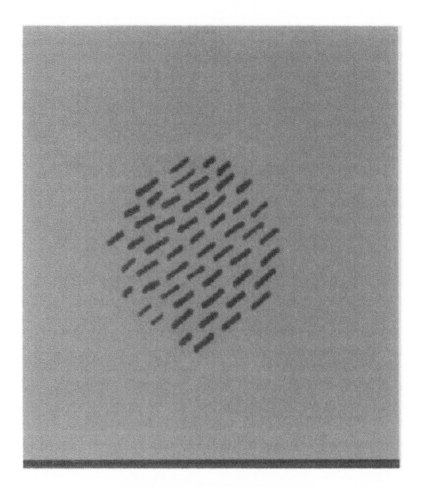

Figure 6.3   Parallel region arrangement.

(5) Circumferential Region Arrangement
Figure 6.5 shows an example of circumferential region arrangement.   In this
arrangement, the orientations of the objects are not the same.   The objects are
concentric in groups to produce many circles or rings.   Each ring has many objects.
This arrangement tends to look like concentric circles.   Again, circumferential
region arrangements can be divided into complete and incomplete classes, with the
emphasis here on the complete class.   Complete circumferential region
arrangements are also found around micro-organisms in soil.

Figure 6.4   Radial region arrangement.

(6)   Random Region Arrangement

Figure 6.6 shows an example of random region arrangement.   Here, the orientations of the objects within the aggregate are random.

(7)   Summary

From the characteristics of the arrangements described above, we can see that the important features to identify different arrangements of objects within aggregates are: collinear or concentric; orientation; and the distances between objects or between objects and some special point.   These features are somewhat related to the straight line Hough transform.   Therefore, for the purpose of recognition and classification of aggregates, we apply the Hough transform to describe the objects and to analyse the arrangements of the objects within aggregates.

Figure 6.5   Circumferential region arrangement.

6.2 EXTENDED HOUGH TRANSFORM

6.2.1 Hough Transform

The Hough transform was proposed by Hough (1962) (see also Duda and Hart 1972) for line detection in an image. Generally, a straight line can be described by the function of x and y in 2-D dimensional space:

$$y = ax + b \qquad\qquad (6.2.1)$$

.

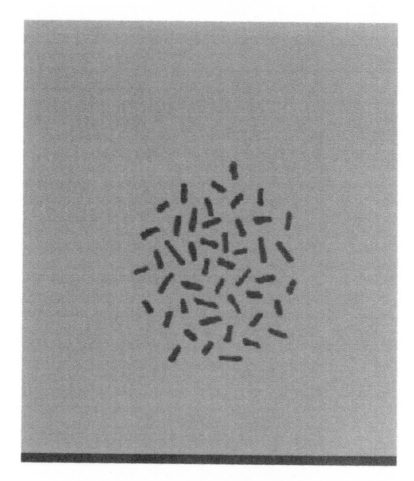

Figure 6.6   Random region arrangement.

where a is the slope of the straight line, and b is the intercept on the y-axis. The Hough transform is a mapping of a set of co-linear points in (x,y) space onto a point in the slope-intercept parameter space (a,b). Thus this, the original form of the Hough transform, is a special case of the general Hough transform described in Chapter 4, Section 4.2.1. Each point on the straight line in (x,y) maps onto a straight line in the parameter space (a,b). The parameters of the straight line in (x,y) being detected are determined by the intersecting point of the straight lines in (a,b). Because both the slope a and the intercept b are unbounded, the application of the naive Hough transform for line detection is not convenient.

Duda and Hart (1972) proposed the angle-radius rather than Hough's slope-intercept parameters to simplify the computation of the Hough transform for line detection. As shown in Figure 6.7, a straight line L in (x,y) space can be expressed by:

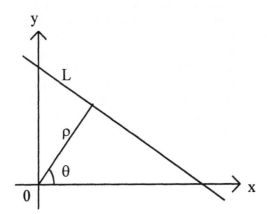

Figure 6.7   Hough transform of a straight line L.

$$\rho = x\cos\theta + y\sin\theta \qquad\qquad (6.2.2)$$

where ρ is the distance from the origin point to the straight line and θ the angle perpendicular to the straight line.   A point on the straight line in (x,y) is a sinusoidal curve in the Hough space (ρ,θ).   The parameters of the straight line being detected in (x,y) are determined by the intersecting point of the curves in (ρ,θ).   Unlike the slope-intercept parameters, the radius parameter ρ is limited within the region of the image being analysed and the angle parameter θ is limited between -90° and +90° (or 0° and 180°).

Because the Hough transform is a powerful and efficient procedure for detecting lines in images, it has been widely used by many scientists, such as O'Gorman and Clowes (1972), Stockman and Agrawala (1977), Guerra and Hambrusch (1989), Schalkoff (1989), Haralick and Shapiro (1992).   In particular, Costa et al. (1990, 1991) used it to find preferred orientation in soil micrographs similar to those of interest here.

6.2.2 Extension of Hough Transform

The general use of the Hough transform in equation (6.2.2) is to detect straight lines in images. The traditional procedure is: first, map all the points of all the objects in an image into curves in the Hough space; then, search for local maxima in the Hough space to determine the parameters of any straight lines in the image (compare Section 4.2.1).

When the traditional procedure is used, points which are collinear in the original image will map into the same maximum in Hough space; thus separate segments of the same straight line in the image are not distinguished. The original motivation behind the proposed extension was to find a method whereby these separate segments would map into different Hough maxima. Let us consider an elongated object in the (x,y) plane as a "cross" as shown in Figure 6.8. Let (x,y) be the position of the centroid and θ be the orientation of the long axis of the object. Then the intersecting point of the "cross" is at (x,y), the long bar of it has the orientation θ, and the short bar is perpendicular to the long bar. The equations of these two bars are given by equation 6.2.2. rewritten as:

$$\rho_1 = -x \sin\theta + y\cos\theta$$
$$(6.2.3)$$

$$\rho_2 = x\cos\theta + y\sin\theta . \qquad\qquad (6.2.4)$$

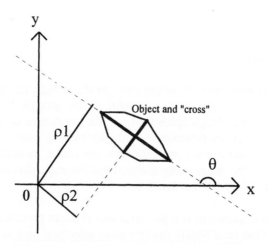

Figure 6.8   Hough transform of a "cross" (object).

Now, in the traditional procedure, when scanning the image, equation (6.2.3) is the equation describing a line in the Hough $O\rho_1\theta$-space. Moreover, equation (6.2.4) now similarly describes a line in a Hough $O\rho_2\theta$-space. Now, combining these two two-dimensional Hough spaces into a three-dimensional Hough space $O\rho_1\rho_2\theta$, each equation considered in isolation defines a sinusoidal surface; and taking both equations simultaneously defines a curve corresponding to the intersection of these two surfaces. The proposed new procedure is: first map all the points of all the objects in the image into curves in the three-dimensional Hough space $O\rho_1\rho_2\theta$; then search for local maxima in this Hough space to determine the parameters (ρ_1,ρ_2,θ) of any elongated objects in the images.

Although the proposed extension of the Hough transform is general and could be extended to grey level images, the immediate problem here is the classification of aggregates of distinct elongated objects. In this case, if there are n objects in the aggregate, n maxima should be found, defining a set of n points in $O\rho_1\rho_2\theta$-space. It will be shown through the example which follows how the set of n points in extended Hough space can be used to classify aggregates.

6.3 SIMPLIFIED EXTENDED HOUGH TRANSFORM

When analysing an aggregate which consists of elongated objects all of which can be identified individually, a simplification of the proposed extension of the Hough transform is possible. This method is fast, because it avoids the need to construct histograms.

In this case, the first step is, for each object individually, to find its preferred orientation θ and the coordinates x and y of its centroid by standard image processing procedures. Next, the corresponding values of ρ_1 and ρ_2 are calculated from equations (6.2.3) and (6.2.4). Then, the point (ρ_1,ρ_2,θ) is plotted in the extended Hough space. Thus, if there are n objects in the aggregate, there will be a set of n points in extended Hough space. Different classes of aggregates will be found to have different distributions of points in extended Hough space.

6.4 ARRANGEMENT FEATURES

As described in Section 6.1, the study was concentrated on the six examples of different arrangements of objects within aggregates, as shown in Figure 6.1 - 6.6. The original images were drawn by hand and then digitised. The digital images were pre-processed to remove the noise which comes from the digitising system and segmented by a simple threshold method to yield binary images. To analyse the arrangements of the objects within aggregates, first the orientation and the position of each object were measured as described in Section 6.4.1 below. Then the simplified version of the new Hough transform was applied to describe the objects in the Hough space.

6.4.1   Orientation and Position

The orientation of an object can be measured by different methods.   In Chapter 3, various methods (directed vein, convex hull, principal component transform, and moments), are introduced for orientation measurement of an object.   Here, for the simplified trial of the arrangement analysis, the method of moments is used.   This is because when the moment method is used, both the orientation and the position of an object can be measured at the same time.   Moreover, we have particle analysis software available in the image processing software SEMPER6 in the computer system NIMBUS, which gives features such as the orientations and the positions of particles based on moments.   When this moment method is used, the input is a binary image, in which the pixels of the objects are set to value 1 and those of the background are set to value 0.   The output comprises the positions of the centroids (x,y), and the orientations θ of the objects in the range -90° to +90° (In general, the analysis could be performed on the grey image, each pixel being weighted by its intensity, provided that (1) a base grey level to be treated as zero and (2) a boundary outside which all is zero can be established).   For convenience, the calculations of the centroid and the orientation of an object by the moment method are re-written as:

$$x = M_{10} / M_{00} \tag{6.4.1}$$

$$y = M_{01} / M_{00} \tag{6.4.2}$$

$$\theta = \frac{1}{2} \arctan \frac{M_{00} M_{11} \quad M_{10} M_{01}}{M_{00}(M_{20} - M_{02}) - (M_{10}^2 - M_{01}^2)} \tag{6.4.3}$$

where M_{00} is the order zero moment, M_{10} and M_{01} are the 1st moments, and M_{11}, M_{20}, and M_{02} are the 2nd moments.

The orientations θ and the positions x and y of the individual objects in Figure 6.1 - 6.6, measured by the moment method in these experiments, are given in Tables 6.1 - 6.6 respectively.   In order to normalise the features of the objects within an aggregate, we choose the centroid of the aggregate as the origin point of the co-ordinate system .

6.4.2   Description in Hough Space

Using the Hough transform, an object with the measurements of the orientations θ and the positions x and y in (x,y) space can be mapped into two 2-D Hough space or into one 3-D Hough space by equation (6.2.3) and (6.2.4).   Then the object is described by the parameters θ, ρ_1, and ρ_2 in the Hough space.   This was done for each of the objects in Figure 6.1 - 6.6.   The values obtained are listed in Tables 6.1 - 6.6. and plotted in Figure 6.9 - 6.14.

Table 6.1   The experimental results of parallel vertical-section arrangement.

Particle No.	x	y	θ	ρ_1	ρ_2
1	151.07	91.18	29.06	6.31	176.35
2	164.72	81.21	28.04	-5.76	183.56
3	118.40	75.86	29.90	6.75	140.46
4	95.14	63.27	31.58	4.07	114.18
5	158.15	65.61	32.62	-29.98	168.57
6	132.65	67.96	30.84	-9.66	148.73
7	123.77	50.05	35.48	-31.09	129.84
8	64.73	50.45	29.35	12.25	81.14
9	94.66	50.64	31.89	-7.01	107.12
10	90.59	35.16	32.15	-18.44	95.40
11	56.03	32.14	32.46	-2.96	64.53
12	25.52	31.34	26.83	16.45	36.92
13	61.27	21.12	36.38	-19.34	61.86
14	19.98	14.78	24.95	4.98	24.35
15	33.72	8.32	34.16	-12.06	32.57
16	-20.35	8.04	28.72	16.83	-13.98
17	-14.80	-1.64	25.57	4.91	-14.06
18	1.64	-6.80	33.28	-6.59	-2.36
19	-62.63	-10.92	30.55	22.43	-59.49
20	-47.66	-17.38	23.49	3.06	-50.64
21	-30.77	-21.89	29.02	-4.21	-37.52
22	-97.97	-31.20	29.39	20.90	-100.68
23	-78.85	-33.12	29.51	10.02	-84.94
24	-60.67	-36.06	31.95	1.51	-70.56
25	-132.15	-46.37	28.94	23.36	-138.08
26	-107.70	-48.75	28.90	9.37	-117.85
27	-89.50	-51.56	30.90	1.72	-103.28
28	-170.31	-68.38	28.81	22.17	-182.18
29	-142.60	-65.95	34.84	27.33	-154.71
30	-122.95	-68.90	33.87	11.31	-140.49
31	-152.45	-85.03	29.68	1.62	-174.55

Table 6.2   The experimental results of parallel cross-section arrangement.

Particle No.	x	y	θ	ρ_1	ρ_2
1	-125.24	139.19	46.51	186.66	14.79
2	-144.92	137.43	44.43	199.59	-7.30
3	-128.50	117.86	46.87	174.35	-1.83
4	-147.50	116.53	46.54	187.22	-16.85
5	-110.01	120.04	47.24	162.27	13.45
6	-95.41	115.61	50.63	147.09	28.85
7	-130.69	98.54	43.29	161.34	-27.55
8	-78.38	92.08	45.35	120.47	10.43
9	-96.74	94.22	46.09	135.03	0.78
10	-115.11	91.40	47.13	146.55	-11.33
11	-66.98	86.76	47.32	108.05	18.37
12	-97.67	72.22	47.71	120.84	-12.31
13	-87.47	62.97	48.90	107.31	-10.05
14	-52.86	59.70	46.33	79.46	6.68
15	-38.09	54.50	46.34	65.18	13.13
16	-69.28	62.11	48.58	93.04	0.73
17	-70.90	40.79	49.01	80.27	-15.72
18	-31.07	41.56	45.73	51.26	8.07
19	-58.13	34.46	47.44	66.13	-13.93
20	-51.47	21.09	47.00	52.03	-19.68
21	3.01	17.32	47.16	9.57	14.75
22	-28.18	23.69	44.90	36.67	-3.24
23	-11.65	19.05	45.88	21.62	5.57
24	-32.62	-0.11	50.42	25.07	-20.86
25	9.55	1.39	49.30	-6.33	7.28
26	22.89	-4.64	50.64	-20.64	10.93
27	-17.45	-3.98	46.89	10.01	-14.83
28	-9.52	-19.14	49.47	-5.20	-20.73
29	3.71	-25.34	46.10	-20.25	-15.69
30	36.34	-31.34	48.09	-47.98	0.95
31	20.09	-27.45	48.38	-33.25	-7.19
32	49.81	-35.02	47.35	-60.36	7.99
33	59.24	-46.96	45.95	-75.23	7.43

Table 6.2 (cont.)

Particle No.	x	y	θ	ρ_1	ρ_2
34	18.27	-52.23	45.06	-49.83	-24.06
35	30.45	-58.72	44.85	-63.11	-19.82
36	60.93	-65.18	48.51	-88.83	-8.46
37	79.33	-68.53	47.78	-104.80	2.55
38	39.51	-68.20	45.36	-76.03	-20.76
39	56.99	-88.40	46.52	-102.18	-24.93
40	80.83	-86.05	43.44	-118.05	-0.49
41	97.06	-89.60	45.58	-132.03	3.95
42	108.95	-101.75	45.21	-149.00	4.55
43	123.16	-107.24	46.51	-163.16	6.96
44	75.33	-109.75	44.87	-130.92	-24.04
45	85.36	-120.07	46.65	-144.49	-28.72
46	140.06	-123.43	48.00	-186.67	1.98
47	100.98	-123.93	47.04	-158.35	-21.90
48	122.72	-124.39	43.15	-174.68	4.47
49	101.51	-141.56	42.21	-173.05	-19.91
50	117.36	-145.85	41.52	-186.99	-8.82

Table 6.3   The experimental results of parallel region arrangement.

Particle No.	x	y	θ	ρ_1	ρ_2
1	3.55	96.29	38.99	72.61	63.34
2	-26.97	92.98	36.04	91.05	32.90
3	18.02	89.75	41.21	55.64	72.69
4	-22.58	80.23	34.91	78.72	27.40
5	-7.57	75.49	31.48	68.34	32.96
6	19.56	76.74	39.43	46.85	63.85
7	38.76	72.46	40.22	30.30	76.38
8	-60.35	71.48	35.51	93.24	-7.60
9	-52.48	60.88	42.11	80.36	1.90
10	-35.97	57.48	29.75	67.75	-2.70
11	-10.70	57.28	33.81	53.54	22.99
12	10.15	54.93	39.78	35.73	42.94
13	35.64	52.77	39.89	17.63	61.19
14	-76.01	48.16	27.56	77.86	-45.10
15	54.90	49.63	41.18	1.21	740.00

Table 6.3 (cont.)

Particle No.	x	y	θ	ρ_1	ρ_2
16	12.71	38.96	38.96	22.30	34.38
17	-62.78	38.17	28.37	63.42	-37.10
18	-42.71	35.14	27.77	50.99	-21.41
19	-18.94	34.47	31.05	39.30	1.55
20	29.07	30.18	34.42	8.46	41.04
21	48.47	28.74	35.14	-4.40	56.18
22	-9.12	22.67	38.15	23.46	6.83
23	64.87	23.53	37.74	-21.09	65.71
24	-92.92	21.18	37.50	73.37	-60.82
25	-72.19	16.64	32.54	52.86	-51.91
26	-50.42	14.04	31.59	38.37	-35.59
27	0.06	9.76	35.71	7.89	5.75
28	-31.46	7.51	37.15	24.99	-20.54
29	17.12	6.80	36.61	-4.75	17.80
30	35.49	3.09	35.70	-18.20	30.62
31	65.43	3.10	43.18	-42.51	49.84
32	-79.79	-5.16	40.81	48.25	-63.76
33	-59.81	-7.65	33.41	26.55	-54.14
34	-29.22	-10.31	36.79	9.24	-29.58
35	-10.17	-12.53	33.16	-4.93	-15.37
36	37.25	-17.64	40.49	-37.60	16.87
37	6.42	-18.09	39.46	-18.05	-6.54
38	60.54	-18.47	40.59	-53.41	33.95
39	-56.27	-26.25	28.99	4.31	-61.94
40	-80.64	-31.53	41.37	29.64	-81.35
41	-36.55	-31.54	33.36	-6.25	-47.87
42	-23.35	-39.48	36.66	-17.73	-42.30
43	30.86	-39.21	39.03	-49.90	-0.72
44	6.86	-38.32	38.75	-34.18	-18.64
45	56.36	-40.18	41.19	-67.35	15.95
46	-62.50	-49.58	37.91	-0.72	-79.78
47	-50.07	-59.06	38.74	-14.73	-76.01
48	2.36	-59.20	37.62	-48.33	-34.27
49	-24.58	-58.47	39.91	-29.08	-56.37
50	26.07	-61.24	37.99	-64.31	-17.15
51	-21.00	-78.77	40.33	-46.45	-66.99
52	-2.51	-82.02	39.45	-61.73	-54.06

Table 6.4   The experimental results of radial region arrangement.

Particle No.	x	y	θ	ρ_1	ρ_2
1	-12.19	90.64	-84.86	-4.02	-91.37
2	16.13	92.63	80.98	-1.40	94.02
3	-33.62	82.49	-73.77	-9.22	-88.60
4	42.37	84.55	51.40	19.64	92.51
5	-54.11	75.50	-39.78	23.40	-89.89
6	63.02	72.86	45.18	6.66	96.10
7	-67.77	59.41	-38.73	3.95	-90.03
8	-6.36	57.97	-88.32	-4.66	-58.13
9	66.48	51.86	30.29	11.25	83.56
10	-23.74	51.34	-75.85	-10.47	-55.59
11	38.77	49.19	39.17	13.65	61.13
12	13.20	51.28	63.82	10.78	51.84
13	-42.57	40.58	-30.69	13.17	-57.32
14	-75.49	41.46	-34.21	-8.16	-85.74
15	77.33	29.44	10.80	14.43	81.48
16	46.02	26.09	23.00	6.03	52.56
17	-48.07	22.87	-17.59	7.28	-52.73
18	-83.42	20.12	0.13	20.32	-83.37
19	15.23	26.08	53.25	3.40	30.01
20	-21.35	22.28	-45.67	0.30	-30.86
21	-5.61	22.02	-84.43	-3.45	-22.46
22	65.22	11.05	8.64	1.12	66.14
23	19.55	7.48	8.32	4.57	20.42
24	-24.04	4.89	0.89	5.26	-23.96
25	-62.38	-1.06	5.22	4.62	-62.21
26	73.30	-9.70	-3.80	-4.81	73.78
27	13.06	-9.14	-46.30	3.13	15.63
28	43.33	-11.38	-29.42	11.37	43.33
29	-81.74	-18.02	9.34	-4.51	-83.58
30	-49.14	-16.82	28.53	8.69	-51.20
31	-23.64	-18.36	50.87	6.75	-29.16
32	-2.60	-16.77	-84.54	-4.18	16.45
33	33.60	-26.37	-37.37	-0.56	42.71
34	66.77	-30.80	-32.69	10.14	72.82
35	-73.32	-41.54	34.00	6.57	-84.01
36	-43.62	-40.39	44.74	2.02	-59.42
37	18.93	-40.27	-60.15	-3.62	44.35
38	55.06	-44.51	-37.70	-1.54	70.78

Table 6.4 (cont.)

Particle No.	x	y	θ	ρ_1	ρ_2
39	-18.41	-45.17	73.14	4.52	-48.57
40	3.63	-51.71	-82.69	-2.98	51.76
41	-64.89	-62.14	40.45	-5.19	-89.70
42	43.30	-61.27	-48.06	-8.74	74.52
43	-41.45	-66.85	58.99	1.08	-78.65
44	22.23	-74.29	-74.13	1.07	77.54
45	-10.28	-77.79	77.00	-7.48	-78.11

Table 6.5   The experimental results of circumferential region arrangement.

Particle No.	x	y	θ	ρ_1	ρ_2
1	-34.21	87.76	16.87	93.91	-7.27
2	22.02	86.66	-16.05	89.36	-2.79
3	13.43	62.72	-13.96	64.11	-2.11
4	-83.87	64.27	36.60	101.06	-29.02
5	67.74	61.25	-49.36	91.29	-2.36
6	-46.48	57.83	26.89	72.60	-15.30
7	-8.92	36.78	-15.24	33.14	-18.28
8	53.45	35.13	-60.21	63.84	-3.93
9	-49.45	27.46	35.30	50.99	-24.49
10	-21.01	17.60	13.41	21.99	-16.36
11	-74.67	24.91	47.74	72.01	-31.78
12	28.18	22.86	-53.21	36.26	-1.43
13	-95.79	23.57	69.01	97.88	-12.30
14	8.59	12.22	-42.77	14.80	-1.99
15	-9.41	3.51	-14.00	1.13	-9.98
16	83.76	12.58	83.68	-81.87	21.73
17	-29.27	-5.40	52.35	19.88	-22.16
18	1.62	-6.42	-77.68	0.21	6.62
19	-50.63	-4.63	72.18	46.79	-19.90
20	-92.12	-11.50	84.69	90.66	-19.98
21	-75.28	-6.62	84.02	74.18	-14.42
22	-14.21	-13.71	71.54	9.13	-17.51
23	16.56	-14.53	76.75	-19.45	-10.35
24	37.99	-13.57	-82.31	35.83	18.53
25	60.00	-12.57	86.62	-60.64	-9.01

Table 6.5 (cont.)

Particle No.	x	y	θ	ρ₁	ρ₂
26	-4.08	-24.99	32.95	-18.75	-17.02
27	-26.63	-27.69	-53.76	-37.84	6.59
28	-107.50	-28.82	-76.40	-111.26	2.72
29	-41.89	-37.11	-38.02	-55.04	-10.15
30	-0.61	-39.07	38.16	-30.34	-24.62
31	83.22	-32.85	61.03	-88.72	11.56
32	-59.96	-43.41	-54.04	-74.03	-0.08
33	22.67	-44.20	37.81	-48.82	-9.19
34	49.91	-50.76	42.84	-71.15	2.08
35	-77.66	-47.67	-57.19	-91.10	-2.03
36	-18.55	-63.24	-6.85	-65.00	-10.88
37	-91.36	-69.77	-52.07	-114.95	-1.12
38	16.93	-73.35	23.89	-73.92	-14.22
39	-36.26	-78.27	-23.64	-86.24	-1.82
40	58.37	-78.69	37.45	-97.97	-1.51
41	-52.15	-101.09	-20.91	-113.05	-12.64
42	2.24	-105.39	7.96	-104.69	-12.38

Table 6.6   The experimental results of random region arrangement.

Particle No.	x	y	θ	ρ₁	ρ₂
1	30.26	84.63	-82.35	41.26	-79.85
2	14.25	67.84	-31.01	65.48	-22.74
3	-21.03	61.79	89.18	21.91	61.48
4	57.69	58.39	89.68	-57.36	58.70
5	32.98	54.31	49.54	10.15	62.73
6	-43.05	47.83	37.79	64.18	-4.70
7	4.76	48.22	-72.81	18.80	-44.66
8	59.07	35.84	3.99	31.65	61.42
9	7.07	32.38	19.21	28.25	17.33
10	86.50	35.10	81.57	-80.42	47.41
11	-11.33	35.26	81.19	16.60	33.11
12	36.81	28.21	-65.94	45.11	-10.75
13	-27.82	29.16	83.95	30.74	26.06
14	-56.39	22.56	24.00	43.55	-42.34
15	5.26	12.65	-16.54	13.62	1.44

Table 6.6 (cont.)

Particle No.	x	y	θ	ρ_1	ρ_2
16	21.56	13.44	-85.57	22.53	-11.74
17	37.12	4.64	16.92	-6.36	36.87
18	-11.85	3.97	-78.19	-10.79	-6.31
19	59.43	6.22	-80.97	59.67	3.18
20	82.24	4.51	-51.94	67.54	47.15
21	-30.21	2.28	-51.28	-22.15	-20.68
22	21.99	-7.26	-19.97	0.69	23.14
23	-47.05	-3.80	-71.74	-45.87	-11.14
24	-65.36	-14.86	18.24	6.34	-66.73
25	1.62	-10.78	76.64	-4.07	-10.12
26	63.19	-22.12	9.26	-32.00	58.81
27	40.22	-20.83	52.01	-44.52	8.34
28	-12.72	-29.63	-12.98	-31.73	-5.74
29	15.71	-29.29	57.61	-28.95	-16.32
30	-39.73	-27.24	55.13	17.03	-45.06
31	89.65	-29.73	61.18	-92.88	17.17
32	50.86	-37.32	-6.84	-31.00	54.94
33	1.86	-46.63	-14.76	-44.62	13.68
34	-20.88	-49.75	-79.05	-29.95	44.88
35	30.80	-46.36	-58.33	1.87	55.63
36	-57.92	-50.56	-56.67	-76.18	10.42
37	76.28	-50.17	-74.86	60.52	68.35
38	6.24	-63.57	10.14	-63.68	-5.05
39	-37.39	-62.42	70.92	14.93	-71.21
40	53.32	-62.44	47.27	-81.53	-9.68
41	75.79	-75.36	-18.18	-47.95	95.52
42	-13.87	-77.86	-36.29	-70.97	34.90
43	25.25	-77.25	74.98	-44.41	-68.06
44	47.94	-85.58	-17.48	-67.24	71.43
45	3.82	-91.03	52.95	-57.89	-70.35
46	27.69	-101.01	-2.47	-99.72	32.02
47	-30.08	-97.43	57.45	-27.06	-98.31

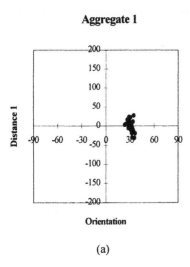

(a)

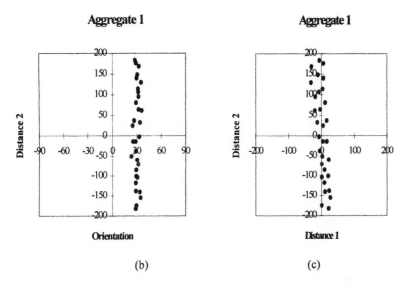

(b)   (c)

Figure 6.9   Distribution of features of vertical-section arrangement in the Hough space.

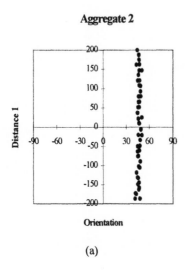

(a)

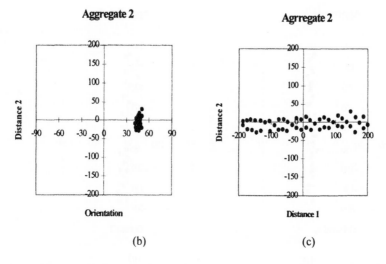

(b)   (c)

Figure 6.10   Distribution of features of cross-section arrangement in the Hough space.

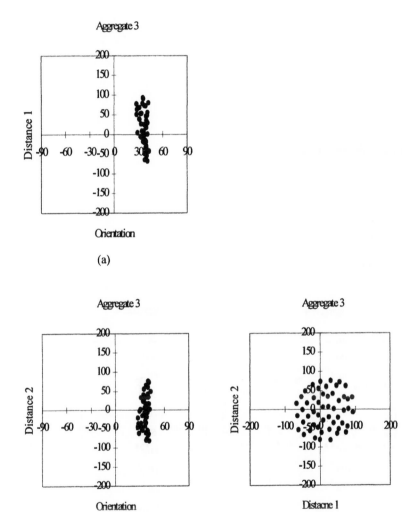

Figure 6.11   Distribution of features of parallel region arrangement in the Hough space.

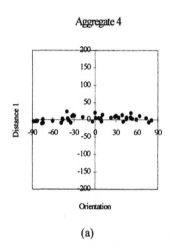

(a)

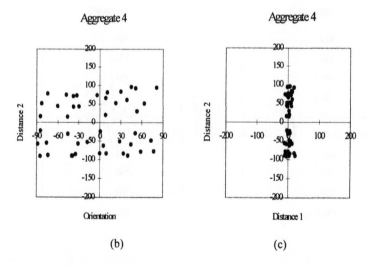

(b)   (c)

Figure 6.12   Distribution of features of radial arrangement in the Hough space.

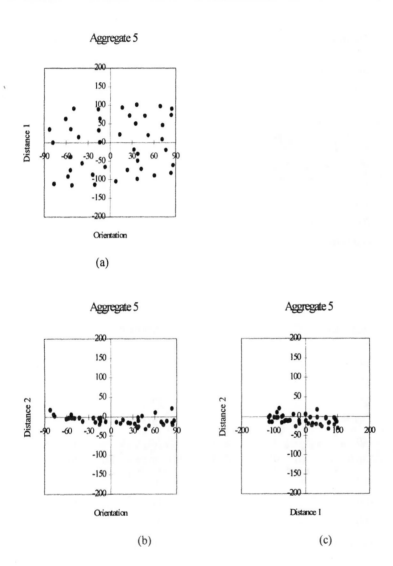

Figure 6.13   Distribution of features of circumferential arrangement in the Hough space.

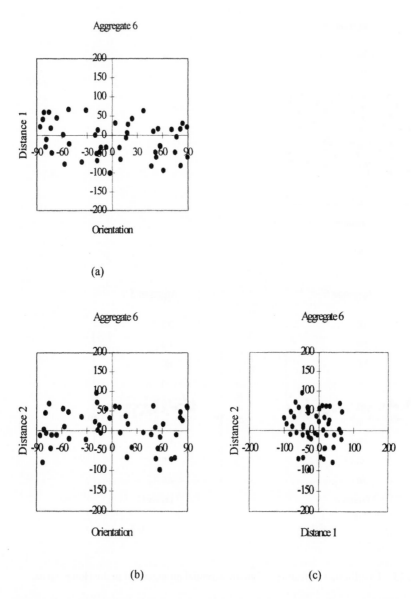

Figure 6.14   Distribution of features of random region arrangement in the Hough space.

For the three parallel arrangements, we can see from Tables 6.1 - 6.3 and Figure 6.9 - 6.11 that the orientations concentrate in a narrow range. However, for the three non-parallel arrangements we can see from Tables 6.4 - 6.6 and Figure 6.12 - 6.14 that the orientations spread over the whole range from -90° to +90°. It seems that, as expected, the consistency ratio (which is akin to the standard deviation of the orientation (see Appendix 6A) can be used to separate parallel from non-parallel arrangements.

Figure 6.9 shows the feature distributions of parallel vertical-section arrangement in Figure 6.1. (a) shows the distance ρ_1 against orientation θ and (b) the distance ρ_2 against θ. From (a) and (b), we can see that θ concentrates in a very narrow range. This means that the orientations of the objects are almost the same, i.e. they are parallel to each other. We can also see that ρ_1 has much more narrow distribution than ρ_2, this implies that the arrangement of the objects form a strip or a band along the direction of the objects. Thus Figure 6.9 corresponds as expected to the fact that the objects are in parallel arrangements and form a band-shaped aggregate, which is thin in the direction perpendicular to θ, and long in the direction parallel to θ.

Figure 6.10 (for the parallel cross-section arrangement in Figure 6.2) is similar to Figure 6.9 in that the orientations are within a narrow range. But on contrary to Figure 6.9, the distribution of ρ_1 is much wider than that of ρ_2. It is clear that the objects are parallel and close to each other to form a band-shaped aggregate, which is long in the direction perpendicular to θ and thin in the direction parallel to θ.

Figure 6.11 represents the parallel region arrangement in Figure 6.3. The fact that both ρ_1 and ρ_2 are in wider range imply that the objects scatter in the directions both perpendicular and parallel to θ.

Figure 6.12 represents the radial region arrangement in Figure 6.4. From Figure 6.12 (a), we know that the widely spread orientations θ are of nearly uniform distribution, and the fact that the distances ρ_1 are narrowly concentrated around a mean of zero indicates that the objects are towards one point to form a radial arrangement. From Figure 6.12 (b) and (c), we can see that the distribution of ρ_2 has a wider range.

Figure 6.13 represents the circumferential region arrangement in Figure 6.5. The distribution of ρ_1 is wider than in Figure 6.12 and the distribution of ρ_2 is narrow. It is clear that the objects lie on circles which are concentric and form an aggregate ring by ring.

Figure 6.14 represents the random region arrangement in Figure 6.6. Obviously, from (a) and (b), the orientations θ are random, and the distances ρ_1 and ρ_2 are in wide range.

Hence, by comparing Figs. 6.9 - 6.11, it seems that the three parallel arrangements can be separated as follows:

Arrangements	Standard deviation of ρ_1	Standard deviation of ρ_2
1. vertical-section	low	high
2. cross-section	high	low
3. region scattered	high	high
4. very small region	low	low

where the scheme has had to be extended to include the possibility of a very small region arrangement.

Similarly, the three non-parallel arrangements can be separated as follows:

Arrangements	Standard deviation of ρ_1	Standard deviation of ρ_2
1. radial	low	high
2. circumferential	high	low
3. random	high	high
4. very small region	low	low

Although the above analysis was based on idealised images, we can see that there do exist quite big differences among the features of different arrangements of objects within aggregates. This means that the features θ, ρ_1, and ρ_2 are suitable for recognition of the six classes of aggregates defined in Section 6.1.2.

6.4.3   Feature Extraction
For the purpose of recognition and classification of aggregates, the features which describe aggregates can therefore be extracted from the measurements θ, ρ_1 and ρ_2 of the arrangements of the objects within aggregates.

(1)   Standard Deviations Θ, P_1, and P_2 of θ, ρ_1, and ρ_2
From Figure 6.9 - 6.14, as discussed above, the parallel arrangements have a dense θ, but the non-parallel arrangements do not; the vertical-section and the radial arrangements have a dense ρ_1 but not ρ_2; the cross-section and the circumferential arrangement have a dense ρ_2 but not ρ_1. Therefore, we adopt the standard deviations Θ, P_1 and P_2 of θ, ρ_1, and ρ_2 as features for classification.

Theoretically, the following properties hold for the six arrangements in the Hough space:
(a) Θ should be 0° for the parallel arrangements;
(b) P_1 should be 0 for the radial arrangement and a very low value for vertical-section arrangement:
(c) P_2 should be 0 for the circumferential arrangement and a very low value for the cross-section arrangement.

Actually, although the objects are not exactly parallel to each other, strictly radial, nor precisely concentric, the properties above still hold roughly. To support this conclusion, some experimental results are listed in Table 6.7, where θ, $\overline{\rho}_1$ and

$\bar{\rho}_2$ are the mean values of θ, ρ_1, and ρ_2, respectively. Thus, the parallel and the non-parallel arrangements can be distinguished by Θ; the three parallel arrangements and the three non-parallel arrangements are classified by P_1 and P_2.

Table 6.7 Features extracted from the features in Hough space.

Arrangements	$\bar{\theta}$	$\bar{\rho}_1$	$\bar{\rho}_2$	Θ	P_1	P_2
Parallel vertical-section	30.42	2.59	3.88	2.95	14.67	111.28
Parallel cross-section	46.62	1.51	-4.53	1.99	116.00	13.96
Parallel region	36.72	14.39	-2.70	3.95	44.52	45.67
Radial region	-6.95	3.11	-4.03	50.67	8.09	66.57
Circumferential region	7.91	-6.27	-8.11	51.64	70.22	11.58
Random region	2.86	-11.00	6.91	56.23	46.03	45.52

(2) The Consistency Ratio R_θ of θ

As discussed previously, the orientations θ are defined in the range from -90° to +90°. However, in some cases, the orientations θ may distribute around the boundary -90° and +90°. In this case, to guarantee the correct classification, the consistency ratio was chosen in preference to the standard deviation of θ. The consistency ratio R_θ of θ is defined in Appendix 6A.

The experimental results of the consistency ratio R_θ of θ for the six arrangements are listed in Table 6.8. From Table 6.8, it is clear that R_θ has a high value for parallel arrangements and a low value for non-parallel arrangements.

(3) The Ratio R_P of the Standard Deviations P_1 and P_2

It is possible to classify the six arrangements by the features Θ, P_1, P_2 and R_θ. However, the two dimensions P_1, P_2 can be reduced to one dimension by their ratio r_P.

$$r_P = P_2 / P_1 . \tag{6.4.4}$$

From Table 6.7, we know that the limits of r_P are 0 and ∞. This is not convenient for decision making in pattern classification. Therefore, instead of the ratio r_P, we use another normalised value of R_P as one of the features for the purpose of classification:

$$R_P = \frac{2}{\pi} \tan^{-1} \frac{P_2}{P_1} \tag{6.4.5}$$

giving limits of 0 and 1 for R_p.   The experimental results of R_p for the six arrangements are given in Table 6.8.   From the results, we can see that R_p has a high value for vertical-section and radial arrangement and a low value for cross-section and circumferential arrangement.

The above ideas can readily be extended to allow other arrangements of objects within aggregates to be analysed.   Some examples of further possible arrangements are now discussed.

Table 6.8   Features extracted for description and classification.

Arrangements	R_θ	R_p
Parallel vertical-section	0.99	0.92
Parallel cross-section	1.00	0.08
Parallel region	0.99	0.51
Radial region	0.03	0.92
Circumferential region	0.06	0.10
Random region	0.11	0.50

6.5   MORE ARRANGEMENTS AND FEATURES

6.5.1   More Arrangements
The four possible arrangements now given as examples are: shear, parallel hollow, radial hollow, and circumferential hollow arrangements.

(1)   Shear Arrangements
An example of shear arrangement is shown in Figure 6.15.   This arrangement seems to be formed by shearing the parallel cross-section arrangement.

(2)   Parallel Hollow Arrangement
An example of the parallel hollow arrangement is given in Figure 6.16.   It seems to be made by digging out the central part of the parallel region arrangement.

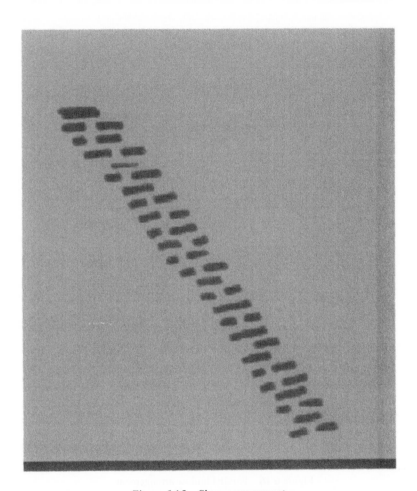

Figure 6.15   Shear arrangement.

(3) Radial Hollow Arrangements
Figure 6.17 shows an example of the radial hollow arrangement. This arrangement can be considered as a radial region with a hollow centre.

(4) Circumferential Hollow Arrangement
Figure 6.18 gives an example of the circumferential hollow arrangement. It seems to be the circumferential region arrangements with a hollow centre.

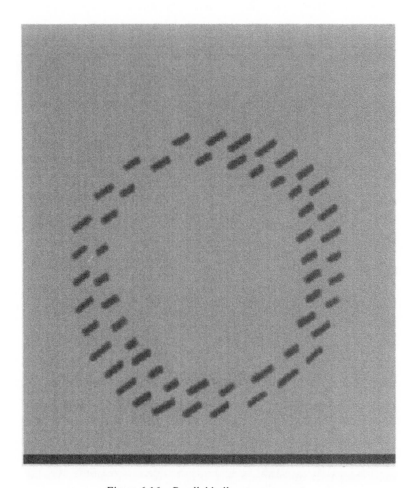

Figure 6.16   Parallel hollow arrangement.

6.5.2 Measurements

These four more arrangements were processed in the same way as the six "basic" arrangements to produce their measurements of θ, x, and y in (x,y) space and their features of θ, ρ_1, and ρ_2 in the Hough space.   The measurements and the features are listed in Tables 6.9 - 6.12, respectively.   The θ, ρ_1, and ρ_2 are plotted in Figure 6.19 - 6.22.   The features extracted similarly are put into Table 6.13 and 6.14.

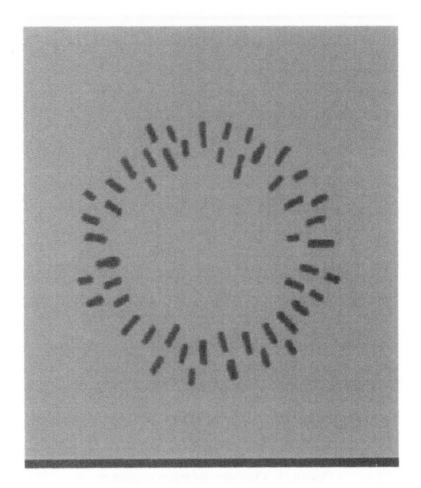

Figure 6.17   Radial hollow arrangement.

From Figure 6.19 - 6.22, it is clear that the distributions of the objects are quite different in the four new arrangements and in the six "basic" arrangements. From Table 6.14, we can know that the first two arrangements of the four can be completely distinguished from the first two of the six in Table 6.8, but are not clearly distinguished from the third of the six. The last two of the four are not very different from the radial and the circumferential arrangements of the six.

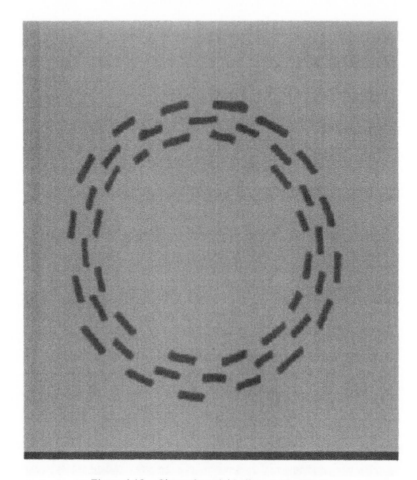

Figure 6.18   Circumferential hollow arrangement.

If the above analysis method, which allows only for the existence of the six "basic" arrangements, were applied, the shear arrangement or the parallel hollow would be probably classified as a parallel region arrangement. The radial hollow and the circumferential hollow arrangements would be classified as radial and circumferential region arrangement, respectively. Hence, more features need to be extracted from θ, ρ_1, and ρ_2 to distinguish the four from the six.

Table 6.9   The experimental results of shear arrangement.

Particle No.	x	y	θ	ρ_1	ρ_2
1	-129.52	148.09	0.57	149.36	-128.05
2	-97.98	135.40	0.18	135.72	-97.54
3	-134.43	133.61	5.67	146.25	-120.57
4	-98.62	122.02	3.66	128.07	-90.63
5	-128.91	120.27	-0.57	118.99	-130.09
6	-74.02	109.27	4.68	114.94	-64.86
7	-109.91	107.03	5.83	117.64	-98.47
8	-84.10	95.14	2.66	98.94	-79.60
9	-60.37	86.56	6.02	92.42	-50.96
10	-94.22	83.72	4.58	90.97	-87.23
11	-69.22	71.92	7.87	80.72	-58.71
12	-40.85	63.36	10.64	69.82	-28.45
13	-68.86	57.76	11.26	70.10	-56.25
14	-26.50	47.44	7.81	50.60	-19.81
15	-56.87	44.66	12.99	56.30	-45.38
16	-22.64	32.41	9.55	35.71	-16.95
17	-52.15	28.93	10.37	37.84	-46.09
18	-4.80	20.85	11.95	21.39 ·	-0.38
19	-36.89	16.91	6.24	20.83	-34.83
20	-8.80	7.85	8.62	9.08	-7.52
21	-33.55	1.99	8.47	6.91	-32.89
22	10.09	-4.73	6.32	-5.81	9.50
23	-18.12	-9.98	11.45	-6.18	-19.74
24	3.80	-18.88	4.45	-19.11	2.32
25	28.20	-27.64	8.38	-31.46	23.87
26	2.65	-34.23	0.21	-34.24	2.52
27	27.60	-44.86	10.60	-49.17	18.88
28	48.64	-55.87	9.13	-62.88	39.16
29	23.66	-60.15	7.38	-62.69	15.74
30	44.42	-71.99	10.94	-79.12	29.95
31	63.06	-81.29	6.85	-88.23	52.91
32	52.51	-95.62	11.31	-104.06	32.73
33	80.79	-104.34	10.57	-117.38	60.28
34	54.47	-110.74	10.60	-118.87	33.18
35	91.84	-117.64	13.42	-135.74	62.02
36	63.55	-125.10	13.48	-136.47	32.64
37	87.45	-131.26	12.46	-147.04	57.07
38	108.41	-140.73	2.22	-144.82	102.88
39	80.01	-146.50	5.01	-152.93	66.90
40	104.33	-155.11	10.25	-171.19	75.07
41	124.41	-163.93	7.96	-179.58	100.50
42	95.00	-170.05	11.40	-185.48	59.51

Table 6.10　The experimental results of parallel hollow arrangement.

Particle No.	x	y	θ	ρ_1	ρ_2
1	-23.81	114.98	25.66	113.95	28.32
2	12.35	116.59	30.84	93.77	70.38
3	36.79	112.02	32.17	75.23	90.78
4	63.81	106.83	35.67	49.57	114.13
5	-0.86	95.83	31.13	82.48	48.80
6	84.47	96.21	32.23	36.33	122.77
7	-74.59	91.60	30.06	116.64	-18.68
8	-44.47	91.47	29.26	101.53	5.92
9	33.67	92.67	30.68	62.52	76.24
10	54.01	83.75	35.31	37.12	92.49
11	103.78	83.16	33.45	12.18	132.43
12	75.57	73.59	29.27	27.25	101.90
13	117.84	68.44	34.45	-10.21	135.89
14	-79.60	64.74	30.74	96.34	-35.32
15	-103.72	64.17	31.80	109.20	-54.33
16	93.50	63.29	39.26	-10.16	112.45
17	104.39	45.85	38.38	-28.87	110.30
18	126.66	42.68	35.06	-37.82	128.19
19	-98.64	39.35	33.50	87.25	-60.54
20	-127.44	32.49	33.78	97.86	-87.86
21	129.52	21.00	30.38	-47.40	122.35
22	102.77	20.49	37.00	-45.49	94.40
23	-106.53	6.56	40.08	73.60	-77.29
24	-130.01	4.15	39.10	85.21	-98.28
25	133.04	-1.15	28.17	-63.82	116.74
26	107.26	-1.27	29.81	-54.43	92.43
27	110.26	-19.97	33.35	-77.31	81.12
28	134.71	-22.87	26.57	-80.71	110.25
29	-128.21	-21.67	36.61	59.06	-115.84
30	-107.04	-23.29	33.01	38.78	-102.45
31	111.05	-39.51	32.37	-92.83	72.63
32	130.84	-45.79	27.91	-101.72	94.18
33	-98.34	-45.12	30.79	11.59	-107.57
34	-125.03	-48.01	37.48	37.99	-128.42
35	103.83	-63.28	31.35	-108.06	55.75
36	-89.14	-67.77	34.39	-5.58	-111.84
37	-118.58	-71.38	36.16	12.34	-137.85
38	118.80	-73.40	33.96	-127.25	57.53
39	-76.27	-87.48	33.02	-31.78	-111.63

Table 6.10 (cont.)

Particle No.	x	y	θ	ρ_1	ρ_2
40	88.69	-94.49	36.58	-128.73	14.92
41	-108.52	-94.47	38.82	-5.57	-143.77
42	112.09	-97.94	40.79	-147.38	20.89
43	-66.02	-99.85	33.24	-47.33	-109.95
44	-94.54	-111.98	36.86	-32.88	-142.81
45	-51.27	-114.68	28.16	-76.91	-99.33
46	58.96	-116.51	33.18	-129.78	-14.41
47	84.61	-120.31	37.49	-146.96	-6.10
48	-35.11	-127.94	32.33	-89.33	-98.09
49	-81.80	-128.93	36.49	-55.00	-142.45
50	-8.00	-129.79	30.96	-107.18	-73.62
51	22.10	-132.52	35.11	-121.12	-58.14
52	-65.32	-141.96	32.06	-85.64	-130.72
53	53.04	-141.89	32.50	-148.17	-31.51
54	-43.08	-149.89	28.50	-111.17	-109.37
55	-13.85	-152.63	34.44	-118.04	-97.75
56	14.65	-152.95	35.15	-133.49	-76.08

Table 6.11   The experimental results of radial hollow arrangement.

Particle No.	x	y	θ	ρ_1	ρ_2
1	21.31	126.18	73.26	15.93	126.97
2	-35.78	123.92	-64.59	20.85	-127.29
3	-55.61	124.09	-63.95	4.54	-135.90
4	43.90	122.35	74.22	-8.97	129.67
5	-3.20	123.16	-86.00	5.41	-123.08
6	-21.66	109.15	-84.12	-10.36	-110.79
7	14.37	102.10	79.59	4.32	103.02
8	53.69	103.81	57.46	10.57	116.39
9	78.30	102.14	54.93	-5.39	128.58
10	-58.37	99.98	-56.97	5.56	-115.64
11	-37.59	98.54	-61.97	13.12	-104.65
12	-79.97	90.23	-56.44	-16.76	-119.40
13	33.47	91.22	73.88	-6.82	96.93

Table 6.11 (cont.)

Particle No.	x	y	θ	ρ₁	ρ₂
14	97.10	82.45	27.27	28.79	124.09
15	-56.86	74.54	-54.91	-3.67	-93.68
16	71.43	74.33	47.30	-2.09	103.07
17	-94.23	72.78	-34.76	6.08	-118.91
18	-120.42	63.32	-34.70	-16.50	-135.05
19	116.78	58.28	28.30	-4.03	130.45
20	90.09	55.33	27.30	7.84	105.43
21	-95.88	51.03	-33.72	-10.77	-108.08
22	-119.34	39.52	-16.17	4.71	-125.63
23	112.42	37.71	16.97	3.25	118.54
24	89.16	20.77	10.33	4.44	91.44
25	-114.19	21.43	-6.35	8.66	-115.86
26	117.87	15.74	-0.09	15.94	117.84
27	-101.31	-2.73	6.86	9.39	-100.91
28	105.60	-10.12	-17.43	21.97	103.78
29	-125.25	-19.84	7.01	-4.41	-126.73
30	129.82	-18.88	-16.39	18.51	129.87
31	-96.74	-22.95	20.56	12.48	-98.63
32	90.55	-25.28	-20.97	8.80	93.60
33	113.15	-36.24	-28.77	22.69	116.63
34	-114.97	-41.13	18.88	-1.71	-122.10
35	-87.73	-40.46	32.99	13.83	-95.62
36	95.82	-48.48	-37.40	19.69	105.57
37	82.72	-62.80	-45.61	15.18	102.74
38	-78.87	-64.83	48.26	15.68	-100.89
39	-59.40	-74.89	56.60	8.36	-95.21
40	64.85	-73.90	-60.01	19.23	96.42
41	-35.45	-75.49	59.48	-7.80	-83.03
42	16.18	-81.97	-71.62	-10.49	82.89
43	41.11	-83.26	-75.37	18.75	90.94
44	86.49	-87.97	-57.54	25.76	120.65
45	-24.42	-93.75	74.31	-1.84	-96.86
46	-4.04	-92.45	-87.37	-8.28	92.17
47	59.74	-98.11	-71.61	25.74	111.95
48	-51.53	-104.66	57.21	-13.37	-115.89
49	25.73	-109.39	-77.22	0.90	112.37
50	-16.33	-116.93	87.39	10.99	-117.55

Table 6.12 The experimental results of circumferential hollow arrangement.

Particle No.	x	y	θ	ρ_1	ρ_2
1	27.09	144.75	-5.63	146.71	12.77
2	-31.55	143.48	16.62	146.51	10.80
3	-1.84	131.15	4.36	130.91	8.14
4	-83.53	125.31	33.57	150.60	-0.30
5	43.49	120.88	-21.40	128.41	-3.61
6	69.26	124.74	-27.06	142.59	4.94
7	-56.71	119.01	22.44	131.65	-6.99
8	18.43	114.55	-12.98	115.77	-7.76
9	-29.19	111.17	16.70	114.87	3.99
10	-65.97	94.96	39.73	115.19	9.97
11	78.03	96.72	-45.31	123.49	-13.89
12	-96.93	95.78	50.69	135.68	12.70
13	104.41	89.34	-49.85	137.41	-0.97
14	-124.03	83.40	60.31	149.05	11.03
15	77.77	74.99	-49.67	107.82	-6.84
16	-96.58	73.54	60.88	120.16	17.26
17	103.50	56.73	-64.10	117.89	-5.83
18	-118.61	54.44	73.29	129.25	18.03
19	125.27	40.97	-69.10	131.64	6.42
20	99.61	31.43	-66.63	103.90	10.65
21	-112.09	30.33	79.02	115.82	8.43
22	-138.57	28.76	83.63	140.90	13.22
23	116.95	12.64	-85.35	117.59	-3.11
24	-125.06	0.71	-85.28	-124.58	-11.00
25	104.24	-12.89	80.93	-104.97	3.71
26	135.01	-14.26	88.61	-135.31	-10.97
27	-109.90	-25.81	-76.75	-112.89	-0.07
28	117.54	-29.17	77.19	-121.09	-2.38

Table 6.12 (cont.)

Particle No.	x	y	θ	ρ_1	ρ_2
29	-132.50	-36.03	-74.20	-137.30	-1.42
30	92.08	-47.79	64.50	-103.68	-3.50
31	-111.33	-53.76	-60.74	-123.41	-7.52
32	121.66	-60.14	67.20	-135.46	-8.31
33	-83.43	-69.99	-46.23	-108.66	-7.17
34	97.05	-72.58	47.42	-120.57	12.22
35	69.46	-80.48	39.52	-106.28	2.36
36	-117.29	-85.39	-49.64	-144.67	-10.88
37	-85.78	-95.08	-39.40	-127.92	-5.93
38	-25.14	-103.81	-11.08	-106.71	-4.72
39	28.89	-103.70	20.79	-107.20	-9.80
40	58.92	-105.25	35.79	-119.83	-13.77
41	86.28	-106.01	42.62	-136.43	-8.30
42	-40.66	-118.27	-14.88	-124.75	-8.92
43	8.30	-123.13	-0.42	-123.07	9.20
44	-68.82	-122.99	-24.43	-140.44	-11.79
45	43.36	-128.14	19.79	-135.25	-2.60
46	-16.07	-141.01	-6.10	-141.92	-0.98

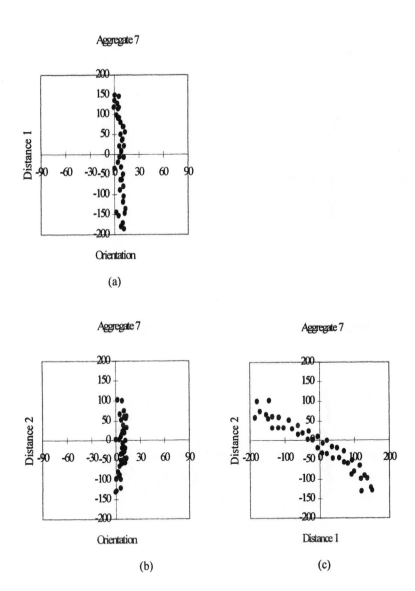

Figure 6.19   Distribution of features of shear arrangement in the Hough space.

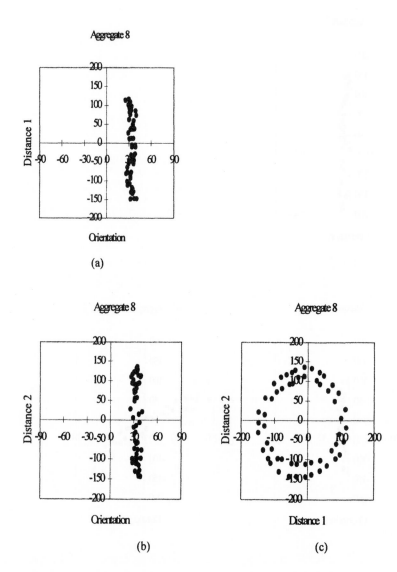

Figure 6.20   Distribution of features of parallel hollow arrangement in the Hough space.

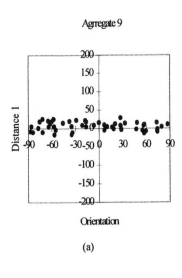

(a)

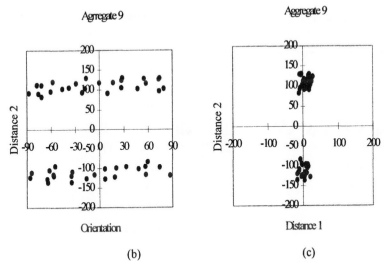

(b)   (c)

Figure 6.21   Distribution of features of radial hollow arrangement in the Hough space.

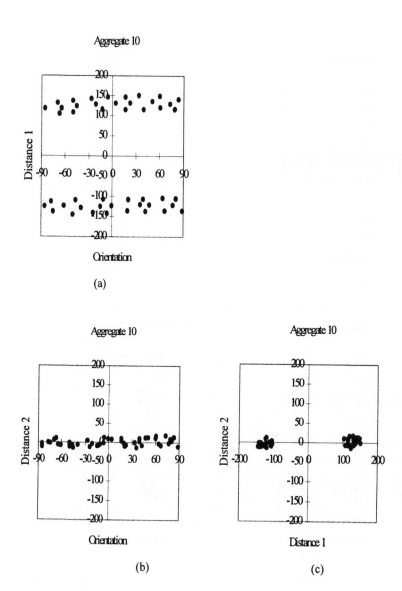

Figure 6.22   Distribution of features of circumferential hollow in the Hough space.

Table 6.13   Features extracted from the features in Hough space.

Arrangements	$\bar{\theta}$	$\bar{\rho}_1$	$\bar{\rho}_2$	Θ	P_1	P_2
shear	7.70	-9.04	-10.41	3.81	101.57	61.98
parallel hollow	33.34	-19.47	-4.96	3.47	81.88	95.06
radial hollow	-5.63	5.89	3.29	53.18	11.84	116.61
circumferential hollow	3.03	2.42	-0.08	52.57	126.69	8.90

Table 6.14   Features extracted for description and classification.

Arrangements	R_θ	R_p
shear	0.99	0.35
parallel hollow	0.99	0.55
radial hollow	0.08	0.93
circumferential hollow	0.03	0.04

6.5.3   More Features

From Figure 6.19 (c), it can be seen that in the shear arrangement ρ_1 and ρ_2 are correlated in the Hough space (Figure 6.19 (c)). This distribution is quite different from that of any of the other parallel arrangements (Figure 6.9-6.11). Hence, we may choose the dot-product of ρ_1 and ρ_2 (normalised as defined below) for an aggregate as the feature to discriminate the symmetry.

Furthermore, comparing Figure 6.20 - 6.22 with Figure 6.9 - 6.14, it is obvious that the hollow arrangements have bimodal or ring-like distributions. The distributions are clearly different from those of the corresponding region arrangements. The characteristic of these distributions is that they have a much higher value of the standard deviation of the modulus of the vectors $v(\rho_1,\rho_2)$ than the corresponding region arrangements. From this point of view, I choose this standard deviation as another feature for the classification.

The following two sections will discuss these two features.

(1)   Symmetry Factor S

As explained above, a normalised dot-product of ρ_1 and ρ_2 for an aggregate can be used as a measure of the symmetry of an arrangement (the normalisation is desirable for classification purposes). Thus the symmetry factor S is defined as:

$$S = \frac{\sum\limits_{i=1}^{N} \rho_{1i}\rho_{2i}}{\sum\limits_{i=1}^{N} (\rho_{1i}^2 + \rho_{2i}^2)} . \qquad (6.5.1)$$

(This form is preferred to the standard correlation coefficient, which in some cases could become 0/0 in this application). The range of S is from 0 to 1/2. If the distribution is symmetric with respect to ρ_1 or ρ_2, S would give a value 0. If it is symmetric with respect to the line in 45° or -45°, S would have the value 1/2.

The experimental values of the symmetry factor S for the ten arrangements are listed in Table 6.15. In Table 6.15, S has the highest value for the shear arrangement and very low values for the parallel and other arrangements. This result agrees with what we desired. Hence, the shear arrangement can be distinguished from the parallel region arrangements.

(2)   Standard Deviation S_r of the Modulus of the Vectors v(ρ_1,ρ_2)
Let r_i be the modulus of the *ith* vector $v(\rho_{1i},\rho_{2i})$:

$$r_i = \sqrt{\rho_{1i}^2 + \rho_{2i}^2} \qquad (6.5.2)$$

and $\bar{r}$ be the mean value of r_i:

$$\bar{r} = \frac{1}{N}\sum_{i=1}^{N} r_i \qquad (6.5.3)$$

then the standard deviation s_r of the modulus of the vectors is:

$$s_r = \sqrt{\frac{1}{N}\sum_{i=1}^{N} (r_i - \bar{r})^2} . \qquad (6.5.4)$$

To classify the hollow type arrangements, we prefer to choose the normalised standard deviation S_r by the mean $\bar{r}$ of the vectors as one another of the features:

$$S_r = s_r / \bar{r} . \qquad (6.5.5)$$

The range of S_r is from 0 to 1. S_r has much lower value for the dense distributions than the scattered ones. The experimental results of S_r for the ten arrangements are listed in Table 6.15. From this table, it is clear that the hollow type arrangements have much lower values of S_r than the corresponding region arrangements.

The computer program *arrnanal.cpp* of the algorithm for the arrangement analysis, written in language C++ by the author, was listed in Computer Programs at the end of this book.

Table 6.15   Features extracted for description and classification.

Arrangements	S	S_r
parallel vertical-section	0.08	0.55
parallel cross-section	0.02	0.55
parallel region	0.04	0.37
radial region	0.02	0.38
circumferential region	0.05	0.47
random region	0.08	0.42
shear	0.41	0.57
parallel hollow	0.01	0.13
radial hollow	0.03	0.12
circumferential hollow	0.04	0.11

6.6   DESCRIPTION AND CLASSIFICATION OF ARRANGEMENTS

6.6.1   Description

Theoretically, there may exist many sorts of arrangements of objects within aggregates.   In practice, we may be concerned with some particular arrangement classes.   Some other arrangements may be classified into these particular classes. In the study of soil microstructure, we take account of the ten particular classes mentioned above.   From the discussion above, we set up a 4-dimensional pattern space (R_θ, R_p, S, S_r) to describe the ten classes.   Each aggregate is projected onto one point in the pattern space.

The values of R_θ, R_p, S, and S_r for the artificial examples of each of the ten arrangements are given in Table 6.16.   Bar charts for the ten arrangements in the pattern space are plotted in Figure 6.23, grouped according to features in Figure 6.23 (a), and according to arrangements in Figure 6.23 (b).

Table 6.16   Features extracted for description and classification.

Arrangements	R_θ	R_p	S	S_r
parallel vertical-section	0.99	0.92	0.08	0.55
parallel cross-section	1.00	0.08	0.02	0.55
shear	0.99	0.35	0.41	0.57
parallel hollow	0.99	0.55	0.01	0.13
parallel region	0.99	0.51	0.04	0.37
radial region	0.03	0.92	0.02	0.38
radial hollow	0.08	0.93	0.03	0.12
circumferential region	0.06	0.10	0.05	0.47
circumferential hollow	0.03	0.04	0.04	0.11
random region	0.11	0.50	0.08	0.42

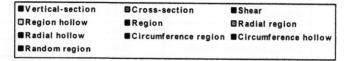

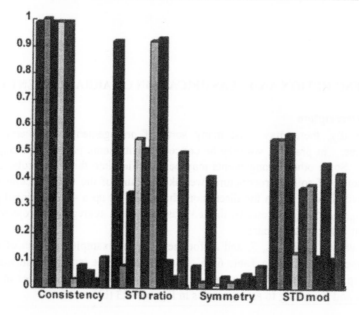

Figure 6.23 (a)   Bar chart for the patterns. Consistency: R_θ,   STD ratio: R_p, Symmetry: S,   STD mod: S_r.

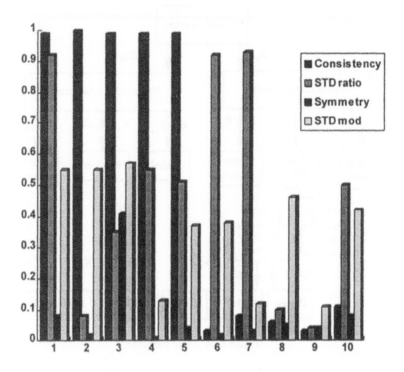

Figure 6.23 (b).   Bar chart for the patterns.   1. Parallel vertical-section;
2. parallel cross-section;   3. shear;   4. parallel hollow;   5. parallel region;
6. radial region;   7. radial hollow;   8. circumferential region;
9. circumferential hollow;   10. random region.
Consistency: R_θ,   STD ratio: R_P,   Symmetry: S,   STD mod: S_r .

6.6.2   Classification

Table 6.16 and Figure 6.23 suggest that aggregates in real soil micrographs, as represented in the above-defined feature space, may tend to be clustered according to the arrangements of particles within the aggregates. This suggests the possibility of automatically discriminating between the arrangements by feature-space pattern recognition methods.   One possibility would be a tree classifier (using threshold values) such as the one shown in Figure 6.24.   Although this is not necessarily the kind of classifier that would be used in practice, it is described here because it gives some insight into the structure of the pattern space defined by the four features used.

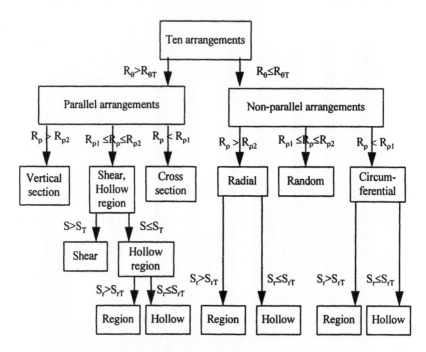

Figure 6.24   Tree classifier.

First of all, the ten arrangements would be classified by R_θ into two groups: parallel arrangements which have very high values of R_θ, and non-parallel arrangements which have very low values of R_θ. The classification rule is:

$$R_\theta > R_{\theta T} \qquad \text{Parallel arrangements}$$
$$R_\theta \leq R_{\theta T} \qquad \text{Non-parallel arrangements}$$

where $R_{\theta T}$ is the boundary between the two classes.

In the parallel group, the arrangements would first be distinguished by R_p into the vertical-section arrangement with a very high value of R_p, cross-section arrangement with a very low value of R_p and the other three arrangements with medium values of R_p. The classification rule in this stage is:

$$R_p > R_{p2} \qquad \text{Vertical-section arrangement}$$
$$R_{p2} \geq R_p \geq R_{p1} \qquad \text{Shear,Hollow,and Region arrangements}$$
$$R_p < R_{p1} \qquad \text{Cross-section arrangement}$$

where R_{P1} and R_{P2} are the boundaries between the three classes. Then, the three arrangements left would be discriminated by S into the shear arrangement which has a very high value of S and the other two arrangements which have very low values of S. The classification rule is:

$$S > S_T \qquad\qquad \text{Shear arrangement}$$
$$S \le S_T \qquad\qquad \text{Hollow and Region arrangements}$$

where S_T is the boundary between the two classes. Finally, the last two parallel arrangements would be classified by S_r into the region scattered arrangement with a high value of S_r and the region hollow arrangement with a low value of S_r. The classification rule is:

$$S_r > S_{rT} \qquad\qquad \text{Region arrangement}$$
$$S_r \le S_{rT} \qquad\qquad \text{Hollow arrangement}$$

where S_{rT} is the boundary between the two classes.

In the non-parallel group, similarly, the arrangements would first be distinguished by R_P into two radial arrangements which have very high values of R_P, two circumferential arrangements which have very low values of R_P, and the random arrangement which has a medium value of R_P:

$$R_P > R_{P2} \qquad\qquad \text{Radial arrangements}$$
$$R_{P2} \ge R_P \ge R_{P1} \qquad\qquad \text{Random region arrangement}$$
$$R_P < R_{P1} \qquad\qquad \text{Circumferential arrangements}$$

Because there is no significant difference among the values of S for the four non-parallel arrangements, there is in this case no need for any classification according to S, and we proceed directly to classification according to S_r. The two radial arrangements would be discriminated by S_r into the radial region arrangement with a high value of S_r and the radial hollow arrangement with a low value of S_r:

$$S_r > S_{rT} \qquad\qquad \text{Radial region arrangement}$$
$$S_r \le S_{rT} \qquad\qquad \text{Radial hollow arrangement}$$

Finally, the two circumferential arrangements would be similarly classified by S_r into the circumferential region arrangement with a high value of S_r and the circumferential region hollow arrangement with a low value of S_r:

$$S_r > S_{rT} \qquad\qquad \text{Circumferential region arrangement}$$
$$S_r \le S_{rT} \qquad\qquad \text{Circumferential hollow arrangement}$$

6.6.3   Further Development

Some other arrangements in addition to the ten we introduced above might be also classified as proposed here, using either the tree classifier or another classifier. Some other features might be needed.

Because I just present the basic and the starting work for the automatic analysis of the arrangements of the objects within an aggregate and the automatic classification of the aggregates, I will not present the further development of the method in this chapter.

6.7   SUMMARY

A method based on Hough transform for feature measurement to describe the arrangements of the objects within an aggregate, and using the extracted features to describe aggregates, has been proposed and has been demonstrated using artificial samples of ten different aggregate structures.   The measurements of an object in (x,y) space are the orientation θ and the position x and y of the object.   The feature measurements in the Hough space mapped by the Hough transform are the orientation θ and the distances ρ_1, and ρ_2.   The extracted features are the consistency ratio R_θ of θ, the ratio R_P of the standard deviation of ρ_1 and ρ_2, the symmetry factor S, and the standard deviation S_r of the modulus of the vectors. Other aggregate structures might also be recognised and classified automatically by this method: additional features might be required.

Based on the experiments and reasoning discussed above, the following conclusions were drawn:

1. The simplified version of the Extended Hough Transform proposed in Section 6.3 provides a possible method of automatic analysis and classification of the arrangements of objects within aggregates when these individual objects can be separated.

2. In more difficult cases, the extended Hough transform proposed in Section 6.2 might provide the basis for an alternative approach.

3. The extended Hough transform is itself worthy of future study.

4. The alternative treatments of the measured parameters suggested in Section 6.5 may be found to be useful in future work.

References

Baver, L. D. (1948) *Soil Physics*, Chapman-Hall, Ltd.

Brewer, R. (1964) *Fabric and Mineral Analysis of Soils*, John Wiley.

Burnham, C. P. (1970) The micromorphology of argillaceous sediments: particularly calcareous clays and siltstones, in Micromorphological Techniques and Applications. *Osmond, D. A. and Bullock, P. (eds.), Technical Monograph, No. 2*, Rothamsted Experimental Station, pp. 83-96.

Costa, L. D. F. and Sandler, M. B. (1990) Implementation of the binary Hough transform in pipelined multi-transputer architectures. *Pritchard, D. J. & Scott C. J. (eds.), Applications of Transputers 2*, IOS Press, pp. 150-155.

Costa, L. D. F., Leng, X., Smart, P., and Sandler. M. B. (1991) Analysis of clay microstructure by transputers. *Durrani, T. S., Sandham, W. A., Soraghan, J. J., & Forbes, S. M. (eds.), Applications of Transputers 3, Vol. I*, IOS Press, pp. 317-322.

Duda, R. O., and Hart, P. E. (1972) Use of Hough transformation to detect lines and curves in pictures, *Communications of the ACM*, Vol. 15, pp. 11-15.

FitzPatrick, E. A. (1984) *Micromorphology of Soils*, Chapman and Hall.

Guerra, C. and Hambrusch, S. (1989) Parallel algorithms for line detection on a mesh, *J. Parallel Distrib. Comput.* Vol. 6, pp. 1-19.

Haralick, R. M. and Shapiro, L. G. (1992) *Computer and Robot Vision*. Addison-Wesley Publishing Company.

Hough, P. V. C. (1962) *A method and means for recognising complex patterns*, US. Patent, No. 3,069,654. (Known only through Duda and Hart 1972, Stockman et al. 1977.)

Krumbein, W. C. and Sloss, L. L. (1955) *Stratigraphy and Sedimentation*, W. H. Freeman and Co.

Kubiena, W. L. (1938) *Micropedology*, Collegiate Press Inc.

Kubiena, W. L. (1953) *The soils of Europe*, Thomas Murby.

O'Gorman, F. and Clowes, M. B. (1976) Finding picture edges through collinearity of feature points, *IEEE Trans. on Computers*, Vol. C-25, pp. 449-454.

Pettijohn, F. J. (1957) *Sedimentary Rocks*. Harper & Row.

Schalkoff, R. J. (1989) *Digital Image Processing and Computer Vision*, John Wiley & Sons Inc.

Smart, P. (1966) Particle arrangements in kaolin. *Clays Clay Minerals*, Vol. 15, pp. 241-254.

Smart, P. (1971) Soil structure in the electron microscope. *Te'eni, M. (ed.), Structure, Solid Mechanics and Engineering Design, The proceedings of the Southampton 1969 Civil Engineering Materials Conference, Part 1*, Wiley-Interscience.

Smart, P. and Tovey, N. K. (1981) *Electron Microscopy of Soils and Sediments: Examples*, Academic press.

Stockman, G. C. and Agrawala, A. K. (1977) Equivalence of Hough curve detection to template matching. *Commu. of the ACM*, Vol. 20, pp. 820-822.

Van Olphen, H. (1963) *An introduction to clay colloid chemistry for clay technologists, geologists, and soil scientists*, Interscience.

Appendix 6A   The Consistency Ratio R_θ of θ

Let x_i and y_i be the components of a unit vector v_i with orientation θ_i:

$$v_i = x_i + jy_i \qquad (6A.1)$$

$$x_i = \cos\theta_i \qquad (6A.2)$$

$$y_i = \sin\theta_i \qquad (6A.3)$$

where $j = \sqrt{-1}$ is the unit imaginary. Then the summation Mod_s of the modulus of all the vectors is given by:

$$Mod_s = \sum_{i=1}^{N}\sqrt{x_i^2 + y_i^2} = \sum_{i=1}^{N}\sqrt{\cos^2\theta_i + \sin^2\theta_i} = \sum_{i=1}^{N}1 = N \qquad (6A.4)$$

where N is the number of the vectors. The composition vector V_c of the all vectors is:

$$_c = X + jY \qquad (6A.5)$$

$$X = \sum_{i=1}^{N}x_i \qquad (6A.6)$$

$$Y = \sum_{i=1}^{N}y_i \cdot \qquad (6A.7)$$

The modulus Mod_c of the composition vector then is:

$$Mod_c = \sqrt{X^2 + Y^2} . \qquad (6A.8)$$

Thus, the consistency ratio R_θ is defined as:

$$R_\theta = Mod_c / Mod_s . \qquad (6A.9)$$

If required, the preferred orientation is:

$$\Theta = \arctan\frac{Y}{X} . \qquad (6A.10)$$

7

Conclusions

The work presented here was aimed principally at a need for analysing objects as recorded in two-dimensional images which might be conventional photographs, optical micrographs, or electron-micrographs. In particular, the work concentrated on feature measurements, where the features were extracted from individual objects such as particles, leaves, industrial spare parts; and the work was intended to complement a parallel study which was concentrating on field or industrial measurements.

The SPCH algorithm for finding the convex hull of a feature, which was presented in Chapter 3, was found to be efficient and is believed to be reliable.

Use of the convex hull of an object led to a rapid method of extracting a set of measurements to describe the shapes of objects, such as leaves of plants. These measurements are invariant with respect to coordinate rotation, translation, and scaling, and the range of each measurement as presented has been arranged to be between 0 and 1.

Use of the convex hull of an object also led to a rapid method of extracting the orientation of the object, i.e. the direction of its elongation. In Chapter 5, this was found to be in general agreement with the perhaps more accurate estimates found by the principal component method and the method of moments, which were in general slower.

The Circular Hough Transform was successfully applied to the measurement of the roundness (sharpness of corners) of two-dimensional objects (particles), see Chapter 4. Estimates of Roundness and Sphericity from two-dimensional views have traditionally been used in the subjective classification of objects; so this use of the Circular Hough Transform together with a measurement of sphericity (given by the Convex Hull, Principal Components, or Method of Moments) places this traditional concept of classification on an objective basis.

In the course of the above, five methods of implementing the Circular Hough Transform were compared from the points of view of memory requirement, speed and accuracy; and methods of dealing both with noise in the image and with very sharp corners were implemented.

The method of Directed Vein, which was also presented in Chapter 5, was found to be faster than the above methods for finding the orientation of a simple object. However, it is based on a different concept and actually estimates the direction of internal preferred orientation in objects for which this is strong. It might, therefore, be sometimes appropriate to use this method in parallel with one of the others when classifying objects.

An extension of the linear Hough transform was suggested in Chapter 6, the basic idea being to separate co-linear objects, which are thrown together in the original method.

Also in Chapter 6, a method of automatic analysis and classification of the arrangements of elongated objects within aggregates was proposed on the basis of the extended linear Hough transform. For cases in which individual objects can be separated, a simplified and less-demanding version of this proposed method was implemented and tested satisfactorily.

Taken together, the methods developed or tested here, provide a useful toolkit for analysing the shapes, orientation, and aggregation of objects (particles) such as those seen in two-dimensional images of soil structure at various scales.

Computer Programs

===

```
/*
  File name:      edgfoll.cpp
  Version         199807
  Author:         Dr. D. Luo
  Description:  This program is used for finding the boundary of the binary
    image of an object. The input binimg is the binary image of an object,
    start the start point of edge following and binvalue the pixel value of
    the binary image. The output bndry is the boundary containing the boundary
    points of the object.
*/
/* ---------- Starting the program of edge following ---------- */
void EdgFoll(Image *binimg,Point start,int binvalue,Boundary *bndry)
{
  int m,m0,m1,m2,n,n0,n1,n2,count1,code,temp,maxcount;

  maxcount=bndry->size;
  m=start.x; n=start.y;
  m0=m1=m2=m; n0=n1=n2=n;
  count1=1;
  bndry->x[count1]=m; bndry->y[count1]=n;
  if (binimg->image[n+1][m-1]==binvalue) { code=11;}
  else {
    if (binimg->image[n+1][m]==binvalue) { code=12;}
    else {
      if (binimg->image[n+1][m+1]==binvalue) {code=13;}
      else {
        if (binimg->image[n][m+1]==binvalue) {code=14;}
        else {
          code=20;
          }
        }
      }
    }
  temp=code;
  while(temp<20) {
    code=temp;
    switch(code) {
      case 1:
        if (binimg->image[n+1][m-1]==binvalue) {temp=11;}
```

```
    else {temp=2;}
    break;

  case 2:
    if (binimg->image[n+1][m]==binvalue) {temp=12;}
    else {temp=3;}
    break;

  case 3:
    if (binimg->image[n+1][m+1]==binvalue) {temp=13;}
    else {temp=4;}
    break;

  case 4:
   if (binimg->image[n][m+1]==binvalue) {temp=14;}
   else {temp=5;}
   break;

  case 5:
   if (binimg->image[n-1][m+1]==binvalue) {temp=15;}
   else {temp=6;}
   break;

  case 6:
   if (binimg->image[n-1][m]==binvalue) {temp=16;}
   else {temp=7;}
   break;

  case 7:
   if (binimg->image[n-1][m-1]==binvalue) { temp=17;}
   else {temp=8;}
   break;

  case 8:
   if (binimg->image[n][m-1]==binvalue) {temp=18;}
   else {temp=1;}
   break;

  case 11:
   m--; n++; count1++;
   if (count1>maxcount-1) {
    printf("The number of boundary points exceeds memory size!\n");
    exit(1);
    }
```

```
  bndry->x[count1]=m;  bndry->y[count1]=n; temp=7;
  break;

case 12:
  n++; count1++;
  if (count1>maxcount-1) {
    printf("The number of boundary points exceeds memory size!\n");
    exit(1);
    }

  bndry->x[count1]=m; bndry->y[count1]=n; temp=1;
  break;

case 13:
  m++; n++; count1++;
  if (count1>maxcount-1) {
    printf("The number of boundary points exceeds memory size!\n");
    exit(1);
    }
  bndry->x[count1]=m; bndry->y[count1]=n; temp=1;
  break;

case 14:
  m++; count1++;
  if (count1>maxcount-1) {
    printf("The number of boundary points exceeds memory size!\n");
    exit(1);
    }
  bndry->x[count1]=m;  bndry->y[count1]=n; temp=3;
  break;

case 15:
  m++; n--; count1++;
  if (count1>maxcount-1) {
    printf("The number of boundary points exceeds memory size!\n");
    exit(1);
    }
  bndry->x[count1]=m; bndry->y[count1]=n;
  if (m!=m0 || n!=n0){temp=3;}
  else {temp=19;}
  break;

case 16:
  n--; count1++;
```

```
      if (count1>maxcount-1) {
        printf("The number of boundary points exceeds memory size!\n");
        exit(1);}
      bndry->x[count1]=m; bndry->y[count1]=n;
      if (m!=m0 || n!=n0) {temp=5;}
      else {temp=20;}
      break;

   case 17:
      m--; n--; count1++;
      if (count1>maxcount-1) {
        printf("The number of boundary points exceeds memory size!\n");
        exit(1);
        }
      bndry->x[count1]=m; bndry->y[count1]=n;
      if (m!=m0 || n!=n0) {temp=5;}
      else {temp=20;}
      break;

   case 18:
      m--; count1++;
      if (count1>maxcount-1) {
        printf("The number of boundary points exceeds memory size!\n");
        exit(1);
        }
      bndry->x[count1]=m; bndry->y[count1]=n;
      if (m!=m0 || n!=n0) {temp=7;}
      else {temp=20;}
      break;

   case 19:
      if (binimg->image[n+1][m+1]==binvalue) {temp=13;}
      else {
        if (binimg->image[n][m+1]==binvalue) {temp=14;}
        else {temp=20;}
        }
      break;

   default:
      break;
      }
    }
  bndry->length=count1;
}
```

```
/* ---------- End of the program of edge following ---------- */


/*
    File name:      simpoly.cpp
    Version         199807
    Author:         Dr. D. Luo
    Description: This program is used for finding the simple polygon of an object  in
a
    binary image. The input binimg is the boundary or the binary image of an object
    and binvalue the pixel value of the boundary or the binary image. The output
    polygon is the simple polygon containing the vetices of the polygon of the object.
*/
/* ---------- Starting the program of finding simple polygon ---------- */
void SimPoly(Image *binimg,int binvalue,Boundary *polygon)
{
  int l,m,m1,m2,n,n1,n2,nn,count1,maxcount,temp;

  m1=binimg->xmin;
  m2=binimg->xmax;
  n1=binimg->ymin;
  n2=binimg->ymax;
  maxcount=polygon->size;

/* ----- Building chain 1 ----- */
  l=1;
  n=n1;
  while (binimg->image[n][m1]!=binvalue)
    n++;
  polygon->x[l]=m1;
  polygon->y[l]=n;
  nn=n;
  if (n!=n1) {
    m=m1+1;
    while ((n!=n1) && (m<=m2)) {
      n=n1;
      while ((n<=nn) && (binimg->image[n][m]!=binvalue))
        n++;
      if (n<nn){
        l++;
        polygon->x[l]=m;
        polygon->y[l]=n;
        nn=n;
      }
```

```
    m++;
    }
  }
  count1=l;
/* ----- End of building chain 1 ----- */

/* ----- Building chain 2 ----- */
  l=maxcount-1;
  n=n1;
  while (binimg->image[n][m2]!=binvalue) {
    n++;
  }
  polygon->x[l]=m2;
  polygon->y[l]=n;
  nn=n;
  if (n!=n1) {
    m=m2-1;
    while ((n!=n1) && (m>=m1)) {
      n=n1;
      while ((n<=nn) && (binimg->image[n][m]!=binvalue)) {
        n++;
      }
      if (n<nn){
        l--;
        polygon->x[l]=m;
        polygon->y[l]=n;
        nn=n;
      }
      m--;
    }
  }
  temp=l;
/* ----- End of building chain 2 ----- */

/* ----- Linking chain 1 & 2 ----- */
  if (polygon->x[temp]==polygon->x[count1])
    count1--;
  for (l=1;l<=maxcount-temp;l++){
    polygon->x[count1+l]=polygon->x[temp+l-1];
    polygon->y[count1+l]=polygon->y[temp+l-1];
  }
  count1=count1+maxcount-temp;
/* ----- End of linking chain 1 & 2 ----- */
```

```
/* ----- Building chain 3 ----- */
 l=count1+1;
 n=n2;
 while (binimg->image[n][m2]!=binvalue) {
   n--;
   }
 if (n==polygon->y[count1])
   l--;
 polygon->x[l]=m2;
 polygon->y[l]=n;
 nn=n;
 if (n!=n2) {
   m=m2-1;
   while ((n!=n2) && (m>=m1)) {
   n=n2;
   while ((n>=nn) && (binimg->image[n][m]!=binvalue)) {
     n--;
     }
   if (n>nn){
     l++;
     polygon->x[l]=m;
     polygon->y[l]=n;
     nn=n;
     }
   m--;
   }
  }
 count1=l;
/* ----- End of building chain 3 ----- */


/* ----- Building chain 4 ----- */
 l=maxcount-1;
 n=n2;
 while (binimg->image[n][m1]!=binvalue) {
   n--;
   }
 polygon->x[l]=m1;
 polygon->y[l]=n;
 nn=n;
 if (n!=n2) {
   m=m1+1;
   while ((n!=n2) && (m<=m2)) {
     n=n2;
```

```
    while ((n>=nn) && (binimg->image[n][m]!=binvalue))
      n--;
    if (n>nn){
      l--;
      polygon->x[l]=m;
      polygon->y[l]=n;
      nn=n;
      }
    m++;
    }
  }
 temp=l;
/* ----- End of building chain 4 ----- */


/* ----- Linking chain 3 & 4 ----- */
  if (polygon->x[temp]==polygon->x[count1])
   count1--;
  for (l=1;l<=maxcount-temp;l++){
   polygon->x[count1+l]=polygon->x[temp+l-1];
   polygon->y[count1+l]=polygon->y[temp+l-1];
   }
  count1=count1+maxcount-temp;
/* ----- End of linking chain 3 & 4 ----- */


/* ----- Linking head and tail ----- */
  if (polygon->y[1]!=polygon->y[count1]){
   count1++;
   polygon->x[count1]=polygon->x[1];
   polygon->y[count1]=polygon->y[1];
   }
/* ----- End of linking head and tail ----- */


  polygon->length=count1;


}
/* ---------- End of the program of finding simple polygon ---------- */
/*
```

File name: **conhull.cpp**
Version   199807
Author: Dr. D. Luo
Description: This program is used for finding the convex hull of a simple
  polygon. The input *polygon* is the simple polygon of an object. The output
  convexhull is the convex hull of the polygon.
```
*/
```

```
/* ---------- Starting the program of finding convex hull ---------- */
void ConHull(Boundary *polygon,Boundary *convexhull)
{
  int l,m,p1,p2,count1;

  for (l=1;l<=2;l++) {
    convexhull->x[l]=polygon->x[l];
    convexhull->y[l]=polygon->y[l];
  }
  count1=polygon->length;

/* ----- Start constructing convex hull ----- */
  l=2;
  for (m=3;m<=count1;m++){
    p1=(polygon->y[m]-convexhull->y[l])*(convexhull->x[l]-convexhull->x[l-1]);
    p2=(convexhull->y[l]-convexhull->y[l-1])*(polygon->x[m]-convexhull->x[l]);
    while ((l>=2) && (p1<p2)) {
      l--;
      p1=(polygon->y[m]-convexhull->y[l])*(convexhull->x[l]-convexhull->x[l-1]);
      p2=(convexhull->y[l]-convexhull->y[l-1])*(polygon->x[m]-convexhull->x[l]);
    }
    l++;
    convexhull->x[l]=polygon->x[m];
    convexhull->y[l]=polygon->y[m];
  }
  convexhull->length=l;
/* ----- End of constructing convex hull ----- */
}
/* ---------- End of the program of finding convex hull ---------- */
```

Chapter 4
===
```
/*
  File name:      cirhft.cpp
  Version:        199807
  Author:         Dr. D. Luo
  Description:    This program is used for Finding circles fitting to the corners of
the boundary
```
of an object by Circular Hough Transform.   The input *binimg* is a binary image with pixel

values *binval* and boundary point values *bndval*.   The output *hfimg* is an image with pixel

values equal to the radius *r* at the center (*a,b*) of the circle detected.

```
*/
/* ---------- Starting the program of circular Hough transform ---------- */
void CircleHFT(Image *binimg,int binval,int bndval,Image *hfimg)
{
  int i,i1,i2,j,j1,j2,k,k1,r,max,min,minr,len;
  double x,y,dx,dy;

  int bndsz=65535;
  MatrixI hfcir(3,bndsz);
  Boundary boundary(bndsz);

  int width=binimg->width;
  int heigh=binimg->heigh;
  int radl=2,radh=(width>heigh)?width:heigh;
  VectorI radthre(radh),radhis(radh);
  int thirough=2;

/* ----- Store boundary points ----- */
  k=0;
  for (j=0;j<heigh;j++)
   for (i=0;i<width;i++) {
    if (binimg->image[i][j]==bndval) {
     k++;
     if (k>bndsz) {
      cout<<"The size of boundary exceeds memory size !\n";
      exit(1);
      }
     boundary.x[k]=i;
     boundary.y[k]=j;
     }
    }
  len=k;
  boundary.length=k;

/* ----- Set Threshold for each circle. ----- */
  for (i=radl;i<=radh;i++) {
   j1=0;
   i1=1;
   j=i;
   while(j<=i-thirough-1 && j>=0) {
    k=i1;
    r=i;
    while(k<=radh && r<=i) {
     x=(double)(k);
```

```
     y=(double)(j);
     r=(int)(sqrt(x*x+y*y)+0.5);
     if(r==i)
       j1++;
     k++;
     }
   i1=k-1;
   j--;
   }
 radthre.vector[i]=2*j1+1;
   }
/* ----- End of setting threshold ----- */

/* ----- Hough transform ----- */
 i1=binimg->xmin;
 i2=binimg->xmax;
 j1=binimg->ymin;
 j2=binimg->ymax;
 k1=0;
 for (j=j1;j<=j2;j++)
   for (i=i1;i<=i2;i++)
     if (binimg->image[i][j]==binval) {
       max=0;
       min=radh;
       for (k=1;k<=radh;k++)
         radhis.vector[k]=0;
       k=1;
       r=radl;
       while(k<=len && r>=radl) {
         x=(double)boundary.x[k];
         y=(double)boundary.y[k];
         dx=(i-x);
         dy=(j-y);
         r=(int)(sqrt(dx*dx+dy*dy)+0.5);
         if (r>=radl && r<=radh) {
           radhis.vector[r]++;
           if (r>max)
             max=r;
           else {
             if (r<min)
               min=r;
           }
         }
         k++;
```

```
        }
      if (r>=radl) {
      minr=radh;
      for (k=min;k<=max;k++)
        if (radhis.vector[k]>=radthre.vector[k]) {
          if (k<minr)
            minr=k;
          }
        k1++;
        hfcir.matrix[1][k1]=i;
        hfcir.matrix[2][k1]=j;
        hfcir.matrix[3][k1]=r;
        hfimg->image[i][j]=255-minr;
        }
      }

  hfcir.nrow=k1;

/* ----- End of Hough Transform ----- */
};

/* ----------End of the program of circular Hough transform ---------- */
```

Chapter 5
==
```
/*
  File name:        pct.cpp
  Version:          199807
  Author:           Dr. D. Luo
  Description:  This progrm is used for principal component transform.
    The input srcmtrx is a source matrix[j][i] containing j vectors of
    i components. The output destmtrx is a destinate matrix[j][i]
    transformed from srcmtrx, eignvec the eignvalue[i] and eignvec the
    eignvector[k][i].
*/
/* ---------- Starting the program of principal component transform ---------- */
void PCT(MatrixR *srcmtrx,MatrixR *destmtrx,MatrixR *eignvec,VectorR
*eignval)
{
  int ncol,nrow;
  int i,j,m,rtt,rpt,swp,nlp=100;
  double sum,summn,swp1,swp2,tmp1,tmp2,theta,cs,sn;
```

```
ncol=srcmtrx->ncol;
nrow=srcmtrx->nrow;

MatrixR scatmtrx(ncol,ncol);
VectorR mean(ncol),diff(ncol),diag(ncol);
VectorI ordr(ncol);

/* ----- Start finding length, width, thickness by PCT, OK 96.07.30. ----- */

/* ----- Calculation of mean vector ----- */
  for (i=0;i<ncol;i++) {
    mean.vector[i]=0;
    for (j=0;j<nrow;j++)
      mean.vector[i]+=srcmtrx->matrix[j][i];
    mean.vector[i]/=nrow;
    }
/* ----- End of calculation of mean vector ----- */

/* ----- Calculation of scatter matrix ----- */
  for (i=0;i<ncol;i++)
    for (j=0;j<ncol;j++) {
      scatmtrx.matrix[i][j]=0;
      for (m=0;m<nrow;m++)
          scatmtrx.matrix[i][j]+=((srcmtrx->matrix[m][j]-mean[j])*(srcmtrx-
>matrix[m][i]-                              mean[i]));
      }
/* ----- End of calculation of catter matrix ----- */

/* ----- Starting calculation of eigen values and eigen vectors ----- */
for (j=0;j<ncol;j++)
    for (i=0;i<ncol;i++) {
      if (i==j)
          eignvec->matrix[j][i]=1;
      else
        eignvec->matrix[j][i]=0;
      }
  for (i=0;i<ncol;i++) {
    eignval->vector[i]=scatmtrx[i][i];
    diag.vector[i]=eignval->vector[i];
    diff.vector[i]=0.0;
    }
rtt=0;
  for (rpt=1;rpt<=nlp;rpt++){
    sum=0.0;
```

```
for (i=0;i<ncol-1;i++)
  for (j=i+1;j<ncol;j++)
    sum+=fabs(scatmtrx[j][i]);
if (sum==0.0)
  goto end;
if (rpt<4)
  summn=0.2*sum/(ncol*ncol);
else
  summn=0.0;
for (i=0;i<ncol-1;i++)
  for (j=i+1;j<ncol;j++){
    swp1=100.0*fabs(scatmtrx[j][i]);
    if ((rpt>4) && (fabs(eignval->vector[i])+swp1)==fabs(eignval->vector[i]) &&
      (fabs(eignval->vector[j])+swp1)==fabs(eignval->vector[j])) {
      scatmtrx.matrix[j][i]=0.0;
      }
    else {
      if (fabs(scatmtrx[j][i])>summn){
        swp2=eignval->vector[j]-eignval->vector[i];
        if ((fabs(swp2)+swp1)==fabs(swp2)) {
          tmp1=scatmtrx[j][i]/swp2;
          }
        else {
          theta=0.5*swp2/scatmtrx[j][i];
          tmp1=1.0/(fabs(theta)+sqrt(1.0+theta*theta));
          if (theta<0)
            tmp1=-tmp1;
          }
        cs=1.0/sqrt(1.0+tmp1*tmp1);
        sn=tmp1*cs;
        tmp2=sn/(1.0+cs);
        swp2=tmp1*scatmtrx[j][i];
        diff.vector[i]-=swp2;
        diff.vector[j]+=swp2;
        eignval->vector[i]-=swp2;
        eignval->vector[j]+=swp2;
        scatmtrx.matrix[j][i]=0.0;
        for(m=0;m<i;m++){
          swp1=scatmtrx[i][m];
          swp2=scatmtrx[j][m];
          scatmtrx.matrix[i][m]=swp1-sn*(swp2+swp1*tmp2);
          scatmtrx.matrix[j][m]=swp2+sn*(swp1-swp2*tmp2);
          }
        for (m=i+1;m<j;m++){
```

```
            swp1=scatmtrx[m][i];
            swp2=scatmtrx[j][m];
            scatmtrx.matrix[m][i]=swp1-sn*(swp2+swp1*tmp2);
            scatmtrx.matrix[j][m]=swp2+sn*(swp1-swp2*tmp2);
            }
          for (m=j+1;m<ncol;m++){
            swp1=scatmtrx[m][i];
            swp2=scatmtrx[m][j];
            scatmtrx.matrix[m][i]=swp1-sn*(swp2+swp1*tmp2);
            scatmtrx.matrix[m][j]=swp2+sn*(swp1-swp2*tmp2);
            }
          for (m=0;m<ncol;m++){
            swp1=eignvec->matrix[i][m];
            swp2=eignvec->matrix[j][m];
            eignvec->matrix[i][m]=swp1-sn*(swp2+swp1*tmp2);
            eignvec->matrix[j][m]=swp2+sn*(swp1-swp2*tmp2);
            }
          rtt++;
          }
         }
        }
   for (i=0;i<ncol;i++){
    diag.vector[i]+=diff[i];
    eignval->vector[i]=diag[i];
    diff.vector[i]=0.0;
    }
 }

end:
  for (i=0;i<ncol;i++)
   ordr.vector[i]=i;
  for (i=0;i<ncol-1;i++)
   for (j=i+1;j<ncol;j++)
    if (eignval->vector[ordr[i]]<eignval->vector[ordr[j]]) {
      swp=ordr[i];
      ordr.vector[i]=ordr[j];
      ordr.vector[j]=swp;
      }
/* ----- End of calculation of eigen values and eigen vectors ----- */
/*
  Now, eignval->vector[ordr[i]] is the i-th eigenvalue in descending order,
  and eignvec->matrix[j][ordr[i]] is the j-th component of the corresponding
eigenvector.
*/
```

```
/* ----- Ordering eignvalue and eignvector ----- */
  for (i=0;i<ncol;i++)
    diff.vector[i]=eignval->vector[ordr[i]];
  for (i=0;i<ncol;i++)
    eignval->vector[i]=diff[i];
  for (j=0;j<ncol;j++)
    for (i=0;i<ncol;i++)
      scatmtrx.matrix[j][i]=eignvec->matrix[ordr[j]][i];
  for (j=0;j<ncol;j++)
    for (i=0;i<ncol;i++)
      eignvec->matrix[j][i]=scatmtrx[j][i];
/* ----- End of ordering eignvalue and eignvector ----- */

/* ----- Performance of transform ----- */
  for (j=0;j<nrow;j++)
    for (i=0;i<ncol;i++) {
      destmtrx->matrix[j][i]=0;
      for (m=0;m<ncol;m++)
          destmtrx->matrix[j][i]+=srcmtrx->matrix[j][m]*eignvec->matrix[i][m];
    }
  destmtrx->ncol=ncol;
  destmtrx->nrow=nrow;
/* ----- End of performance of transform ----- */
}
/* ---------- End of the program of principal component transform ---------- */


/* File name:        dv.cpp
   Version:          199807
   Author:           Dr. D. Luo
   Description: This program is used for measurement of the orientation of an objet
by directed vein
      method.   The input chncd is the chain code of the boundary of the object. The
parameter
      iterate is the iterate times (>=0). The output is the orientation returned from the
program.
   */
/* ---------- Starting the program of directed vein method ---------- */
void Modify(VectorI *chncd)
{
  int i,k,r,d,len;

  len=chncd->length;
  for (i=0;i<len-1;i++) {
```

```
  k=chncd->vector[i]/8;
  r=chncd->vector[i]-k*8;
  d=chncd->vector[i+1]-r;
  if (d<-3) {
    chncd->vector[i+1]+=(k+1)*8;
    }
  else {
    if (d>3)
         chncd->vector[i+1]+=(k-1)*8;
    else
         chncd->vector[i+1]+=k*8;
    }
  }
}

void Smooth(VectorI *chncd,int iterate)
{
  int i,j,len;

  len=chncd->length;
  if (iterate!=0) {
    for (j=1;j<=iterate;j++) {
     for (i=0;i<len-1;i++)
          chncd->vector[i]+=chncd->vector[i+1];
     len--;
     }
    }
  chncd->length=len;
}

void Module4(VectorI *chncd,int iterate)
{
  int i,k1,k2,len;

  len=chncd->length;
  k1=1;
  if (iterate!=0)
    for (i=1;i<=iterate;i++)
      k1*=2;
  k2=k1*4;
  for (i=0;i<len;i++) {
    chncd->vector[i]%=k2;
    if (chncd->vector[i]<0)
         chncd->vector[i]+=k2;
```

```
    }
}

void Segment(VectorI *chncd,VectorI *encd)
{
  int i,j,len;

  len=chncd->length;
  j=0;
  encd->vector[j]=1;
  for (i=1;i<len;i++) {
    if (chncd->vector[i]==chncd->vector[i-1])
      encd->vector[j]++;
    else{
      j++;
      chncd->vector[j]=chncd->vector[i];
      encd->vector[j]=1;
    }
  }
  chncd->length=j+1;
  encd->length=j+1;
}

double Orient(VectorI *chncd,VectorI *encd,int iterate)
{
  int i,k1,k2,k3,c,g,len,scale;
  double angle;

  len=chncd->length;
  scale=100;
  k1=1;
  if (iterate!=0)
    for (i=1;i<=iterate;i++)
      k1*=2;
  k1*=scale;
  k2=k1*2;
  k3=k1*4;
  for (i=0;i<len;i++)
    chncd->vector[i]*=scale;
  for (i=1;i<len;i++) {
    c=abs(chncd->vector[i]-chncd->vector[0]);
    if (c>k2) {
      if (chncd->vector[i]<=chncd->vector[0])
          chncd->vector[i]+=k3;
```

```
      else
            chncd->vector[0]+=k3;
      }
    g=encd->vector[0]+encd->vector[i];
    chncd->vector[0]=(chncd->vector[0]*encd->vector[0]+chncd->vector[i]*encd-
>vector[i])/g;
      encd->vector[0]=g;
      if (chncd->vector[0]>=k3)
        chncd->vector[0]-=k3;
      }
    angle=(double)chncd->vector[0]*45/encd->vector[0];
    if (angle>180.0)
      angle-=180.0;
    return angle;
}

double DV(VectorI *chncd,int iterate)
{
    int len=chncd->length;
    VectorI encode(len),*encd;
    encd=&encode;

    Modify(chncd);
    Smooth(chncd,iterate);
    Module4(chncd,iterate);
    Segment(chncd,encd);
    return Orient(chncd,encd,iterate);
}
/* ---------- End of the program of directed vein method ---------- */
```

Chapter 6

===

```
/*
    File name:       arrnanal.cpp
    Version:         199807
    Author:          Dr. D. Luo
    Description:      This program is used for automatic analysis of arrangements of
aggregate objects
        by 2-D linear Hough Transform from the (x,y) coordinates and the orientatin θ
of each object.
        The input parameter ipar contains x and y coordinates and orientations θ of
objects. The output
        ofea contains measured features for recognition and classification of aggregates.
```

```
*/
/* ---------- Starting the Program of arrangement analysis ---------- */
void ArrnAnal(MatrixR *ipar,MatrixR *ofea)
{
  int i,j,n0;
  int ncol=3,nrow=ipar->nrow,npara=0;
  double s0,x,y,theta,consr;
  MatrixR mtrx(ncol,nrow);
  VectorR mean(ncol),mnsqrt(ncol),hlfbw(ncol),ndens(ncol),dens(ncol);
  VectorR cr(5),modr(4),var(3),sum(6),sum2(4);

  double dg=3.14159265/180;

/* ----- Hough transform ----- */
  for (j=0;j<nrow;j++) {
    theta=dg*ipar->matrix[j][2];
    mtrx.matrix[j][2]=ipar->matrix[j][2];
    mtrx.matrix[j][0]=-ipar->matrix[j][0]*sin(theta)
                    +ipar->matrix[j][1]*cos(theta);
    mtrx.matrix[j][1]=ipar->matrix[j][0]*cos(theta)
                    +ipar->matrix[j][1]*sin(theta);
  }
/* ----- End of Hough transform ----- */

  cout<<"\n\n";
  cout<<"linear Hough Transform:\n";
  cout<<"Nobj  x     y     Angle Thou1  Thou2\n";
  for (j=0;j<nrow;j++) {
    cout<<j+1<<"\t";
    for (i=0;i<3;i++)
      cout<<ipar->matrix[j][i]<<"\t";
    for (i=0;i<2;i++)
      cout<<mtrx[j][i]<<"\t";
    cout<<"\n";
  }
  cout<<"\n\n";

/* ----- Calculating mean vector ----- */
  for (i=0;i<3;i++) {
    mean.vector[i]=0;
    for (j=0;j<nrow;j++)
      mean.vector[i]+=mtrx[j][i];
    mean.vector[i]/=nrow;
  }
```

```
/* ----- End of alculating mean vector ----- */

  ++npara;
  for (i=0;i<3;i++)
   ofea->matrix[npara][i]=mean[i];

  cout<<"Param  Thou1  Thou2  Angle  Total\n";
  cout<<"Mean:  ";
  for (i=0;i<3;i++)
   cout<<mean[i]<<"\t";
  cout<<"\n";

/* ----- Calculating mean square root ----- */
  s0=0;
  for (i=0;i<3;i++) {
   mnsqrt.vector[i]=0;
   for (j=0;j<nrow;j++)
    mnsqrt.vector[i]+=mtrx[j][i]*mtrx[j][i];
   mnsqrt.vector[i]-=mean[i]*mean[i]*nrow;
   s0+=mnsqrt[i];
   mnsqrt.vector[i]=sqrt(mnsqrt[i]/nrow);
   }
  s0=sqrt(s0/(3*nrow));
  theta=log(mnsqrt[0]/mnsqrt[1]);
/* ----- End of calculating mean square root ----- */

  ++npara;
  for (i=0;i<3;i++)
   ofea->matrix[npara][i]=mnsqrt[i];
  ++npara;
  ofea->matrix[npara][0]=s0;
  ++npara;
  ofea->matrix[npara][0]=theta;

  cout<<"Mnsqrt: ";
  for (i=0;i<3;i++)
   cout<<mnsqrt[i]<<"\t";
  cout<<"\n";
  cout<<"\t"<<s0<<"\n";
  cout<<"\t"<<theta<<"\n";

/* ----- Calculating half bandwidth ----- */
  for (i=0;i<3;i++) {
   hlfbw.vector[i]=sqrt(-2*mnsqrt.vector[i]*mnsqrt.vector[i]*log(0.1));
```

```
    }
/* ----- End of calculating half bandwidth ----- */

  ++npara;
  for (i=0;i<3;i++)
   ofea->matrix[npara][i]=hlfbw[i];

  cout<<"Hlfbw: ";
  for (i=0;i<3;i++)
   cout<<hlfbw[i]<<"\t";
  cout<<"\n";

/* ----- Calculate the number N0 of objects whithin band and the densities ----- */
  for(i=0;i<3;i++) {
   n0=0;
   for (j=0;j<nrow;j++)
    if (fabs(mtrx[j][i]-mean[i])<=hlfbw[i])
         n0+=1;
   ndens.vector[i]=n0;
   dens.vector[i]=hlfbw[i]/n0;
   }
/* ----- End of calculate the number N0 of objects whithin band and the densities ---
-- */

  ++npara;
  for (i=0;i<3;i++)
   ofea->matrix[npara][i]=ndens[i];
  ++npara;
  for (i=0;i<3;i++) {
   ofea->matrix[npara][i]=dens[i];
   }
  cout<<"DnsNo: ";
  for (i=0;i<3;i++)
   cout<<ndens[i]<<"\t";
  cout<<"\n";
  cout<<"Dnsty: ";
  for (i=0;i<3;i++)
   cout<<dens[i]<<"\t";
  cout<<"\n";

/* ----- Mod ratio ----- */
  for (i=0;i<6;i++)
   sum.vector[i]=0;
  for (i=0;i<4;i++)
```

```
  sum2.vector[i]=0;
 for (j=0;j<nrow;j++) {
  for (i=0;i<3;i++)
   var.vector[i]=mtrx[j][i]*mtrx[j][i];
   var.vector[3]=mtrx[j][0]*mtrx[j][1];
   sum2.vector[0]+=var[0]+var[2];
   sum2.vector[1]+=var[1]+var[2];
   sum2.vector[2]+=var[0]+var[1];
   sum2.vector[3]+=var[0]+var[1]+var[2];
   sum.vector[0]+=sqrt(var[0]+var[2]);
   sum.vector[1]+=sqrt(var[1]+var[2]);
   sum.vector[2]+=sqrt(var[0]+var[1]);
   sum.vector[3]+=sqrt(var[0]+var[1]+var[2]);
   sum.vector[4]=var[3];
   sum.vector[5]=fabs(var[3]);
   }
 for (i=0;i<3;i++)
  var.vector[i]=mean[i]*mean[i];
 cr.vector[0]=nrow*sqrt(var[0]+var[2])/sum[0];
 cr.vector[1]=nrow*sqrt(var[1]+var[2])/sum[1];
 cr.vector[2]=nrow*sqrt(var[0]+var[1])/sum[2];
 cr.vector[3]=nrow*sqrt(var[0]+var[1]+var[2])/sum[3];
 cr.vector[4]=fabs(sum[4])/sum[5];
 for (i=0;i<4;i++){
  modr.vector[i]=sqrt((sum2[i]-sum[i]*sum[i]/nrow)/nrow);
  }
/* ----- End of Mod ratio ----- */


 ++npara;
 for (i=0;i<3;i++)
  ofea->matrix[npara][i]=cr[i];
 ++npara;
 for (i=3;i<5;i++)
  ofea->matrix[npara][i-3]=cr[i];
 ++npara;
 for (i=0;i<3;i++)
  ofea->matrix[npara][i]=modr[i];
 ++npara;
 ofea->matrix[npara][0]=modr[3];
 ++npara;
 ofea->matrix[npara][0]=modr[2]*nrow/sum[2];

 cout<<"ccr:   ";
```

```
  for (i=0;i<3;i++)
    cout<<cr[i]<<"\t";
  cout<<"\n";
  for (i=0;i<2;i++)
    cout<<"\t"<<cr[i]<<"\t";
  cout<<"\n";
  cout<<"Modr:   ";
  for (i=0;i<3;i++)
    cout<<modr[i]<<"\t";
  cout<<"\n";
  for (i=0;i<1;i++)
    cout<<"\t"<<modr[i]<<"\t";
  cout<<"\n\n";

/* ----- Consistent ratio ----- */
  x=0; y=0;
  for (j=0;j<nrow;j++) {
    theta=dg*2*ipar->matrix[j][2];
    x+=cos(theta);
    y+=sin(theta);
    }
  consr=sqrt(x*x+y*y)/nrow;
  if (x!=0.0)
    theta=atan(y/x)/2/dg;
  else
    theta=3.141159265/2/2/dg;
/* ----- End of consistent ratio ----- */

  ++npara;
  ofea->matrix[npara][0]=theta;
  ofea->nrow=npara;
  cout<<"Consistent Ratio of Hough space:\n"<<theta<<"\n\n";
}
/* ---------- End of the Program of arrangement analysis ---------- */
```

Index

A

additive noise 11
aggregates 160
arc detection 89
area 54-55
arrangement 160
    circumferential 163
    circumferential hollow 189
    parallel cross-section 160
    parallel hollow 188
    parallel region 161
    parallel vertical-section 160
    radial region 162
    random region 164
    radial hollow 189
    shear 188
arrangement analysis 159-209
    arrangement examples 160-164, 188-190
    classification 207-210
    description 170,185-186,205-207
    feature extraction 186-188
arrangement classification 207
arrangement description 170, 205
arrangement features 169-188
arrangement feature extraction 186-188
    consistency ratio 187
    orientation 169
    standard deviation 186-187,204-205
    symmetry factor 203-204
arrnanal.cpp 205

B

basic method 85, 93-94
boundary 48-52, 74-75
boundary detection 11
boundary points 48
boundary segmentation 18, 20-22

gradient operator 15, 20-21,
    Laplacian-Gaussian filter 21,
    Laplacian operator 21
    template operator 21-22
Butterworth filter
    high pass 14-15
    low pass 13

C

centre gradient method 85
centre method 85, 96-99
central moment 137
chain code of direction 126-127
    modified 127
    modulo-4 128
    smoothing 127
    segmentation 128
circle detection 89
circle fitting 89
circular Hough transform 85, 89, 92-106
    basic algorithm 93-94
    centre method 96-99
    directional gradient algorithm 94-96
    gradient centre method 100-101
    radius method 101-104
    threshold function 102, 104-106
cirhft.cpp 104
classifier 2
classification method 23
clustering analysis 5
clustering method 23
conhull.cpp 44
consistency ratio 187
constrained least-square filter 12-13
contrast adjusting 16
contrast enhancement 23
convex deficiencies 55-58
convex hull 34-46,121, 122, 130
    definition 34
    finding 34-46
    orientation 130
    Sklansky's algorithm 43

SPCH algorithm 35
convex polygon 34
convex set 34
convolution 11
coordinate transform 50
criteria 4
curvature 56, 58, 89
curvature description 33
curve detection 92-93

D
data analysis 1,5
decision making 4
description function 49-52
    coordinate system 50
    coordinate transform 50-51
design set 3
diagonal matrix 133
directed vein 121-130, 157
    chain code 126-127
    image 123-125
    orientation 125-126,128
directed vein orientation 125
    algorithm 126
    definition 1 125
    definition 2 129
direction chain codes 33
directional gradient method 85, 94-96
double boundary 23 ,156

E
edge detection 11
    edge segmentation 20-22
edge following 23
edge segmentation 20-22
edgfoll.cpp 59
eigenvalues 123
eigenvectors 123
enhancement 1, 13-18
    equalisation 16, 18
    sharpening 14-15
    smoothening 13-14
equalisation 13, 16-18
    histogram equalisation 16

histogram specification 16-17
    intensity equalisation 17
error 12
extended Hough transform 165,168

F
feature extraction 52,56-58186-188
    consistency ratio 187
    convex deficiencies 57
    curvature 56, 58
    horizontal symmetry 56-57
    measurements 54-56
    orientation 169
    shape factor 57
    standard deviation 186-187,204-
    width 56
    205
    symmetry factor 203-204
feature measurements 1
feature space method 2
field measurements 1
filtering 4, 11
Fourier boundary encoding 33
Fourier transform 12
fractal boundary 71,74-75
fractal geometry 71
fractal region 72,75
fractals 71-77
    applications 71
    definition 7172
    dimension 74
    multi-fractals 74
    self-similarity 73
    shape representation 74-75
fractal texture 72

G
Gaussian filter 13
    low pass filter 13
gradient centre method 100-101
gradient filter 108
gradient operator 15, 20-21
Graham's algorithm 35

H
half widths 54
hierarchic method 5
hierarchic image segmentation 23
hierarchic representation 33
high pass filter 15
    Butterworth filter 14-15
histogram 16
histogram equalisation 16
histogram specification 16-17
homogeneity 16
horizontal symmetry 56-57
Hough transform 85, 90-92,168-169
    algorithm 91-92
    circular 92
    definition 91

I
image acquisition 11, 14
image blur 14
image coding 71
image compression 71
image enhancement 11,13-18
    equalisation 16-17
    sharpening 14-15
    smoothing 13
image equalisation 16-18
image processing 1-7
    applications 1
    enhancement 11,13-18
    equalisation 16-18
    restoration 11-13
    segmentation 18-23
image restoration 11-13
    constrained least-square filter 12-13
    inverse filter 12
    wiener filter 12
image segmentation 18-23
    region segmentation 18-19
    boundary segmentation 19-22
integrating 23
intensity bands 19
intensity equalisation 16, 17

intensity gradient 11
intensity linear stretching 16
inverse filter 12
inverse Fourier transform 12
irregular shape 27
irregular structure 71

K
k-curvature algorithm 89

L
Laplacian-Gaussian filter 21
Laplace operator 15, 21
least square error 89
limit-band frequency 14
linear transform 11
longest diagonal 50
low pass filter 13
    Butterworth filter 13
    Gaussian filter 13

M
matrix 123, 132
mean filter 13
mean square root error 108
measurements 1, 3, 54-56
    area 54-55
    convex deficiencies 55-56
    feature measurements 1
    field measurements 1
    half widths 54
    perimeter 55
    vertical half-symmetry 54
medial axis transform 33
median filter 13
moments 121-131, 136-140
    central 137-138
    orientation 138-140
    theory 137
multi-dimensional feature space 3
multi-fractals 74
multi-level thresholding 19

N

noise 11-12
nominal filter cut-off frequency 13
non-linear diffusion 23
non-linear transform 11
non-self-intersecting 41,44

O
object analysis 6, 11
object classification 6
object description 6
object detection 11-23
object labelling 23
object modelling 71
object orientation 128, 130, 135, 138, 169
orientation
    arrangement 169
    convex hull 130
    directed vein 125-126,128
    moments 138-140
    principal component transform 135-136
orientation analysis 121-152
    convex hull 130
    directed vein 123-130
    moment 136-140
    principal component transform 131-136
out-of-focus 14

P
pattern 3
pattern analysis 3
pattern classification 11
pattern generating mechanism 3
pattern recognition 2-7
    applications 2
    classifier 2
    criteria 4
    decision making 4
    design set 3
    feature space method 2
    measurements 3
    pattern 3

pattern generating mechanism 3
    statistical approach 3
    structural method 2
    syntactic method 2
    system design 3
    training samples 3-4
pattern vector 59
perimeter 55
piecewise approximation 33
point spread function 11
polygon 37
    finding 37
    properties 40
    simple polygon 37
Prewitt operator 21
principal component transform 59, 121, 122, 131-136
    orientation 135-136
    theory 132-135

R
radial method 85, 101-104
random shape 47
ratio of noise to signal 12
rectification 1
recursive thresholding 19
reflection of illumination 14
refraction of illumination 14
region growing 11, 19
region splitting 11, 19
region detection 11
    region segmentation 18-19
region segmentation 18-19
    multi-level thresholding 19
    recursive thresholding 19
    region growing 19
    region splitting 19
    thresholding 18-19
regular shape 27
representation 4
restoration 11-13
    constrained least-square filter 12-13
    inverse filter 12

Wiener filter 12
Robert operator 21-22
roundness 89
    definition 89
roundness analysis 85-116

S
scatter matrix 123
segmentation 1, 4, 19-23
    (edge) boundary 20-22
    others 23
    region 18-19
self-similarity 73
shadow correction 17
shape analysis 27-78
    convex hull based 47-59
    fractals based 74-75
shape classification 59
shape factor 57
shape ratio 30
shape representation 27-33, 47-
    52, 74-75
    boundary 48
    convex hull 47-52
    description function 51
    fractals 74-75
sharp corners 106
sharpening 13, 14-16
    Butterworth high pass filter 14-15
    gradient operator 15
    Laplace operator 15
sharpness 89
sharpness analysis 85-116
    see roundness analysis
similarity measure 23
simple polygon 35, 37-46, 83
    finding 37-39
    properties 40-42
simpoly.cpp 39
Sklansky's algorithm 34-36, 43-44
smoothening 13-14
    Butterworth low pass filter 13
    Gaussian low pass filter 13
    mean filter 13

median filter 13
Sobel operator 21
SPCH algorithm 35-47
special shape 27
sphericity 27-31
stair-climbing algorithm 35,37-39,83
standard deviation 17, 186-187.204-
    205
star-shaped polygon 35
statistical approach 3
straight line Hough transform 167
structural method 2
surface fitting 23
symmetry factor 203-204
syntactic method 2
system design 3

T
template matching 11
template operator 22
    Prewitt operator 21
    Robert operator 21-22
    Sobel operator 21
texture segmentation 5, 23
threshold function 104-106
thresholding 11, 18-19
training samples 3-4
transform matrix 132
transpose matrix 133

U
unit matrix 134

V
validity 44-47
vector 59
vertical half-symmetry 54

W
weight function 14
width 54, 56
Wiener filter 12
window function 13,19

DIGITAL SIGNAL PROCESSING: Software Solutions and Applications
J.M. BLACKLEDGE and M.J. TURNER, Department of Mathematical Sciences, Faculty of Computing Science and Engineering, De Montfort University, Leicester

ISBN: 1-898563-48-9   *ca.* 200 pages   1998

This text is for advanced undergraduates and postgraduates reading electronic engineering, computer science and/or applied mathematics. Complete with CD-ROM it delivers the necessary mathematical and computational background and some of the processing techniques used for Digital Signal Processing (DSP). The book's appeal lies in its emphasis on software solutions for which source code is provided.

SIGNAL PROCESSING IN ELECTRONIC COMMUNICATION
MICHAEL J. CHAPMAN, DAVID P. GOODALL, and NIGEL C. STEELE, School of Mathematics and Information Sciences, University of Coventry

ISBN 1-898563-30-6   288 pages   1997

This text develops the theory of communication from a mathematical viewpoint for advanced undergraduates and graduates, and professional engineers and researchers in communications engineering.

DIGITAL FILTERS AND SIGNAL PROCESSING IN ELECTRONIC ENGINEERING: Theory, Applications, Architecture, Code
S.M. BOZIC and R.J. CHANCE, School of Electrical and Electronics Engineering, University of Birmingham

ISBN 1-898563-58-6   *ca.* 200 pages   1998

From industrial and teaching experience the authors provide an unusual blend of theory and practice of digital signal processing (DSP) for advanced under-graduate and postgraduate engineers readhing electronics in a fast-moving and developing area driven by the information technology revolution. This is a source book of research and development for design engineers of embedded systems in real-time computing, and applied mathematicians who apply DSP techniques in telecommunications, aerospace (control systems), satellite communications, instrumentation, and medical technology (ultrasound and magnetic resonance imaging).

Printed and bound by CPI Group (UK) Ltd, Croydon, CR0 4YY

03/10/2024

01040339-0013